encyclopedia
SCIENCE
PROJECTS

Written by
Pam Robson and Mick Seller

Illustrated by
Ian Moores and Ian Thompson

SHOOTING STAR PRESS

This edition produced in 1994 for Shooting Star Press Inc
230 Fifth Avenue, Suite 1212, New York, NY 10001

© Aladdin Books Ltd 1994

Designed and produced by
Aladdin Books Ltd, 28 Percy Street, London W1

Some of the material in this book was previously published in the Science Workshop series

CONTENTS

ABOUT THIS BOOK

Introduction

Science projects with practical experiments

CALENDARS

Before the invention of the clock, people had to rely on nature's timekeepers - the Sun, the Moon and the stars. The daily movement of the Sun across the sky provided the simplest unit, the solar day. The time period of a year was estimated by watching the seasons, and the constancy of the lunar cycle led to the division of each year into months. Traditionally, calendars were controlled by priests. They were devised either by counting days or by following the phases of the Moon. Nowadays, the Gregorian calendar is most common. This was worked out by Pope Gregory XIII in the 1580s.

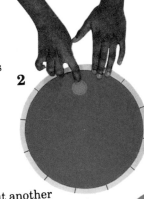

DAY BY DAY

1. Cut out two circles of cardboard. The largest should be 12 in across, the other 11in across. Stick one on top of another and divide into 12 equal pieces to indicate the months.

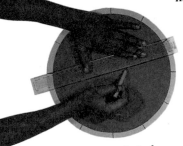

2. Cut out 12 paper circles of 0.5in across. Find out the number of days for each month and write them around the edge of each small circle. Now stick them in order around the large circle. The first day of the month should be nearest the edge as shown.

3. Cut another cardboard circle 10.5in across. Cut a hole, radius 0.5in, to correspond with the position of the paper circles. Cover the hole with stiff, transparent plastic. Attach a red arrow marker, as shown.

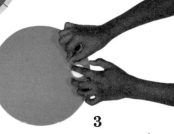

4. Cut out a cardboard circle, radius 0.5in. Carefully make a tiny "window," to view the date through. Position it over the 0.5in hole, and fix it to the plastic with a paper fastener, so it turns.

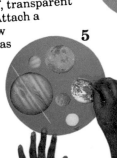

5. Decorate your calendar before joining the separate sections together. Position the smaller circle centrally over the larger circle and join them together with a paper fastener. Rotate your calendar until it is set on the correct day for the current month.

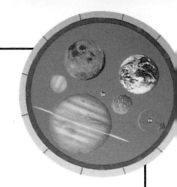

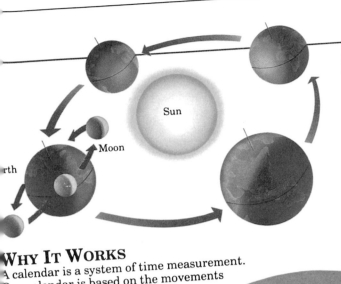

Sun

Moon

rth

orbit

WHY IT WORKS

A calendar is a system of time measurement.
Our calendar is based on the movements
of the planets. The Earth rotates
once every 24 hours, or once a
day. The Moon orbits the
Earth once every month,
and the Earth takes 365
days, or 1 year to
orbit the Sun.

BRIGHT IDEAS

Design a tally system for
marking off the days,
using symbols instead of
numbers. Can you think of a
way to group a certain
number of tally marks
together to make a single tally
mark that represents that
larger number? We say 7 days
equal one whole week. Days
and weeks are units of time.

Find out how and when
different cultures
celebrate New Year. How do
their calendars work?

Bright ideas
for further
projects

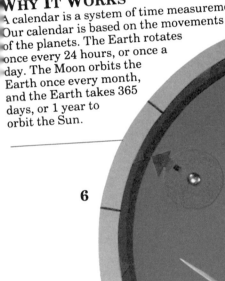

6

6. View the date
through the
"window." Remember
to turn the small wheel
daily. Each revolution of the
0.5in circle is equivalent to
one month, as represented on
the calendar. For each new
month rotate the large circle.

7

THE WORKSHOP

A science workshop is a place to test ideas, perform experiments, and make discoveries. To prove many scientific facts you don't need a lot of fancy equipment. In fact, everything you need for a basic workshop can be found around your home or school. Read through these pages and then use your imagination to add to your "home laboratory." Make sure that you are aware of relevant safety rules and look after the environment. A science experiment is an activity that involves the use of certain basic rules to test a hypothesis. A qualitative approach involves observation. A quantitative approach involves measurement. Remember, one of the keys to being a creative scientist is to keep experimenting. This means experimenting with equipment as well as with ideas, to give you the most accurate results. In this way, you will build up your workshop as you go along.

MAKING THE MODELS

Before you begin, read through all the steps. Then make a list of the things you need and gather them together. Next, think about the project so that you have a clear idea of what you are about to do. Finally, take your time in putting the pieces together. You will find that your projects work best if you wait while glue or paint dries. If something goes wrong, retrace your steps. And, if you can't fix it, start over again. Every scientist makes mistakes, but the best ones know when to begin again!

GENERAL TIPS

There are at least two parts to every experiment: experimenting with materials and testing a science "fact." If you don't have all the materials, experiment with others instead. For example, if you can't find any sand, use sawdust or shredded paper instead. Once you've finished experimenting, read your notes thoroughly and think about what happened, evaluating your measurements and observations. See what conclusions you can draw from your results.

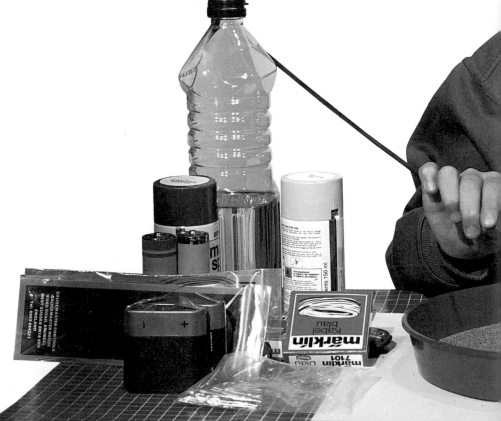

WORKSHOP SAFETY

Make sure that an adult knows what you are doing at all times. Cutting and filing can be dangerous so always ask an adult to do these for you. In any experiments that use electricity, always use a battery of 1.5 volts. Never use main-line electricity! Always be careful with sharp items. If you spill any water, wipe it up right away. Slippery surfaces are dangerous. Clean up your workshop when you finish!

EXPERIMENTING

Always conduct a "fair test." This means changing one thing at a time for each stage of an experiment. In this way, you can always tell which change caused a different result. As you go along, record what you see and compare your results with what you thought would happen before you began. Ask questions such as "why?" "how?" and "what if?" Then test your project and write down the answers you find. Compare your results to those of your friends or classmates.

AIR
AND
WATER

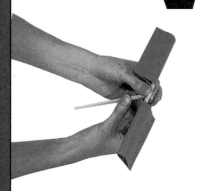

CONTENTS

INTRODUCTION

Air cannot be seen, it has no taste and we can't hold it. Air is a rich mixture of different gases which includes the oxygen we breathe. Air surrounding the Earth is like a heavy blanket pushing down on us; this is called air pressure. Air movements over the face of the Earth are familiar to us as breezes, winds or even hurricanes. The power of moving air is quite considerable; it can sail ships, turn a wind turbine, or heated, can land a balloon. One of the strongest properties of air, is that it can be compressed so that large amounts can be stored in small spaces, as for example, in a diver's cylinder.

We can't live without air but neither can we live without water. Water can stretch, curve, run up or downhill but always settles at the lowest level possible. Water can be liquid, solid (ice) or gas (steam). In the form of ice it expands, which is why pipes sometimes burst in the winter. Water is a potential source of energy. Tides, waves and currents can all be exploited. Hydroelectric powerstations convert energy from falling water into electricity and steam can be used to drive engines.

Safety Tips
If you use a hairdryer be careful with plugging and unplugging. Never use a hairdryer with wet hands or near water. Don't leave it on too long and allow it to overheat. Experiments with candles should be done with an adult. Don't leave models or equipment directly on a heater. Remember to take care cutting plastic bottles with scissors and do not use flammable materials, like plastic, if heating is required as part of the experiment. Clean up after any experiment.

ESSENTIAL OXYGEN

Everything around us is either solid, a liquid, or a gas. Gases are the lightest (or least dense) of all. Solid things, like cars, can move through gases. The air around us is a mixture of gases. Most of the air, about four-fifths, is nitrogen. About one fifth is oxygen. Then there are small amounts of other gases, argon, helium, krypton, xenon, neon, and carbon dioxide. Finally, there is some water vapor in the air. Without oxygen we could not breathe, and without oxygen fires would not burn – like us they would suffocate. In about 1670 the English doctor John Mayow proved that fire consumes air. By repeating his experiment, you can also see how a flame uses up a part of the air.

Nitrogen

Oxygen

Other gases

"BREATHING" FIRE

1 To test that fire actually burns air, you need a few household items. Find a bowl made of something that is fireproof (not plastic), three coins, a clean glass jar, modeling clay, and a candle.

2 Push a small lump of clay onto the middle of the bowl. Arrange the coins so that the top of the jar will rest on them without wobbling. Firmly push the candle into the clay and half fill the bowl with water.

3 Ask an adult to help you with this step. Light the candle and then very carefully lower the glass jar over the flame, resting it on the coins. Quickly mark the water level on the side of the jar. Watch the flame closely to see how it changes.

WHY IT WORKS

The flame uses up the oxygen in the air as it burns. Once much of the oxygen is taken up, there is no longer enough to support a flame and the candle goes out. Air pressure pushes on the water outside the jar. Inside the jar, the water is forced into the space left by the oxygen. The water level inside rises by about one-fifth, the fraction of oxygen in the air.

This experiment is not exact. Some of the air escapes from the jar as the flame burns because air expands when heated. As the air cools down it shrinks, or contracts, making extra space for the water to fill.

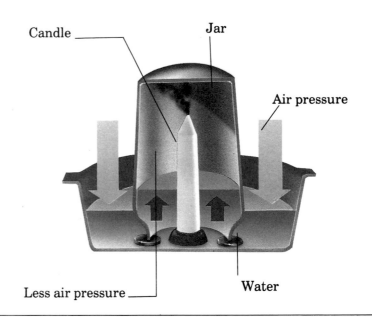

Candle · Jar · Air pressure · Less air pressure · Water

4 Note what happens to the water at the bottom of the bowl. As the candle burns notice if bubbles appear. When the candle goes out see if the water level rises inside the jar. Observe how high it has risen. Mark the side of the glass to show the new water level.

4

BRIGHT IDEAS

Light two candles. Cover one with a small jar and one with a large jar. See which candle burns the longest.

Place a dried pea into the neck of a bottle. Blow hard to make the pea go into the bottle. Notice whether the air pressure inside the bottle is strong enough to keep the pea out.

13

POWERFUL PRESSURE

Although we don't really notice it much, the air is all around us and is pressing on us all the time. Air pressure is caused because air has weight and it is pulled down to Earth by gravity. As it is pulled down it squeezes against things – this is air pressure. Our own blood pressure presses back against the air – if we suddenly took air pressure away, our bodies would explode. This is why spacemen have to wear special pressurized suits: in space there is no air and so no air pressure. Slight changes in air pressure give us a clue about weather changes. We can measure air pressure and so predict the weather with an instrument called a barometer.

WEATHER FORECASTING

1 You can make a simple barometer by using a new balloon, a clean glass jar, a straw, a toothpick, a rubber band, oak tag, and some cardboard. Cut the neck off the balloon. Stretch the balloon over the jar. Hold it in place with the rubber band.

2 Tape the toothpick to the end of the straw. Tape the other end of the straw to the center of the balloon lid. Make a weather picture chart on the oak tag, with the good weather at the top.

3 Fold the sheet of oak tag and cut a cardboard triangle for a support. Fix the weather chart in position. Put the barometer in place and watch the pointer move a little each day.

WHY IT WORKS

Air pressure changes all the time. It pushes on us from all directions because of the endless jostling of gas molecules. When the air pressure rises, indicating good weather, the pressure pushes down on your barometer's lid, making the straw pointer rise. When the air pressure drops, indicating bad weather, the lid swells and the pointer drops. Air temperature also affects pressure. Your barometer is most accurate when kept at a steady temperature.

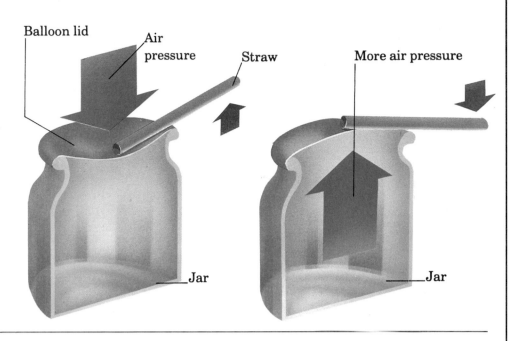

Balloon lid

Air pressure

Straw

More air pressure

Jar

Jar

BRIGHT IDEAS

Try to lift a piece of paper from a tabletop using only a ruler as in the picture. Feel the air pressure try to stop you.

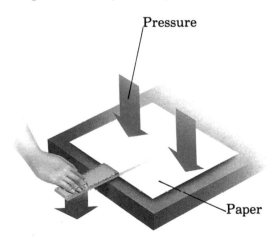

Pressure

Paper

Very carefully hang a ruler from its center by a string so that it balances perfectly. Take two identical balloons and blow one up. Tape the balloons to either end of the ruler. You'll need identical pieces of tape to keep the experiment fair. Notice what happens. Which balloon is the heaviest and why?

Full balloon

Empty balloon

RISING CURRENTS

Have you ever wondered what makes the wind blow?
As the air is warmed by the sun it expands and
becomes lighter. These changes cause the warm air to
rise. At the same time, cooler air moves in, filling up
the space left behind. So, the air is
moving, and moving air is wind. The
rotation of the earth complicates
the pattern, causing wind to swirl.
Satellite images of the earth show
the clouds above us in constant
motion due to these air currents.

MOBILE AIR

1 You can prove that hot air rises with a mobile that spins in the slightest current. Cut some shapes from aluminum foil. For the mobile shown here you need two squares and two circles.

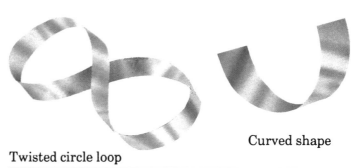

1

2 Turn one of the circles into a spiral like a snail's shell. Make a pinwheel using one of the squares. Twist and cut the other two pieces using your imagination to make interesting shapes. With a needle, thread a length of cotton through each one.

2

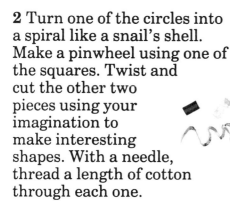

3 Cut a triangle from a piece of cardboard. Decorate one side and tape a stick securely to the other to make the stand. Attach a piece of clay to the bottom of the stick. Make sure the complete stand balances upright evenly.

3

4 Carefully tape the thread lengths to the back of the triangle. Make sure each shape can twist freely. Place your mobile above a radiator, keeping it well away from gas and fire and breezes. Watch the shapes twirl.

4

BRIGHT IDEAS

The spirals turn very nicely in the currents of rising hot air, but would other shapes turn as well? Try a twisted loop, a circle, a strip. Notice which works best. Are the best shapes similar to birds' feathers or the wings of a glider? Do the spirals work better with longer or shorter strings? Is close to the radiator best, or high above it?

Twisted circle loop

Curved shape

WHY IT WORKS

Although dangling at rest when placed elsewhere in a room, your mobile shapes twirl when hung above a radiator. This is because rising warm air pushes upward on the edges of the shapes, causing them to twist and turn like a propeller.

The movements of hot and cold air are called convection currents and cause many winds. The hottest part of the earth is the equator – here the air is heated and it rises. High in the air it travels out toward the poles. At the cold North and South poles the air cools and falls, then travels toward the equator.

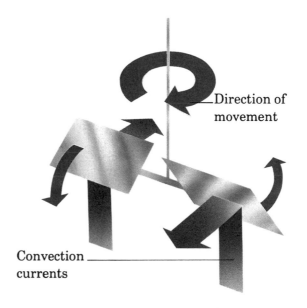

Direction of movement

Convection currents

HOT-AIR FLIGHT

Have you seen a hot-air balloon? More than 200 years ago, two French brothers, Joseph and Jacques Montgolfier, discovered that rising hot air could be captured and used for flight. They made a huge balloon from linen and paper and built a fire underneath it. The balloon trapped the hot air and smoke

rising from the fire and lifted the two men into the air. As the air cooled, the balloon floated back down to the ground. Since that first flight, people have used hot-air balloons for pleasure, for racing, and even for warfare. You can make your own hot-air balloon.

BALLOON LIFT-OFF

1

3

1 To make a balloon that traps hot air to fly, you need four large sheets of tissue paper. Fold each sheet in half and lightly copy this shape on to one using a pencil. When you are happy with the outline cut out your first "panel."

3 Unfold your first panel and spread glue on the edge of one half. Stick the second panel on top and press down. Repeat with the next panel until all four panels are joined into a balloon.

4 Make a small "passenger basket" from a piece of folded oak tag. Attach the basket to the open end of the balloon with four lengths of thread.

2

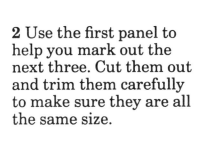

2 Use the first panel to help you mark out the next three. Cut them out and trim them carefully to make sure they are all the same size.

4

5 Take the balloon outside for your first flight. Blow up the balloon with hot air from a hair dryer and watch it lift off.

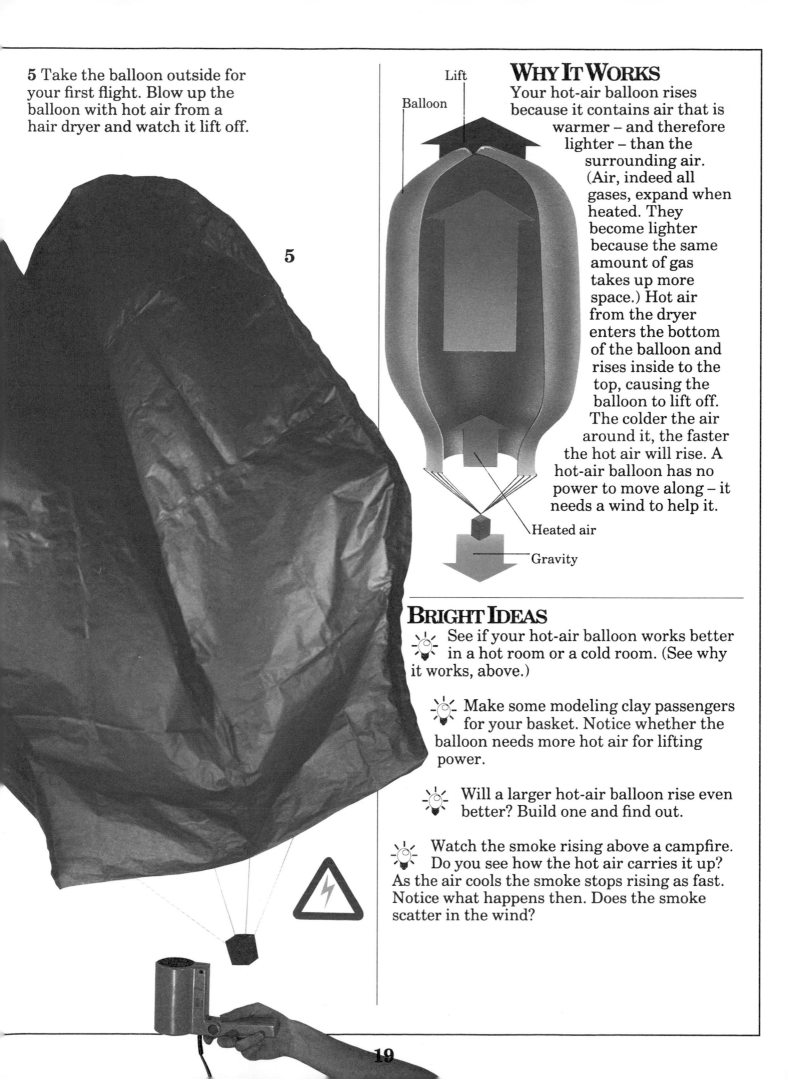

5

Lift

Balloon

Heated air

Gravity

WHY IT WORKS

Your hot-air balloon rises because it contains air that is warmer – and therefore lighter – than the surrounding air. (Air, indeed all gases, expand when heated. They become lighter because the same amount of gas takes up more space.) Hot air from the dryer enters the bottom of the balloon and rises inside to the top, causing the balloon to lift off. The colder the air around it, the faster the hot air will rise. A hot-air balloon has no power to move along – it needs a wind to help it.

BRIGHT IDEAS

See if your hot-air balloon works better in a hot room or a cold room. (See why it works, above.)

Make some modeling clay passengers for your basket. Notice whether the balloon needs more hot air for lifting power.

Will a larger hot-air balloon rise even better? Build one and find out.

Watch the smoke rising above a campfire. Do you see how the hot air carries it up? As the air cools the smoke stops rising as fast. Notice what happens then. Does the smoke scatter in the wind?

Capturing Wind

More than four thousand years ago people were already capturing the wind in sails to move boats through the water. These boats had "square rigged" sails which caught the wind, and oars for rowing when the wind blew the wrong way or when there was no wind at all. About 1,500 years ago, sailors discovered that with a special triangular sail called a "lateen" they could actually sail against the wind. Modern sailboats have tough, nylon sails designed to catch the wind from any angle. A windsurfer's single sail swivels around the board to take the craft in any direction. By trying it out on a simple boat, we can see how a lateen sail works.

5 Fill the bathtub with enough water to float your boat. Place your sailboat in the tub. Use your mouth or a hair dryer at some distance from your boat to blow on the sail, and watch your craft sail away. Both the keel and the rudder keep the boat moving in a straight line.

5

SAIL POWER

1. To make a sailboat, first cut a rectangular hole in the side of a plastic bottle.

2. Secure a blob of modeling clay inside the bottle boat. Use it to hold your straw mast in place.

3. Cut a triangle from a piece of paper and decorate it if you wish. Pierce two holes through your sail. Feed the mast through the holes.

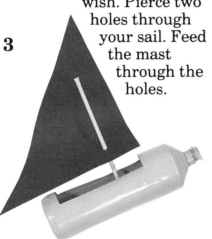

4. Cut a wedge shape from a juice carton for your water-proof keel. Put a chunk of clay on each end and attach it to the boat.

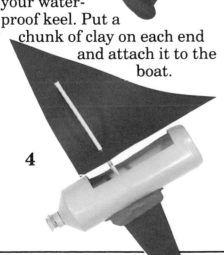

WHY IT WORKS

No matter which way you blow on it, your sailboat can be made to go in any direction. When the wind is directly behind the boat, holding the sail at right angles to the wind channels your boat forward. You can move at right angles, or "across" the wind by again fixing the sail at right angles to the breeze. The boat pictured here is sailing across the wind.

For a "square rigged" boat, the sail is caught in the currents of moving air and pushed along – a bit like you blowing a Ping Pong ball across a table. For a triangular sail the effect is different. The wind blows over the top of the sail and causes low pressure which sucks the sail, and the boat, forward.

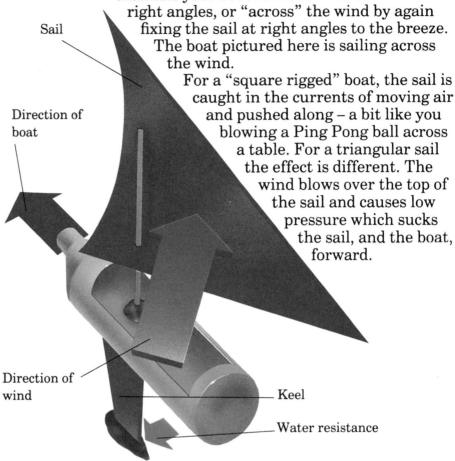

Sail

Direction of boat

Direction of wind

Keel

Water resistance

BRIGHT IDEAS

☀ Which shape do you think is the best for a sail? Experiment with squares, rectangles, circles, and triangles. Once you've found the best shape, try it out in different sizes. Find out if a smaller sail or a larger sail is the best one.

☀ Try blowing on your boat from different directions. Watch how the boat moves every time. Now, keeping the "wind" blowing from one direction, see what happens when the sail is fixed as pictured in the two ways below.

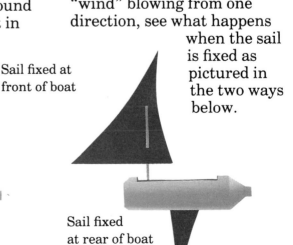

Sail fixed at front of boat

Sail fixed at rear of boat

PRESSURE CHANGES

Even though the rush of wind blows things about, moving air has lower pressure than still air. This is because air molecules have a set amount of energy. When air flows slowly, it has energy left to create sizeable pressure. But when air moves quickly, this motion takes up a lot of energy. Therefore, less energy goes into making pressure and the air pressure drops. Because of this, when air moves between things, the air pressure between them is low and the higher surrounding pressure will push them together. Even the tops of tall buildings bow together a little bit on a windy day. This can be illustrated in the project below using simple materials to simulate skyscrapers on a windy day.

BLOWING BALLS

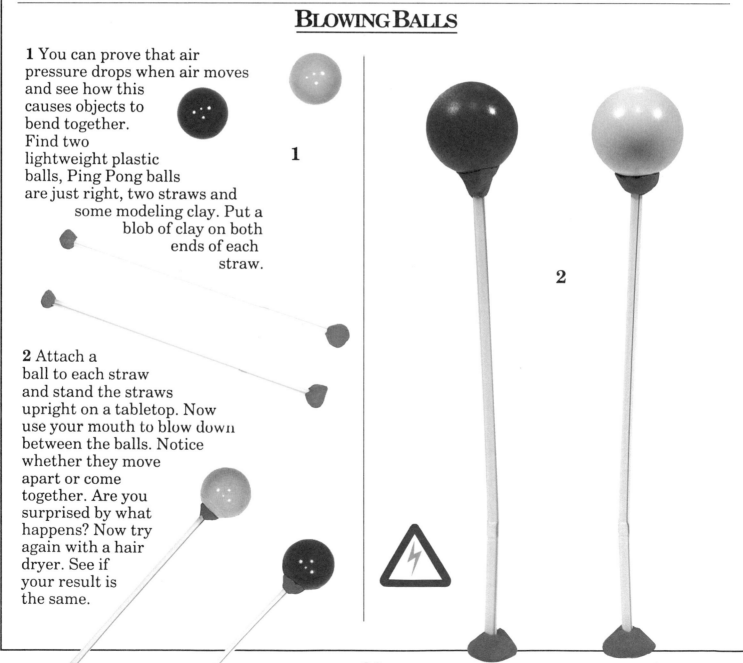

1 You can prove that air pressure drops when air moves and see how this causes objects to bend together. Find two lightweight plastic balls, Ping Pong balls are just right, two straws and some modeling clay. Put a blob of clay on both ends of each straw.

2 Attach a ball to each straw and stand the straws upright on a tabletop. Now use your mouth to blow down between the balls. Notice whether they move apart or come together. Are you surprised by what happens? Now try again with a hair dryer. See if your result is the same.

1

2

22

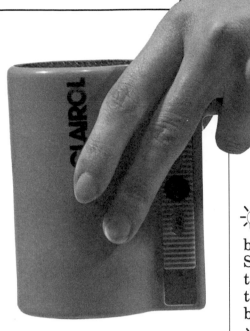

BRIGHT IDEAS

Try blowing the air onto the standing Ping Pong balls from different directions. See if the balls are still drawn together when the air hits them from the side or from below.

Hold two strips of paper about 2 inches apart and blow between them. See how the fast moving air pulls the strips inward.

Hold a strip of paper loosely in front of your mouth and blow over the top. Does the paper rise?

Cut two small flaps in the end of the strip. Bend one flap down. Blow over the paper again. Notice how the flaps change the paper's motion. Rest a piece of paper over a gap between two books. Blow underneath the paper and watch where it goes.

Place a small cardboard disk on a table and see if you can lift it simply by blowing over the top.

WHY IT WORKS

When you direct fast moving air between the balls they come together. This is known as the "Bernoulli effect," named after the Swiss mathematician David Bernoulli. More than 250 years ago, he discovered that when water is forced through a constriction in a pipe, its speed increases, but its pressure drops.

Fast moving air has low pressure, too. As you squeeze fast moving air past the two balls it makes a low pressure pocket between them. The "high pressure" air on either side of the balls pushes them into this pocket, thrusting them together.

High pressure

Fast moving air

Balls move together

Low pressure pocket

Air Cushion

Imagine you are riding your bicycle on a level road and you stop pedaling. What happens? Eventually you slow down and stop. This is because the tires rub against the road, causing friction. The force of friction is strong enough to make the tires stop turning. On a very rough road you would stop more quickly because rough surfaces cause more friction than smooth ones. Air can be used as a cushion to cut down on friction, allowing vehicles to ride almost effortlessly. For example, a hovercraft floats smoothly on air without dragging on the surface of the water or rubbing on the ground as it moves along.

Speedy Hovercraft

1 With this simple model you can see a hovercraft in action. Find a clean plastic container. (A margarine tub is ideal. Heavier sandwich boxes do not work as well.) Ask for help cutting a hole in the middle of the base. Decorate the hovercraft if you wish.

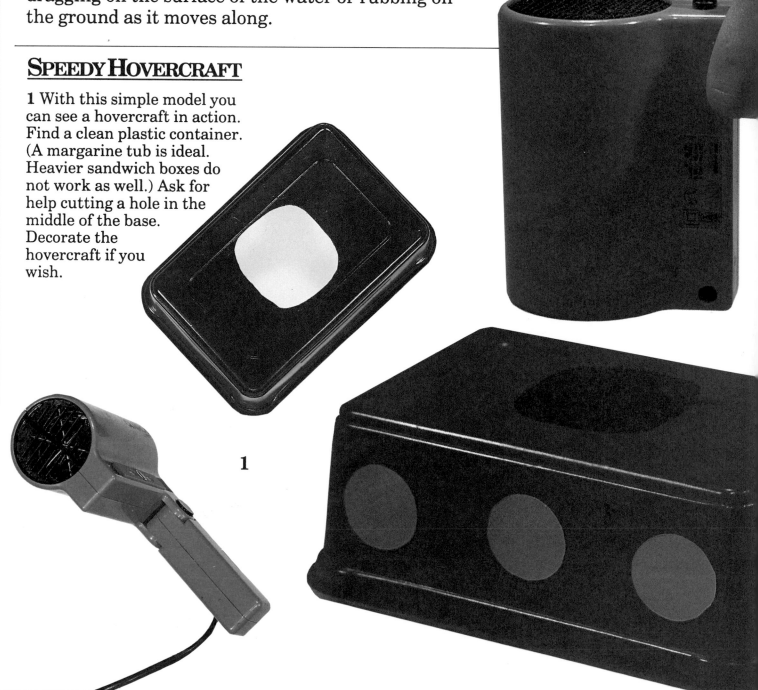

1

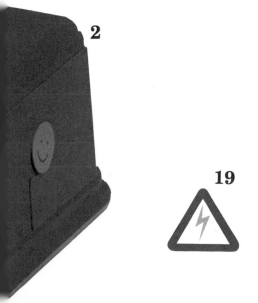

BRIGHT IDEAS

Let's investigate air cushions. Rub your hand very quickly back and forth on a table. Your hand will get hot. This heat is caused by the force of friction. Rub your finger on a dry part of the sink. Does it move easily? Now rub soap on your finger and try again. You will feel the soap acting as a lubricant and reducing friction. Air, too, acts as a lubricant. The smaller the amount of air separating the hovercraft from the surface beneath it, and the slower the air moves, the more friction on your craft. Watch what happens when you use coins to weigh down each corner. Try blowing on your hovercraft now. Does it work as well? When the weight of a vehicle increases the friction increases, too, making it go more slowly.

Coins

Hovercraft

2 Put your hovercraft on a smooth surface with the hole at the top. Blow into the hole with a hair dryer and watch how it floats on a cushion of air. Tap it and see how easy it is to start moving. Now turn the dryer off and tap it again. Does it move as easily?

WHY IT WORKS

The force from the jet of the dryer pushes under the rim of your hovercraft, causing it to rise ever so slightly. Held by a cushion of air, the hovercraft does not push down heavily on the floor or tabletop and can glide freely. Friction, which slows things down, cannot halt the movement of a hovercraft. The air cushion creates a "frictionless surface" beneath the craft, allowing it to move about freely.

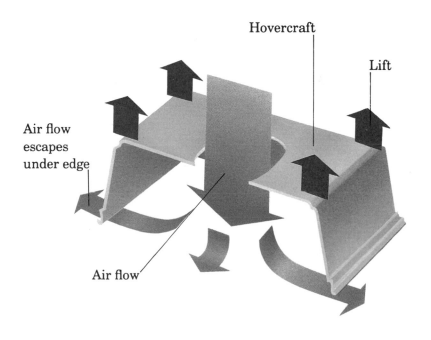

Hovercraft

Lift

Air flow escapes under edge

Air flow

2

19

AIR RESISTANCE

If you open an umbrella and try to run with it on a calm day, you will find it difficult as the umbrella captures the air like a parachute, dragging you back. Whenever we move we have to push the air out of the way and we experience air resistance. Sometimes air resistance is helpful, for example in slowing down a parachute. It becomes a nuisance when it acts against a sports car. Some shapes are "streamlined" to move smoothly through the air. They experience less air resistance because the air does not rub against them too much and block their movement.

STREAMLINED SHAPES

1 You can test the force of air resistance. To make a fair test you need two of the same model cars. Make sure their wheels turn freely.

2 Cut two rectangles from a piece of cardboard. Again, to keep the test fair, make them the same size and shape.

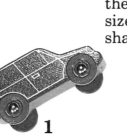

3 Attach the rectangular cardboard to the front end of each car. Fold one smoothly over the top and bend the other one as shown. Tape them in place.

WHY IT WORKS

The shape of your cars makes them roll quickly or slowly. Air flows smoothly over the car with the rounded paper front. This streamlining allows it to roll faster than the car with the square front, which is held back by air resistance, or drag. Drag slows things down, creating ripples of air behind them. These moving ripples, or eddies, lower the air pressure behind the unstreamlined car, keeping it back as it moves.

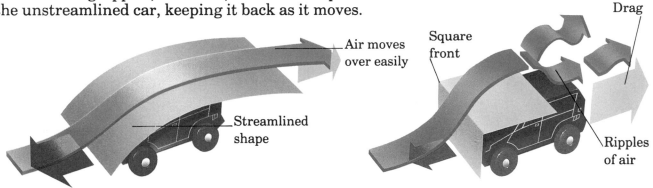

Air moves over easily

Streamlined shape

Square front

Drag

Ripples of air

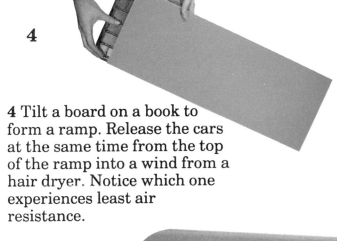

4 Tilt a board on a book to form a ramp. Release the cars at the same time from the top of the ramp into a wind from a hair dryer. Notice which one experiences least air resistance.

BRIGHT IDEAS

Capture air with a simple parachute. Tie four strings to the corners of a large handkerchief. Fix a blob of modeling clay to the strings. Now make a larger parachute from paper, attaching the same piece of clay. It will drop more slowly than the first one because it captures more air.

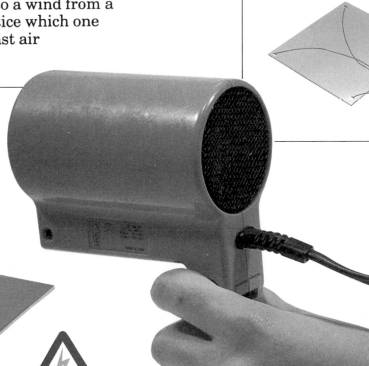

WINGS IN FLIGHT

Birds, insects, bats, and airplanes all need wings to fly. When the Wright brothers made the first powered flight in 1903, it was after years of studying nature's wings. Whether wings are made of something as light as feather or as rigid as metal, it is their shape that gives them lift. This special wing shape is known as an airfoil. Flat on the bottom and curved on top, the airfoil cuts through the air, creating low pressure above which helps the airfoil to rise. You can demonstrate this in the project below.

AIRFOIL

1 To make your own flying wing you need a piece of oak tag measuring about 4in by 6in. Fold the oak tag in two, leaving an overlap of about ½in.

1

2 Push the overlapping ends together. This will make one side of the folded paper curve up. Tape it in place.

2

3

3 Use a pen to pierce holes through the wing (top and bottom) as shown.

4

4 Carefully push a drinking straw through each set of holes.

BRIGHT IDEAS

 Turn your airfoil upside down and test it again. Notice what happens now. Move the hair dryer back from your airfoil. Does it stay up? See how far back you can move the hair dryer before the airfoil drops down.

Make another airfoil double the size. It creates lower pressure above. Try to move the hair dryer even further away.

Larger airfoil

First airfoil

WHY IT WORKS

Your airfoil rises because of its shape. The top surface of the wing is longer than the bottom surface. Air passing over the top of the wing has farther to travel – so it has to go faster. Faster moving air has lower pressure. (Remember the Bernoulli effect!) Low pressure above the wing causes it to lift.

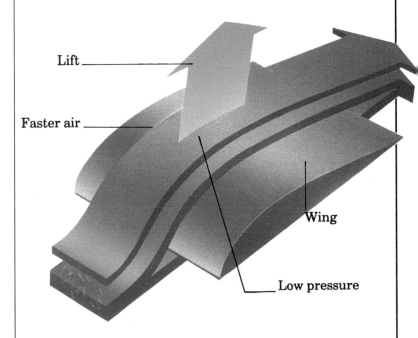

Lift

Faster air

Wing

Low pressure

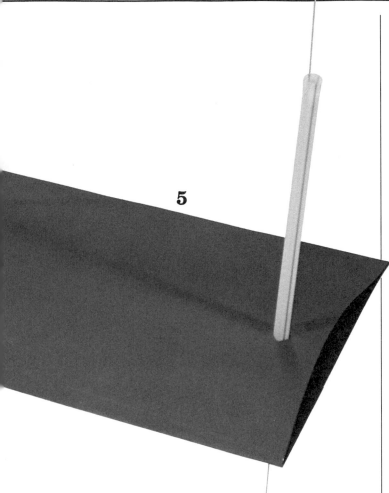

5

5 Pull a long piece of thread through each straw. Pull these tracks tight and fix them straight between a floor and table, so the wing can slide up and down freely. Lift the wing up a little and aim a hair dryer at the folded edge. Turn the dryer on, and watch your wing soar. Make sure you are pointing the dryer straight for the best lift.

AIRSTREAM EVIDENCE

Some things are shaped to move through the air very smoothly, such as rockets, airplanes, and racing cars. Can you think of any more?

Designers use a wind tunnel to test streamlined shapes. Streams of smoke are blown over new models to show how air currents move around them. The flow of smoke tells designers how much air resistance their vehicles will have to face. The straighter the flow of smoke – the less it curls when it hits a surface – the more streamlined the shape is and the better it will move through the air.

Fast moving shapes are also slowed down by drag. The faster a car or an aircraft moves, the more that drag holds it back. A low drag shape in a wind tunnel will have straight smoke streams behind it.

You can use a hair dryer and ribbon instead of smoke to study how streamlined different shapes are.

WIND TUNNEL

1 Make a backdrop for watching airstreams.

2 Cut slits in the side of a cereal box for the backdrop. Push two cardboard triangles through the slits.

1

2

3

3 Carefully make holes through the center of the box and push two thin sticks through them. (These sticks will support shapes for testing, such as your airfoil and a ball.)

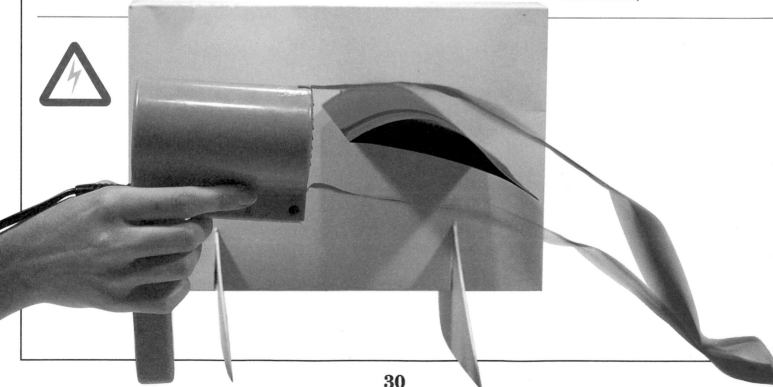

WHY IT WORKS

Your airfoil does not disrupt the lines of smoke – or the ribbons – as they pass over its surface. Instead, the smoke streams continue in almost the same lines as before they struck the wing. This means that the wing can move freely through the air. Air does not rub against it too much, slowing it down by air resistance. (Like water in a swimming pool that seems to push us back if we walk through it, air resistance is a powerful force.)

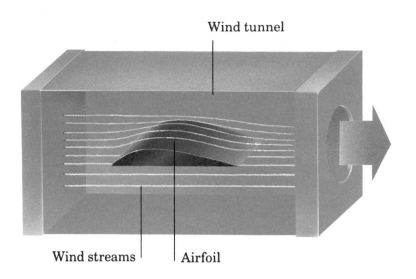

Wind tunnel

Wind streams Airfoil

4 Tape two thin ribbons onto a hair dryer. With the dryer set on "cool," watch how the ribbons blow over your shapes to see the airstreams around them.

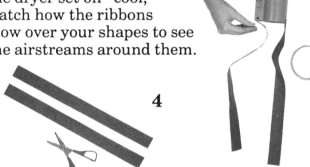

4

BRIGHT IDEAS

See how streams of air move around two different cars. Attach paper fronts to toy cars as shown below. Stand each above a tabletop on a stick of modeling clay. Test each for streamlining.

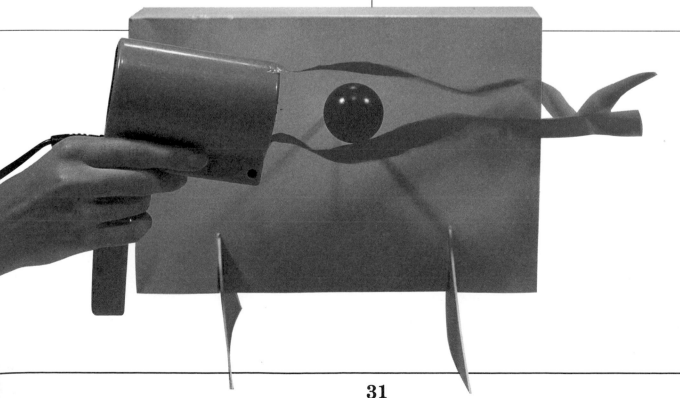

GLIDER FLIGHT

Have you seen a buzzard, a gull, or a kestrel in flight? At times some birds seem to hang in the air without having to flap their wings. Gliders copy these birds, floating on currents of rising air called thermals. Like kites, gliders fly without engine power. However, unlike hot-air balloons, gliders don't just follow the wind. A glider pilot can control the craft by using flaps on the tail and on the wings. The first glider to carry a person was built by an Englishman called Sir George Cayley, in 1853. A state-of-the-art glider, the Space Shuttle gets its lift from the airflow around it. You can make your own simple glider in the project below.

AIRCRAFT DESIGN

1 Study the photographs before you begin. The yellow strips show the flaps and the rudder. The white strips are for double-sided sticky tape.

1

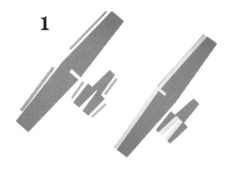

2 Make the wings and tail from light, strong, thin oak tag. Cut out the two blue shapes and the five yellow flaps. Your glider can be whatever size you want.

2

3 Tape on the yellow flaps. Feed a drinking straw through the wings to make an airfoil shape. Use a knitting needle for the body of the glider. Split a 2in piece of straw at one end, and tape it around the tail and onto the knitting needle.

3

BRIGHT IDEAS

💡 Make your glider "roll." The wings give the glider stability – by moving the wing flaps you can shift its balance.

💡 You can make your glider climb and dive by moving the flaps on the tail planes.

💡 A pilot controls the "yaw" with the rudder on the tail. For a yaw to port (a turn to the left), set the rudder as in the picture below. Now try a yaw to starboard (a turn to the right) with your own rudder set as in the picture below.

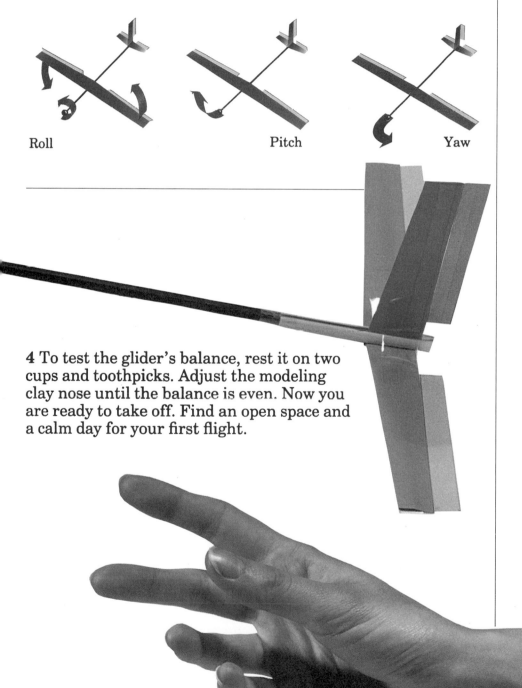

Roll   Pitch   Yaw

4 To test the glider's balance, rest it on two cups and toothpicks. Adjust the modeling clay nose until the balance is even. Now you are ready to take off. Find an open space and a calm day for your first flight.

WHY IT WORKS

Wings and tail flaps help to steer your aircraft. Depending on how these flaps are set (see Bright Ideas), your craft rolls, turns, climbs, or dives as pictured below. This is because the forward motion of the plane is redirected by the force of air hitting the tilted flaps.

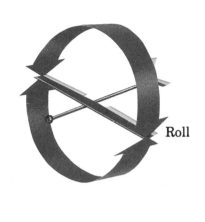

Roll

Yaw

Pitch

PROPELLERS AND FANS

Have you ever heard a news report about a hurricane? The power of the wind can be very dangerous, destroying buildings and ripping up trees. If we catch the wind, it can be very helpful, too. Once, windmills used the wind's energy to drive grinding and threshing machinery. Today, smaller, modern windmills make electricity or pump water. The blades of a windmill use the same principle as airplanes, where the special shape of the wing makes them move smoothly in the air. Like sails on a boat, the blades can also turn to catch the wind from every direction.

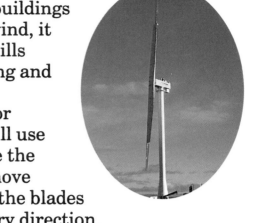

WORKING WINDMILL

1 To put the power of the wind to work, begin by making holes in a juice carton as shown. Push two straws through the holes, with the bottom straw angling upward.

2 Make the blades for the propeller by following steps 1 to 3 of the whirligig project on page 30. You will need two pieces of 6in by 5in oak tag. Make the "tail" from the inside of a ballpoint pen.

3 Your windmill is going to turn a cam that will push a hammer up. The hammer will strike a table. Make these pieces from stiff cardboard as shown above.

5 To put your simple machine together push the propeller pen through the top straw. The cam wire feeds into this straw from the back.

4 Tape the L-shaped wire to the yellow cam. Pierce a small hole in the center of the hammer, push the other wire through, and tape it down. Now fold up the "head" of the hammer.

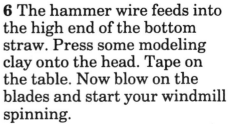

6 The hammer wire feeds into the high end of the bottom straw. Press some modeling clay onto the head. Tape on the table. Now blow on the blades and start your windmill spinning.

BRIGHT IDEAS

💡 Blow on your windmill at different angles as shown here. See which direction makes the blades turn the most quickly and smoothly.

💡 To make a simple paper windmill, you need a square piece of oak tag. Decorate both sides. Cut diagonally from each corner, stopping one-third of the way from the center. Fold down every other point and secure them in the center with a pin. Push the pin through a bead before attaching it to a stick.

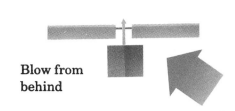

Blow from behind

Blow from front

Blow on side

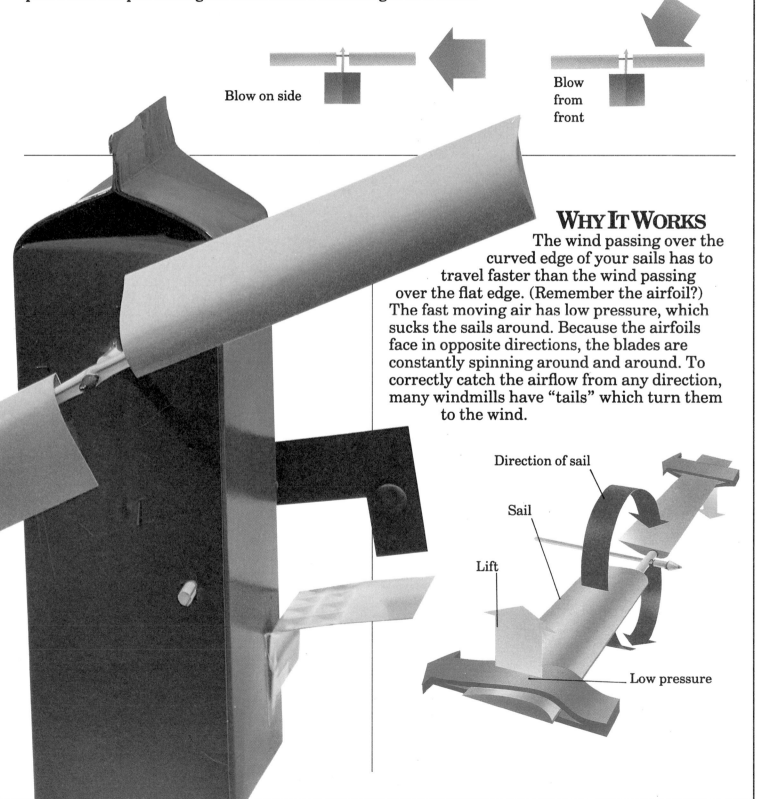

WHY IT WORKS

The wind passing over the curved edge of your sails has to travel faster than the wind passing over the flat edge. (Remember the airfoil?) The fast moving air has low pressure, which sucks the sails around. Because the airfoils face in opposite directions, the blades are constantly spinning around and around. To correctly catch the airflow from any direction, many windmills have "tails" which turn them to the wind.

Direction of sail

Sail

Lift

Low pressure

HELICOPTER ACTION

As any object falls through the air, the air pushes against it. Many trees have winged seeds that use this push to make them spin. The wings are shaped like airfoils, so as they spin they stir up low pressure above them. Higher pressure from the blanket of air below slows their fall as they drift away from the "parent tree." Helicopters also get lift from twirling airfoils. Their rotor blades spin so hard that the low pressure creates enough lift to carry them into the air.

WHIRLIGIG

1 Make two small airfoils from two pieces of oak tag, 4in by 3in. Fold each piece with an overlap.

1

3

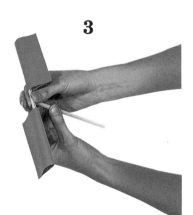

2 Push the overlapping edges together and tape them together. One side will curve up like a wing.

3 Spread a little glue onto each end of a stiff straw or thin stick. With the curved side of the wings pointing up, glue them onto the straw so that they face in different directions.

2

4

4 Tape another straw to the one holding the wings. Use a piece of modeling clay to weigh down the end. This keeps the whirligig level.

5 To send the whirligig spinning, hold it between the palms of your hands. Brush your hands together, pulling one toward you and pushing the other away. As your hands come apart, the whirligig is released, twirling as it flies.

5

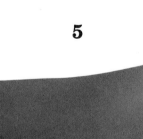

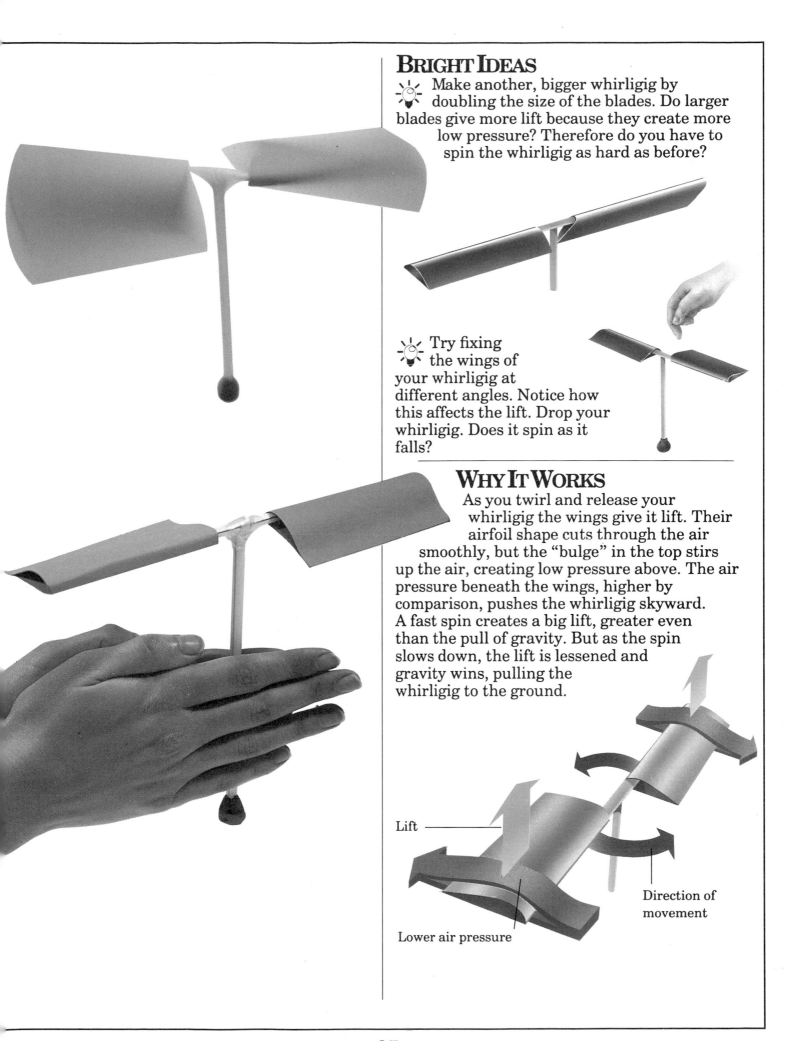

BRIGHT IDEAS

Make another, bigger whirligig by doubling the size of the blades. Do larger blades give more lift because they create more low pressure? Therefore do you have to spin the whirligig as hard as before?

Try fixing the wings of your whirligig at different angles. Notice how this affects the lift. Drop your whirligig. Does it spin as it falls?

WHY IT WORKS

As you twirl and release your whirligig the wings give it lift. Their airfoil shape cuts through the air smoothly, but the "bulge" in the top stirs up the air, creating low pressure above. The air pressure beneath the wings, higher by comparison, pushes the whirligig skyward. A fast spin creates a big lift, greater even than the pull of gravity. But as the spin slows down, the lift is lessened and gravity wins, pulling the whirligig to the ground.

Lift

Lower air pressure

Direction of movement

WATER'S CYCLE

Whether falling from a storm cloud or spurting from a kitchen sink, water moves in an endless cycle between Earth and sky. Year after year, the sun performs a fantastic feat, its energy evaporating 95,000 cubic miles of water from oceans, rivers, lakes, and streams. Rain and snow deliver this water back to Earth. The water cycle is this chain of evaporation and condensation, where water turns to vapor and back to liquid again. Heat accelerates evaporation; cooling leads to condensation. You can illustrate this cycle using hot water and ice.

CLOUDBURST

1 Clean a plastic soda bottle and remove the label. With scissors, carefully cut off the neck and make a wide opening down one side. The opening must be big enough for ice cubes. (Put these in last.)

6

2 From an empty cereal box cut out the forested mountain slope shown here. Make the front tree section lower than the rear sky section. Paint the scene to look like a real mountainside.

2

6 Place an aluminum foil dish inside the bottom of the cereal box as shown. Fill the dish with hot water from a kettle. Be careful!

5 Place another sturdy box behind your mountainscape. (It should be the same height.) Tape the wire "handles" to the top of the box.

3 Make sure that the bottle fits inside the box as shown. It will be your cloud.

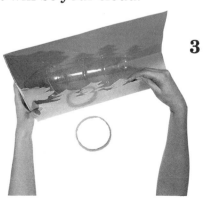

3

5

4

4 Ask a grown-up to cut a wire coat hanger into two lengths. Curve each piece of wire to fit around the plastic bottle. These metal loops will support the ice-filled bottle.

WHY IT WORKS

The sun's heat (1) fills molecules, or tiny particles, of surface water with energy, causing them to rise from the mass of water and escape into the air as water vapor (2). Trapped in the cool air, they condense around dust particles as droplets of water. These droplets join as the air cools, forming clouds (3). When the drops become too big and heavy to stay in the air, rain falls (4). The rainwater runs off the land back into the sea in rivers and streams (5).

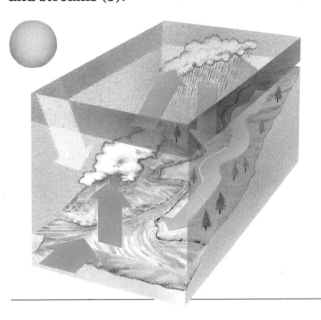

BRIGHT IDEAS

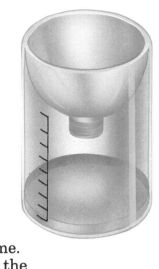

☀ Measure rainfall with a rain gauge. Carefully cut the top off a dishwashing liquid bottle and set it upside down inside the bottom half like a funnel. Mark 1/8- or 1/16-inch divisions from the bottom of the container. Stand it outside in an exposed place. Keep a daily record - remember to empty the gauge every time.

☀ Take two bowls filled to the brim with water. Stand one in a sunny place, the other in the shade. Compare the water levels at the end of each day to measure evaporation.

7

7 As the water evaporates from the dish, water vapor will rise and cool. As it cools, it will condense on the plastic ice-filled bottle. Rain will fall!

FREEZING AND MELTING

Not only does water appear as liquid and vapor, but if cooled to freezing point, water turns into a solid. Unlike most substances which shrink when they turn from liquid to solid, water expands. Water is more dense than ice. This is demonstrated by pipes which burst through the expansion of freezing water. Icebergs also give a good clue to the freezing and melting of water. These huge islands of ice adrift in Polar seas have broken off into the sea from vast glaciers or rivers of ice. As ice is 10 percent less dense than water, the top of an iceberg is only one tenth of the total size of the iceberg. The project below shows how ice floats and how water behaves as it melts.

MELTING ICEBERG

1 Clean a plastic soda bottle and remove the label. With a sharp pair of scissors carefully cut off the top.

2 Fill a plastic bottle with cold water. Add a few drops of food coloring. Shake the bottle to mix the color well.

3 Pour this colored water into an ice-cube tray. Leave the tray in a freezer to freeze overnight.

4 Pour hot tap water into the large plastic bottle. Add a different coloring and stir.

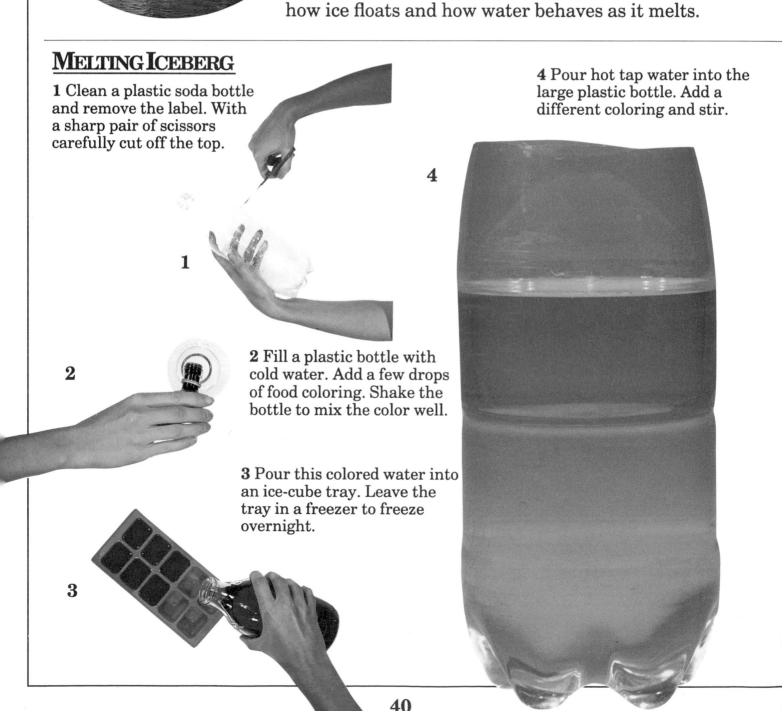

WHY IT WORKS

When the ice cube melts, the water sinks as it regains its original density. Also, cold water is denser, or heavier, than hot water and sinks below it. This also causes the cold water melting from the ice cube to sink first to the bottom of the bottle.

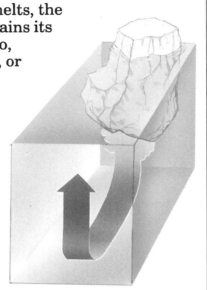

BRIGHT IDEAS

 Fill a small plastic bottle to the brim with water and place it uncovered in the freezer. Wait for the water to freeze. See which takes up more space, the same quantity of liquid water or the frozen water. Try to measure the difference.

Float an ice cube in a full glass of water. See if the glass overflows as the ice melts.

5 Drop a colored ice cube in the hot water. Since ice is less dense than water it will float.

6 Watch the water melting off the ice swirl and sink as it regains its liquid density.

SALTY SOLUTIONS

Most water on the earth's surface is salty from minerals washed out of rocks by pounding rain and rushing rivers. One such mineral is sodium chloride, or common salt. Salt water is buoyant, which means it can hold things up. It helps boats to float better than they would in fresh water. Israel's Dead Sea, pictured here, is too salty for fish, but is ideal for floating. Salt water is more buoyant because the molecules of salt and water are joined tightly together. You can see how these tightly-knit molecules hold things up better than loosely linked fresh water molecules by trying to float things in both salt and tap water.

FLOATING FISH

1

1 To make your fish, cut a 1/2-inch thick slice from a washed, medium-sized potato. Cut a triangular tail fin and a semi-circle from colored cellophane.

2

2 Get an adult to help you make a slit in the potato circle from the center toward the edge. Push the cellophane semicircle through to make balancing fins. Cut another slit along the potato peel for the tail.

3 To make salty water, drop at least 8 large spoonfuls of salt in a plastic bottle three-quarters full of cold water. (Note if there is a change in the water level.) Stir the solution with a straw until no more salt will dissolve.

3

4 Fill a second plastic bottle with the same amount of water as the salt solution. Pour in a few drops of food coloring. Shake it gently to mix the color well.

4

5 Pour the salt solution into a clear bottle from which the top has been cut. Slowly add the colored water by pouring it over the back of a spoon. Place your fish on the water's surface. It will sink no deeper than the surface of salt water.

WHY IT WORKS

Your fish floats in salt water yet sinks in fresh water. This is because the density of the fish is less than the density of the salt water, but more than the fresh water. When you poured salt crystals into the water, the water level did not go up. Instead the salt dissolved and the mixture filled the same space. Therefore, the density of the liquid increased.

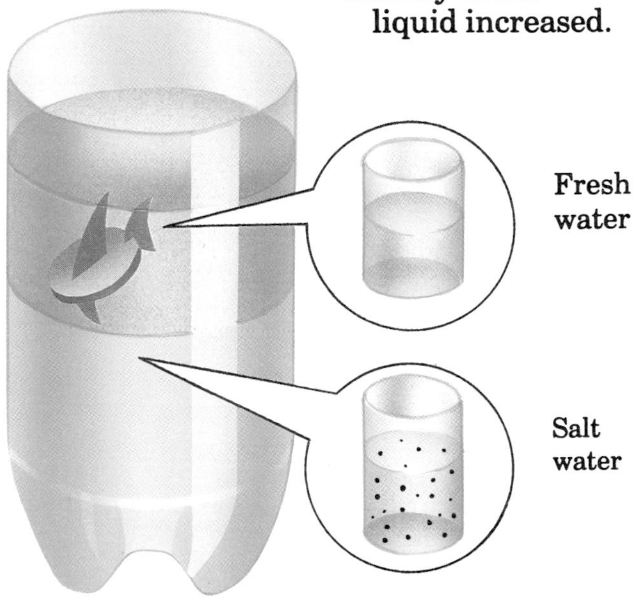

Fresh water

Salt water

BRIGHT IDEAS

You can get the salt back out of the water. Try boiling your solution dry in a saucepan. Be very careful! The salt remains behind. Carefully trap some of the vapor from the boiling solution with the back of a spoon. Watch it condense. The drops of water will be salt-free. Pour all the salt from a salt shaker into a full glass of water. The glass of water will not overflow.

FLOATING LIQUIDS

On a rainy day you will often see oil shimmering on a puddle of water. Like certain objects, liquids, too, can float on other liquids, forming layers as in a salad dressing bottle. Light liquids will float on heavier liquids. Salad oil floats on vinegar because the salad oil is less dense.

Mustard is often added to mix the two solutions as it acts as an emulsifier. Most oils float on water, too. Oil spills can blacken the surface of thousands of miles of water, devastating entire ocean regions and coastlines. One way to disperse a slick and make it mix with water, is to spray it with detergent. You can capture the effect of an oil spill with oil-based paints, water, and paper.

SLICK PICTURES

3 Using a clean stick, swirl the colors around. Do this gently on the water's surface. You can make lots of different patterns. When you have made a pattern that you really like, you are ready to capture it as a picture on white paper.

1

1 To make your oil slick pictures you will need some oil-based paints, thinned with turpentine. Choose bright colors to make exciting prints.

3

4 Lower one sheet of clean, strong paper on top of the paint. Make sure there are no air bubbles. Allow the paint to soak in for a few minutes. Carefully lift the paper off again. Place it on some newspaper to dry.

2

4

2 Fill a deep plastic bowl with cold water. Make sure the bowl is bigger than the sheets of paper you are using for your pictures. (You can add a few drops of vinegar to the water.) Drop small amounts of paint onto the surface of the water.

WHY IT WORKS

Your paints float on the surface because they are less dense than the water below. Liquids of different densities will form into layers in a container, the least dense sitting at the top. To mix the liquids, an emulsifier splits the top layer into tiny droplets that cascade into the layer below. Detergent is an emulsifier that allows oil and water to mix.

BRIGHT IDEAS

☀ Try pulling the blank paper through the surface paint and wiggling it as you do so. You will have a pattern on both sides of the paper.

☀ Squeeze a few drops of dishwashing liquid onto the surface of the paints. Notice how this changes your marbling pattern.

☀ Pour some oil gently onto the surface of cold water in a screw-top jar. Add dishwashing liquid and shake vigorously. Notice what has happened to the two layers in the jar.

☀ To measure the density of liquids, make an hydrometer with a plastic straw and some modeling clay. Adjust the ball of clay on the bottom of the straw until it will float upright in water. Make a mark on the straw at the surface of the water. Now float it in other liquids and observe the change in levels.

5

5 You can keep making pictures until all the paint is used up. The more pictures you make, the paler the colors will become. Experiment with new designs and colors by dropping more paint onto the surface.

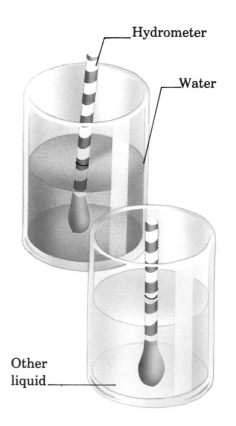

Hydrometer

Water

Other liquid

FLOAT OR SINK?

Enormous aircraft carriers and luxury cruise ships float, yet a single metal screw will sink! Clearly, when it comes to floating, size is not important. Nor necessarily is weight. Whether an object floats or sinks depends on its density and its shape. The Greek mathematician Archimedes noticed that the water level in the bath rose when he got in. He decided that for something to float, the upward push of the water must be the same as the weight of the water displaced, or pushed aside, by the object. Using different objects you can test the rules of floating and sinking.

CRAFTY VESSELS

1 Mold some modeling clay into a solid shape. Try a solid "boat." Drop it into a dish of cold water. Watch it sink to the bottom of the dish. Try other solid shapes, such as a ball.

2 Now use your hands or a rolling pin to roll the clay flat. Curve the edges up to make a boat. Be sure that there are no holes or it will leak!

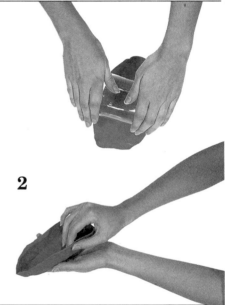

2

3 Half fill a shallow dish with cold water. Gently place your boat onto the surface of the water. It will float easily unless there is a leak. Check how low in the water your boat sits. Mark a water level line on the side of the boat. If you want the boat to carry a load safely, it must sit high in the water.

BRIGHT IDEAS

Can you make your boat even more seaworthy? Mold different shapes. A high-sided shape floats better than a shallow one. Make a long-shaped boat and a round-shaped one. See how many passengers your boat will carry. Try different loads. Mark a safe water level on your craft. This is called a plimsoll line after Samuel Plimsoll.

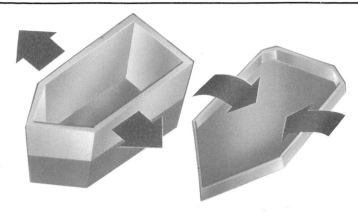

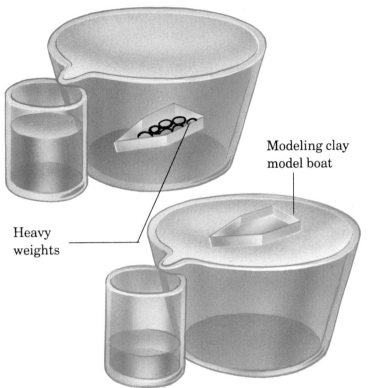

Modeling clay model boat

Heavy weights

WHY IT WORKS

When you dropped a solid piece of clay into the water, it sank. But when you hollowed out the same piece of clay, it floated. This is because by making a boat shape, you changed the density of the solid blob. Solid clay is more dense than water and therefore sinks. But the boat shape holds air which is less dense than water, causing the overall density of the boat to be less dense than the water, thus allowing it to float. An object's shape controls the amount of water it pushes out of the way. If the amount of water pushed aside, or displaced, weighs the same or more than the object, then the object will float. If the amount of water weighs less than the object, it will sink. You can test this by comparing the weights of floating and overloaded boats to the weights of the water they displace.

4

4 Now make a modeling clay passenger. Sit your passenger in the middle of the boat so that it doesn't tip over. (The one shown here is gripping the sides to stay balanced.) Put the boat back in the water and watch it float with the new load. The water level will change. See if it sits lower in the water than the empty boat.

CURVING WATER

A glass of water can be more than full without overflowing. The water seems to puff above the rim of the glass as if held by an invisible skin. Dew drops on a leaf appear to have this skin and so does water at the surface of a still pond. The water strider can glide at great speed over this taut film on the top of water. If you dip the bristles of a paintbrush in water they will spread out. When you lift it out again, they pull together. Each of these effects arise from surface tension, the force between molecules at the surface of all water. You can test its strength yourself.

WATER WALKERS

1 To make your water insects you will need some light-weight aluminum foil and some paper clips. Use sharp scissors to cut the foil into small pieces, one for each paper clip. Make a number of insects so that you can experiment. You can vary the size of your insects.

1

2 Place a paper clip in the middle of one half of each piece of foil. Fold over the other half of the foil so that the paper clip is enclosed. With your fingers, shape six legs on each insect. Look at the insects in the picture opposite.

2

3 Half fill a shallow dish with cold water. Very gently lower each insect onto the water's surface.

3

4. You can position all of your insects on the water at once. To do this you need a paper tissue. Place your insects on the tissue. Holding it firmly at each end, lower the tissue until it rests on the surface of the water.

4

WHY IT WORKS

Water molecules attract each other. Surface molecules have no water molecules attracting them from above so they pull together extra hard at the sides. The result is a force called surface tension - strong enough to support certain insects. Dishwashing liquid reduces this surface tension by breaking down the forces of attraction between the water molecules.

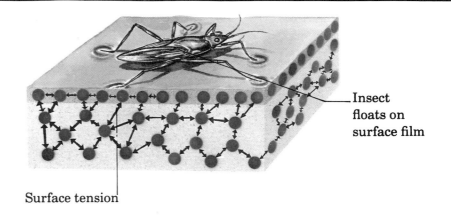

Insect floats on surface film

Surface tension

6 When the water is still, carefully drop some dishwashing liquid onto the surface, just behind each insect. Watch them dart about! To repeat, you need fresh water.

5 The tissue will soak up water and gradually sink to the bottom. But the insects will rest on the surface. Before making your insects dart over the water make sure the liquid is absolutely still.

6

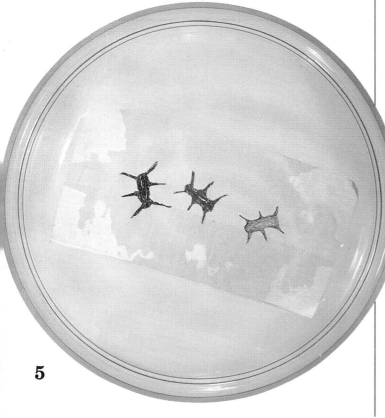

5

BRIGHT IDEAS

🔆 Float your insects together in the center of the bowl and carefully drop some dishwashing liquid on the water between them. Watch the skaters dart away.

🔆 Sprinkle talcum powder onto a shallow dish full of water. Touch the water in one spot with dishwashing liquid and see what happens.

Dishwashing liquid

RISING ACTION

An invisible force called gravity pulls everything towards the earth. However, there are times when water can flow against this force. Plants and trees contain tubes through which water is drawn upward, carried from the roots to the leaves and flowers. In the same way, flowers in a vase take up water through their stems. This process is called capillary action. You can make a closed paper flower unfurl its petals by using the force of capillary action.

PAPER PETALS

1 Take a square piece of smooth writing paper or thin cardboard and fold it in half lengthwise to make a shape twice as long as it is wide. Do not use shiny paper.

2, 3 Fold your rectangular shape in half so that it forms a square. Now fold your square diagonally to make a triangle.

4 Draw a petal shape on your triangle as shown in the picture. The straight edge is the thickest fold in the paper. Cut out your shape carefully with a pair of sharp scissors. Open it up and you will have a flower.

5 Roll up each petal with a pencil to make each curl tightly. Your flower is now closed up. Make two or three flowers. Experiment with different shapes and sizes.

6 Brighten up your flower by decorating it. This one has a red circle glued in the center.

1

2

3

4

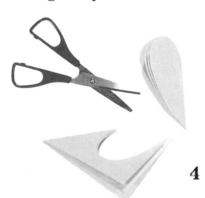

5

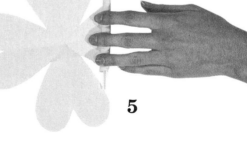

6

7 Fill a shallow bowl with clean, cold water. Gently place your flower on the surface.

7

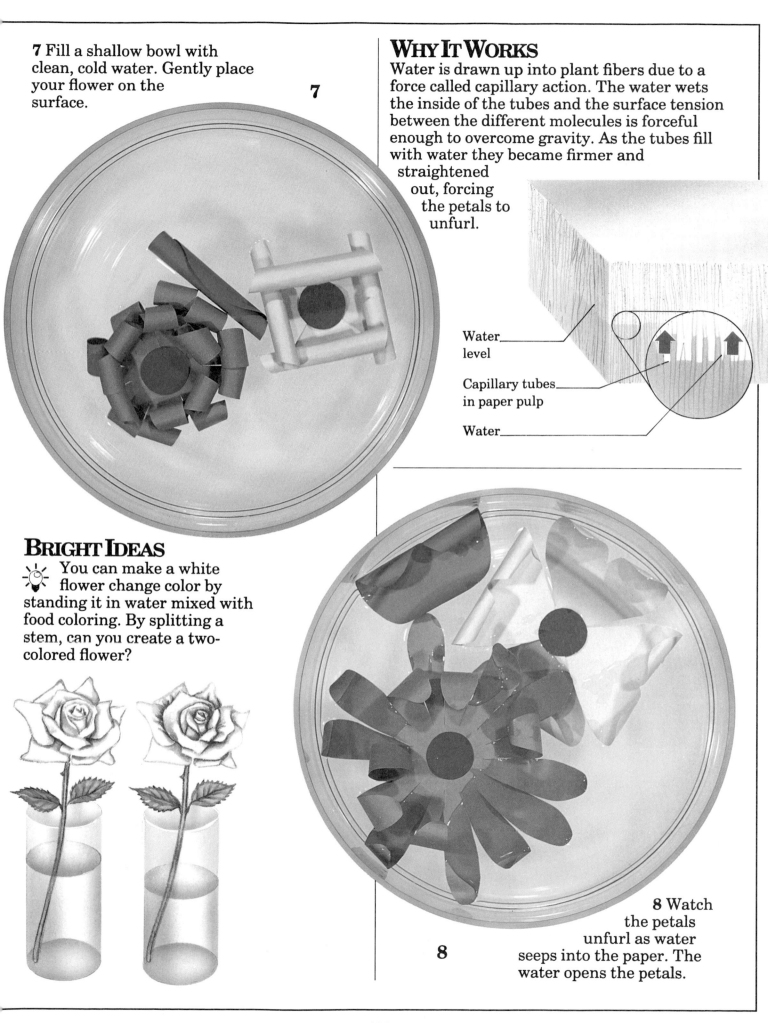

WHY IT WORKS

Water is drawn up into plant fibers due to a force called capillary action. The water wets the inside of the tubes and the surface tension between the different molecules is forceful enough to overcome gravity. As the tubes fill with water they became firmer and straightened out, forcing the petals to unfurl.

Water level

Capillary tubes in paper pulp

Water

BRIGHT IDEAS

You can make a white flower change color by standing it in water mixed with food coloring. By splitting a stem, can you create a two-colored flower?

8 Watch the petals unfurl as water seeps into the paper. The water opens the petals.

8

DIVING DEEP

Submarines were once the creation of science fiction. Today, underwater vessels map the ocean floor, repair oil rigs, and fire torpedoes. There is even a home for aquanauts beneath the sea! To dive and resurface, submarines have borrowed their design from nature. Some jellyfish, usually seen at the surface, can sink into the deep by deflating the air sac that aids their propulsion. In the same way, submarine tanks take in water to go down and replace it with air to rise up again. This kind of diving and resurfacing is possible because water is heavier than air, and water-filled objects will always sink. Try it yourself with a jellyfish that takes in water to dive and expels it to resurface.

PLUNGING JELLYFISH

1 To make the jellyfish, you will need a bendable plastic straw, a paper clip and some modeling clay. Bend the ribbed part of the straw and cut the long side to the same length as the short side.

1

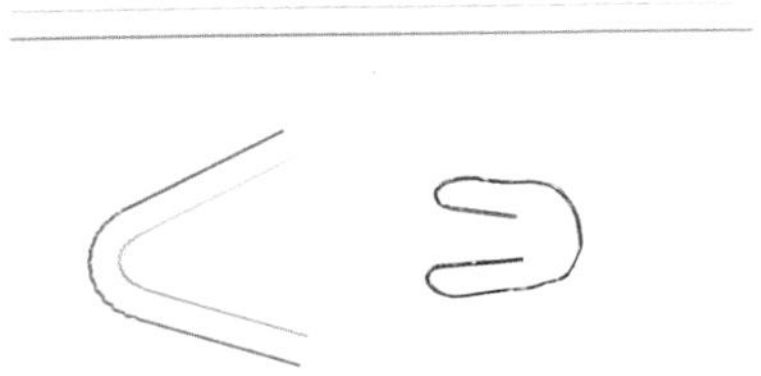

2 Bend a paper clip as shown here. Insert the bent paper clip into each end of the straw. Push the paper clip firmly inside, making sure that it will not slide out.

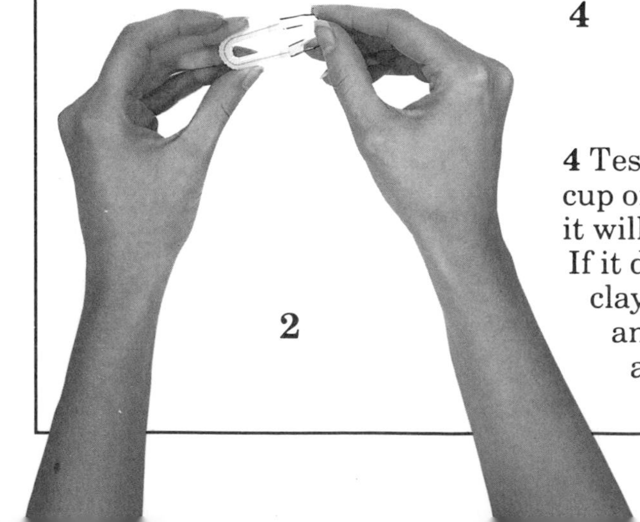

2

3 Roll out three thin strips of clay. Loop and pinch each one around the paper clip.

3

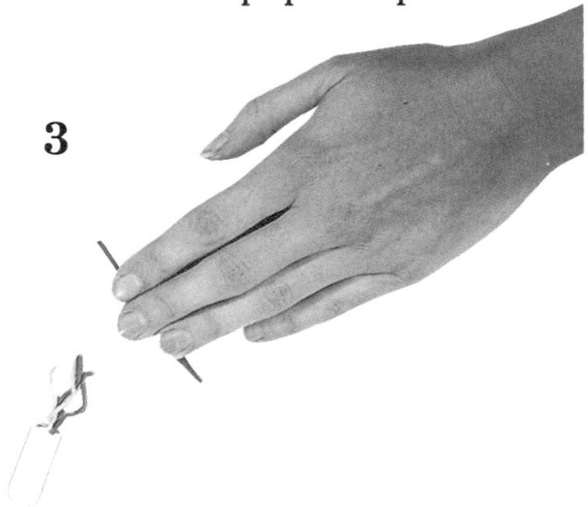

4

4 Test your jellyfish in a clear cup of water to make sure that it will float the right side up. If it doesn't, try adding more clay. This will give it weight and balance. Place it to sit as shown here.

5 Float your jellyfish in a large bottle full of water. Screw on the top.

5

WHY IT WORKS

When you squeeze the bottle, water is pushed into the plastic straw, compressing the air. Because water weighs more than air, the jellyfish gets heavier, causing it to sink.

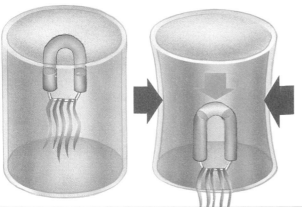

BRIGHT IDEAS

💡 Instead of using a screw-top bottle, try using a deep plastic container to house your jellyfish. Stretch plastic wrap over the top and secure with a rubber band. Apply some pressure to the cling film. Which works best?

💡 Make a deep-sea diver using an eye dropper partially filled with water.

💡 Try floating a plastic bottle filled with varying amounts of water. Try filling it half full or three-quarters full. See how easy it is to submerge with these different amounts of water.

6 Squeeze the sides of the plastic bottle hard. The jellyfish will sink to the bottom as water enters the straw, compressing the air inside it. This makes the jellyfish heavier.

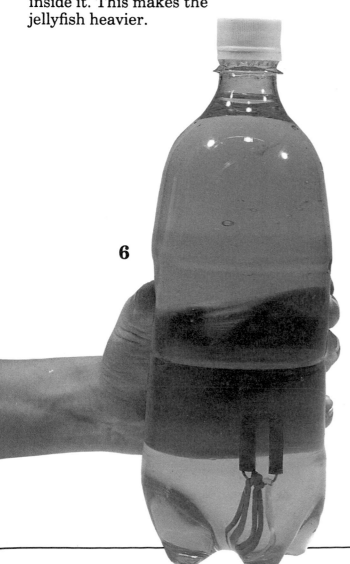

7 Releasing the pressure on the sides of the bottle allows the jellyfish to rise to the surface again. The compressed air inside the straw expands again, forcing the water back out. The jellyfish becomes lighter and therefore more buoyant.

HYDRAULIC MUSCLE

Water can be made to lift heavy things. Because water and other liquids cannot be squeezed, if they are thrust through pipes, they will carry a powerful force. In the 17th century, Blaise Pascal was the first person to discover the principles of hydraulics. Hydraulic lifts are machines that use the natural pushing power of liquids to raise loads. Most modern hydraulic lifts use oil instead of water. Excavating machines operate hydraulic rams. Cars have hydraulic brakes. In the 1930's, the fire services reached greater heights by introducing hydraulically operated turntable ladders. Today, disabled skiers make use of a hydraulic skibob with hydraulic suspension. You can make your own hydraulic lift simply by linking two water-filled containers.

LIQUID LIFT

1 Using sharp scissors, carefully cut the tops off two bottles. Make them the same height.

2 Pierce a hole in the side of each bottle about 2 inches from the bottom. Link the two bottles by inserting the plastic straw into the holes. Use the clay as a seal; there should be no leaks when the bottles are filled with water.

3 You need a balloon, a plastic cup, and some clay. Place the clay inside the cup.

4 Fill the bottles with cold water to the level shown in the picture, about three-quarters full. You can add food coloring to see the water levels more clearly. Place the weighted cup on the surface of the water in one of the containers. Experiment with different weights of clay. It must float. This will be your load.

WHY IT WORKS

Unlike air, liquids cannot be compressed, or squeezed; any pressure that is applied to them passes through the liquid in every direction without loss of strength. When you push down on one side of your water lift, the water has no place to go but up the other side. Pressure from the rising water raises the load.

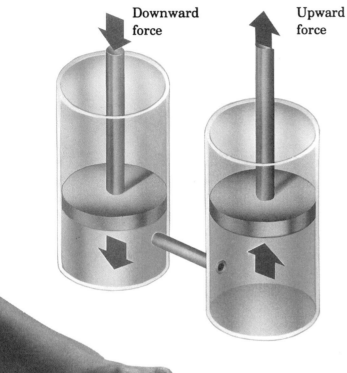

Downward force

Upward force

BRIGHT IDEAS

Increase the load to be lifted. Try several different weights. Test to see if they can be raised as high as each other. Push the balloon down to the same level every time!

Now make a different type of water lift. Replace one bottle with a taller, narrower bottle. See if a load in this new bottle can be raised higher. Notice what happens if you put the load in the other side.

Try making an oil lift. Pour the water out of both containers and replace it with cooking oil. Does this lift work as well or better than the water lift? Oil is messy stuff, so be sure to clean up thoroughly!

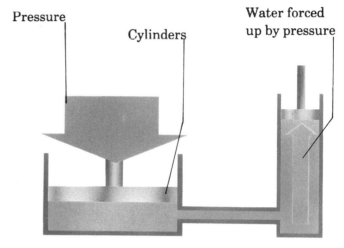

Pressure

Cylinders

Water forced up by pressure

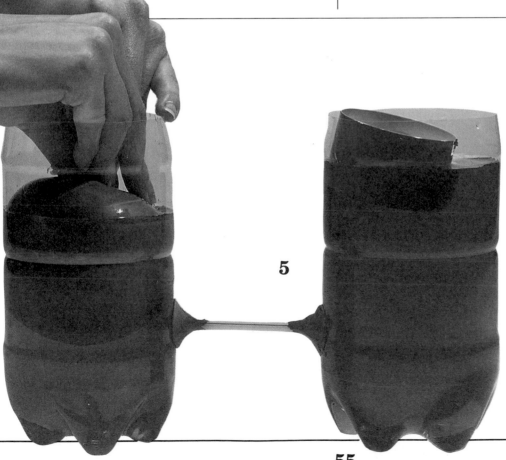

5

5 Position the inflated balloon on the surface of the water and gently push it down. As you push the water down on one side it rises up the other side, lifting the load. The balloon acts as a piston. To raise the load even higher, you need to put more pressure on the balloon. Note the water levels in both bottles. If the water under the balloon goes down by a certain amount, observe how far it goes up on the other side.

Soaring Fountains

Water naturally flows downhill. The pull of gravity draws it down as low as possible. To spurt upward, like the fountain pictures here, water must be put under pressure. When hot rock from the earth's core superheats underground water, a hot, steamy fountain called a geyser bursts skyward. Old Faithful in Yellowstone National Park, rises 150 feet into the air every 70 minutes because of this pressure. A natural fountain will only rise as high as the water table that it feeds. Some natural fountains are fed by water from high lakes. You can make a fountain and also prove that water pressure increases with depth by building the two projects shown here.

Liquid Jets

1 You need a plastic soda bottle, two plastic straws, a plastic tray, and some modeling clay. Cut off the bottom of the bottle.

2 Seal the mouth closed with modeling clay. Poke a straw through it as shown. Fit another straw to the end of the first one.

4 Place the tray and bottle inside a shallow container. Half fill the bottle with water. The pressure of this reservoir will cause a fountain to spurt through the straw if there are no airlocks in the straw.

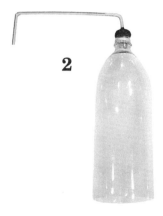

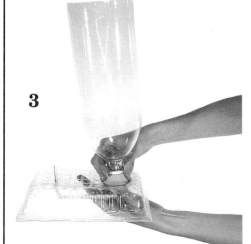

3 Pierce two holes in the plastic tray, one at each end of the base. Turn the bottle upside down and feed straws through the holes. Seal the bottle in position with clay. Also secure the free end of the straw to the tray in the same way.

BRIGHT IDEAS

Add more water to the reservoir. What do you notice about the height of the jet from your fountain?

You can prove that the pressure of water increases with depth. Cut the top off a plastic bottle and make holes at different levels along one side. Put the bottle in a deep-sided dish. With your fingers, cover the holes and have a friend pour water in the bottle. When the bottle is full release your fingers. See how water pressure from above forces longer jets of water through the lower holes.

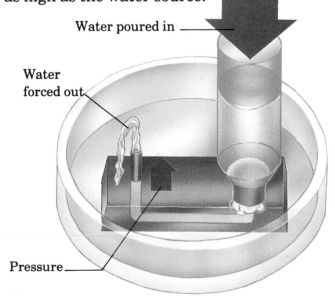

WHY IT WORKS

Pressure from the water in your fountain reservoir pushes the water through the straw, causing it to leap into the air. The deeper you fill the reservoir, the greater the water pressure becomes and the higher the water will shoot up, striving to get as high as the water source.

Water poured in

Water forced out

Pressure

WATER ENGINEERING

For thousands of years people have used water's pushing power to drive machines. Since Roman times wooden waterwheels have powered millstones to grind corn. Later, waterwheels became the main power source for industry. One of the largest machines in the world, the modern water turbine, was developed from the waterwheel. Water turbines are harnessed to generators to produce hydroelectric power. With all waterwheels, the flow of water is directed around wheel blades to start the wheel spinning. The constant movement from the revolving wheel can then be put to work. You can make a waterwheel go to work for you. This one raises a bucketful of water.

WATER ENGINEERING

1 Cut the bottom from a dishwashing liquid bottle to make a waterwheel. Cut out 4 evenly-spaced flaps around the sides of the bottle and fold them out as shown.

2

1

2 Make a hole in the base of the waterwheel and insert a straw. Secure it in place with clay. Cut a section from a soda bottle large enough for the waterwheel to sit inside. Pierce two holes on either side of the bottle for the straw to pass through.

3

3 Fit the waterwheel into the cutout section of the bottle, easing the straw through the holes. Poke toothpicks through the straw to secure it in place.

4 Make two holes through the top of the bottle and insert a pencil or chopstick. Tape a short piece of straw to the end of the pencil.

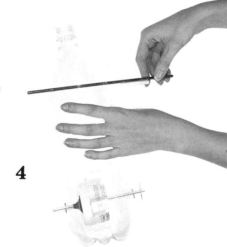

4

5 Make a bucket from a bottle cap. Glue a matchstick across the top. Tie it to thread.

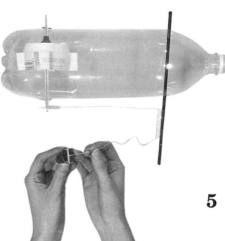

5

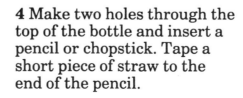

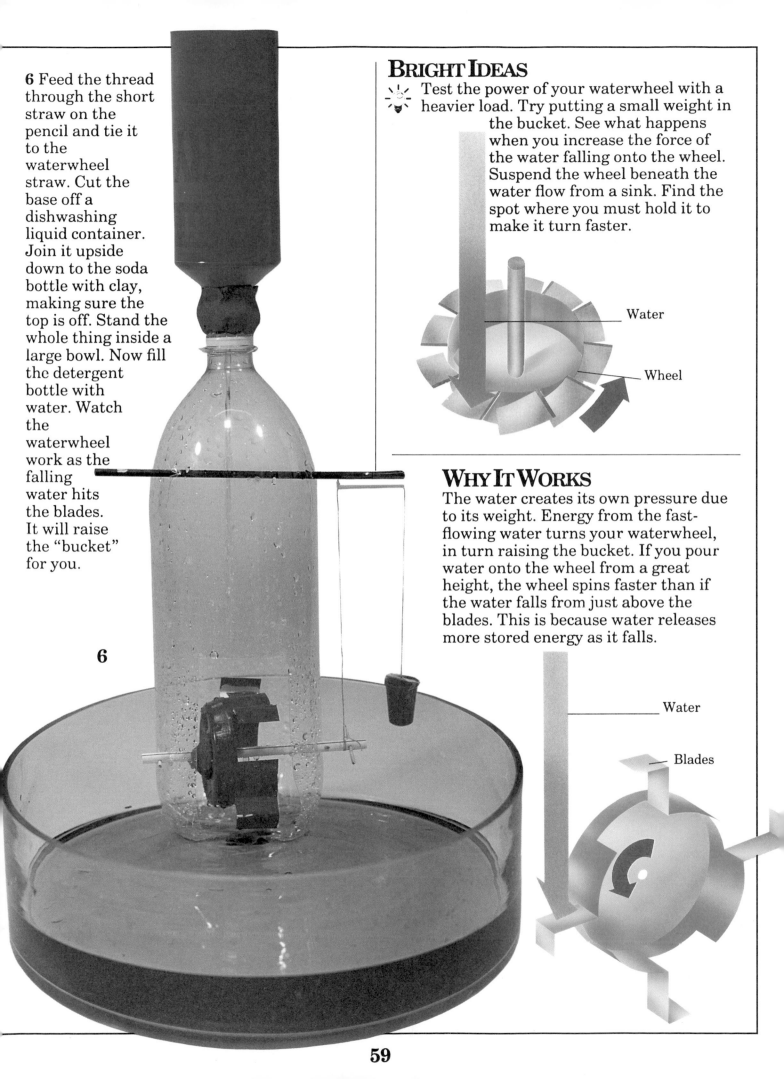

6 Feed the thread through the short straw on the pencil and tie it to the waterwheel straw. Cut the base off a dishwashing liquid container. Join it upside down to the soda bottle with clay, making sure the top is off. Stand the whole thing inside a large bowl. Now fill the detergent bottle with water. Watch the waterwheel work as the falling water hits the blades. It will raise the "bucket" for you.

6

BRIGHT IDEAS

Test the power of your waterwheel with a heavier load. Try putting a small weight in the bucket. See what happens when you increase the force of the water falling onto the wheel. Suspend the wheel beneath the water flow from a sink. Find the spot where you must hold it to make it turn faster.

Water

Wheel

WHY IT WORKS

The water creates its own pressure due to its weight. Energy from the fast-flowing water turns your waterwheel, in turn raising the bucket. If you pour water onto the wheel from a great height, the wheel spins faster than if the water falls from just above the blades. This is because water releases more stored energy as it falls.

Water

Blades

PADDLE POWER

The first paddles used for moving vessels in water were probably simple oars. By the early nineteenth century the first steam-powered ships were fitted with paddles. As the paddle circled around and around, it pushed back the water with its blades. This action propelled the vessel forward. It was Isaac Newton who first stated that for every action, such as the paddle pushing against the water, there is an equal and opposite reaction – the vessel being propelled forward. The British engineer Isambard Kingdom Brunel built the first iron ship to be driven by a screw propeller which, like the paddle, pushes the water backward and the ship forward. Today, paddle steamers, like the one pictured here, still carry tourists on the Mississippi River. You can make a model boat that is powered the same way.

SPEEDY BOATS

1 Take a small plastic bottle with a top and cut a hole in one side large enough for a cardboard tube. This cardboard tube will be the funnel of your paddle steamer.

2 Tape two sticks or pencils on either side of the bottle. They should stick out about 2 inches past the bottom of the bottle.

3 Cut two rectangles from a fruit juice carton. Make sure they are smaller than the base of the bottle.

4 Make a slit halfway down the middle of each. Slide them together to form a paddle.

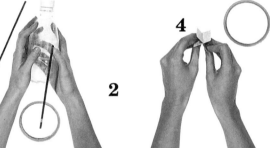

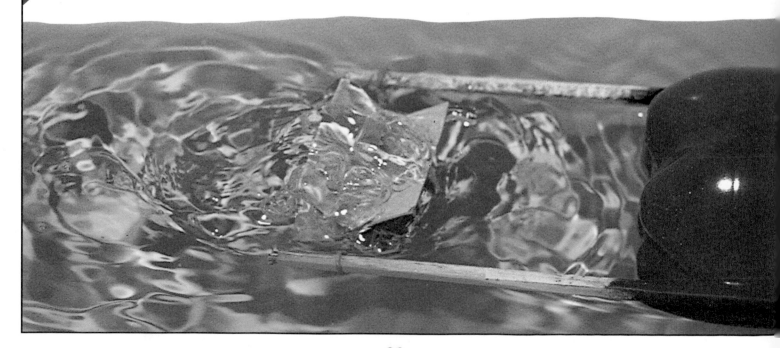

WHY IT WORKS

The paddleboat is driven by the potential, or hidden, energy stored in the rubber band. As the rubber band unwinds, the paddle turns, pushing the water backward and the boat forward. The potential energy has been changed into kinetic, or moving, energy.

BRIGHT IDEAS

☀ Find out how far the boat travels in relation to the number of turns that you give the paddle. You can make a graph to show the results. See if winding up the paddle in or out of the water makes any difference.

☀ Twist the paddle clockwise and note what happens when the boat moves. Now twist it counterclockwise. Attach a different rubber band to your boat. Notice if a tighter rubber band changes the boat's motion.

☀ Make a propeller-driven boat. See if it goes farther or faster than a paddle-driven boat. Race your two different types of boat together in the bathtub.

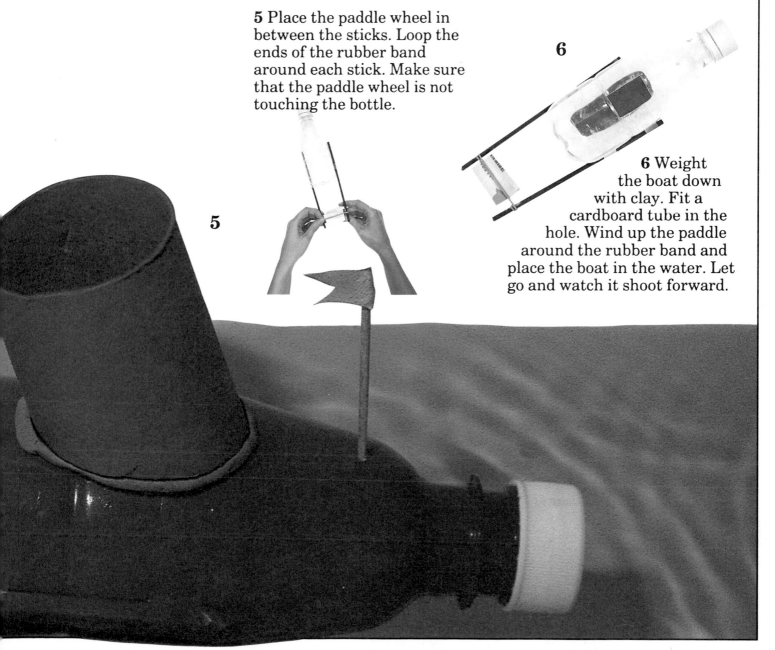

5 Place the paddle wheel in between the sticks. Loop the ends of the rubber band around each stick. Make sure that the paddle wheel is not touching the bottle.

6 Weight the boat down with clay. Fit a cardboard tube in the hole. Wind up the paddle around the rubber band and place the boat in the water. Let go and watch it shoot forward.

STEERING AND BALANCE

The Vikings used a single, hand-operated steering oar at the stern, or back, of their ships. Always on the right-hand side, it led to the term steerboard, or starboard. Stern rudders were first used over 1,000 years ago on flat-bottomed Chinese junks. Modern propeller-driven submarines are steered by tail rudders. To maneuver up and down, they use hydroplane fins which look like airplane wings. Dolphins are propelled by their tail fins – the other fins are for balance and steering.

RUDDER DESIGN

1 For your rudder, slide a pipe cleaner inside a straw, leaving a piece sticking out at the top for the handle and a piece at the bottom.

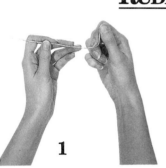

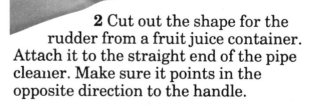

2 Cut out the shape for the rudder from a fruit juice container. Attach it to the straight end of the pipe cleaner. Make sure it points in the opposite direction to the handle.

3 Attach the finished rudder to the back of your paddleboat with modeling clay. Wind the paddle counterclockwise to propel the boat through the water. Once it is moving, use the handle of the rudder to change the direction in which it travels. Keep a record of what happens. When you push the handle to the right, observe which way the rudder turns. At the same time, notice which way this makes the boat turn.

3

BRIGHT IDEAS

If you want to turn the boat to starboard, which way must you turn the rudder? See if you can make your boat do a complete turn by operating the rudder.

Make a "submarine" and fit four adjustable curved fins to the sides. To maneuver, or turn, your vessel, experiment with the fins. With the back fins and the front fins curving in the same direction, gently drop the submarine in water. Now test what happens when the fins are fixed in different directions. For example, try the front fins curving up and the back fins curving down.

WHY IT WORKS

If the rudder is pointing in the same direction as the flow of water, the ship moves straight ahead (3). If the flow strikes the rudder at an angle (1,2), the ship turns. As the force of the flow tries to push the angled rudder back to parallel, it is met with resistance - an opposing force that turns the boat.

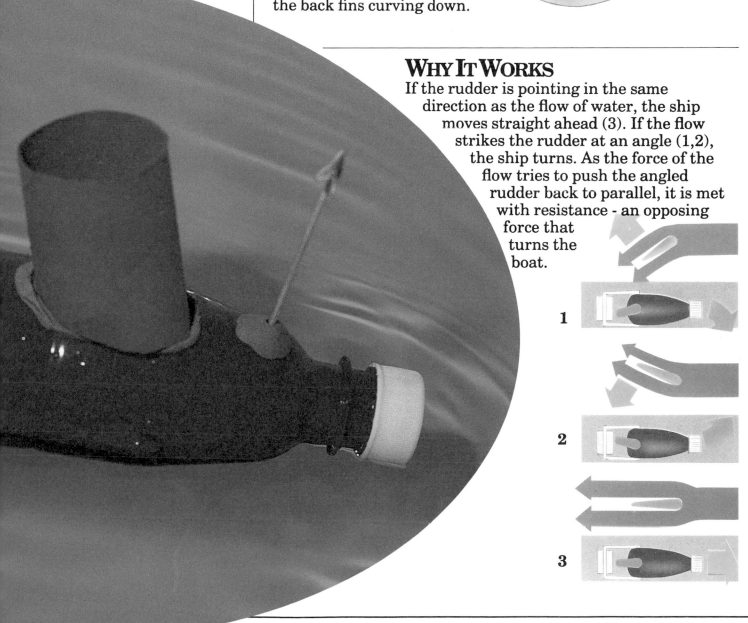

1

2

3

ELECTRICITY AND MAGNETISM

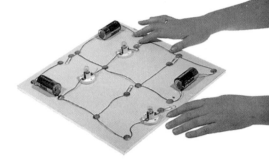

CONTENTS

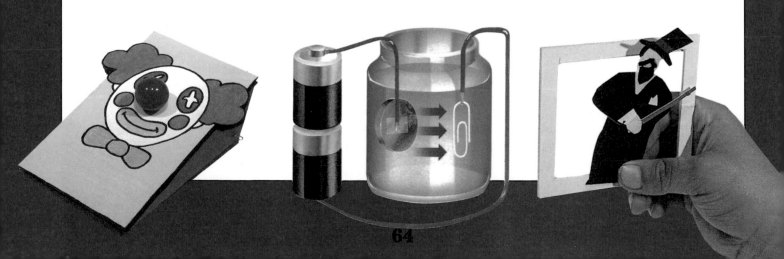

INTRODUCTION

We are accustomed to living with the convenience of electricity. It can be converted into light and heat. We use it to power machines for cooking, cleaning, washing, communication, and travel. We have natural electricity in our bodies which carries signals and messages along nerves. Electricity can be costly to produce and its production can drain the planet of resources and harms the environment.

Magnetism is a force that acts between magnets and is all around us. We rely on magnetism to produce large amounts of electricity. Magnets can be found in telephones, televisions and radios. The age of science began once sailors had learnt how to magnetize a compass needle and the magnetic north and south poles had been located.

Safety Tips

Electricity can be dangerous. NEVER use mains electricity for your experiments but instead use a 1.5 volt battery. Filing an iron nail to make iron filings can also be dangerous so you should ask an adult to do this for you. Water and electricity are a dangerous combination – keep them apart and always make sure your hands are dry. Do your experiments with an adult close by and ask for help with dangerous things like cutting and bending a coat hanger.

Remember to clean up after any experiment.

NATURAL ELECTRICITY

Thousands of years ago, the Greeks noticed that a type of stone called amber attracted light-weight objects, like feathers, after it was rubbed. The Greek word for amber is "elektron." Some materials, such as plastic, do not let electricity pass through, but if they rub against another material, a charge of static electricity can be produced. Static means staying in the same place. We experience static daily – you may hear a crackling sound when you take off your sweater. Sometimes a spark is produced. Rubbing or friction causes static. You can generate your own static and watch the frogs jump.

ACTIVE AMPHIBIANS!

1. Fold a piece of tissue paper a number of times and cut out the shape of a frog. This way you can cut out several frogs at the same time.

3. Cut a bird shape out of yellow cardboard. Attach it to a Ping Pong ball by threading string through both.

4. Tie the other end of the string to the end of the stick. Make sure that the bird rests on top of the ball.

2. Cut out two lily pad shapes from green cardboard. Cut out some flowers, too. Put the lily pads on the cardboard. Place the frogs on one lily pad.

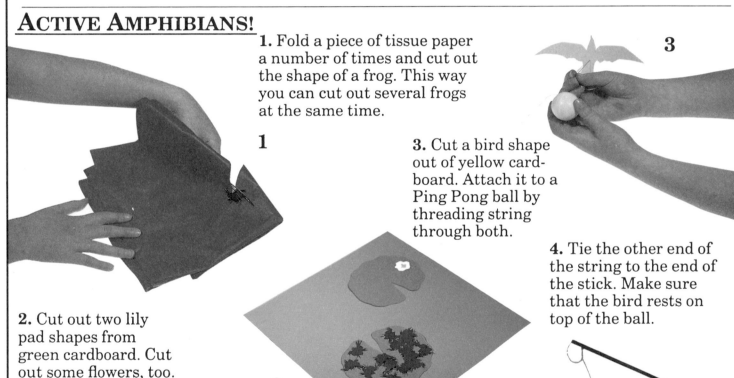

5. A short distance away from the tissue paper shapes, rub the ball against the woolen cloth. Do this quite vigorously. This makes the ball negatively charged.

WHY IT WORKS

Most materials are made of atoms that are electrically neutral. However, if atoms gain tiny particles called electrons, they become negatively charged. If they lose electrons, they become positively charged. Like charges will repel, unlike charges will attract. When the Ping Pong ball is rubbed on the woolen cloth, it gains electrons and becomes negatively charged. The tissue paper frogs, which are not charged, jump toward the ball when it is close by. Each time the frogs jump, they are charged in a process called induction.

Ping Pong ball

Woolen material

BRIGHT IDEAS

Rub a balloon on woolen material, then hold it against a door. Now let go of the balloon. Notice what happens. How long does the effect of static electricity last?

Make a water bow. Rub a plastic spoon on wool. Hold the spoon near a stream of water from a tap. The water will bend toward the spoon. See what happens if the water touches the spoon.

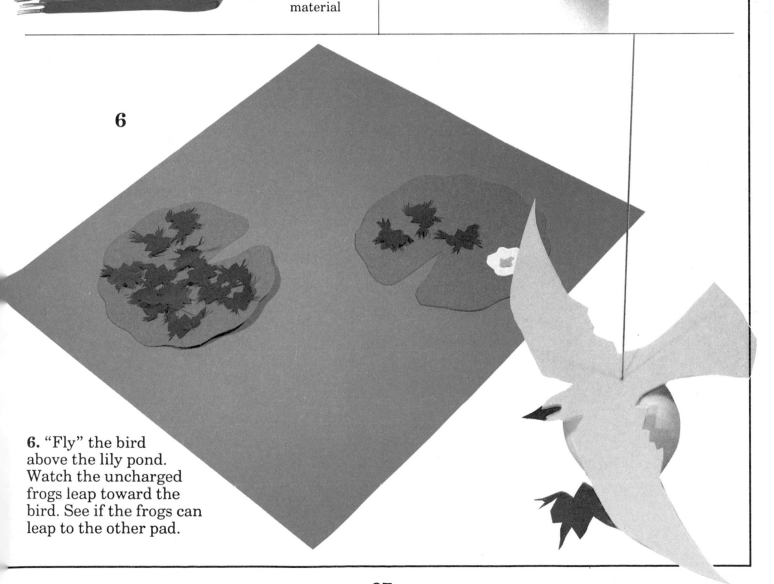

6. "Fly" the bird above the lily pond. Watch the uncharged frogs leap toward the bird. See if the frogs can leap to the other pad.

6

THUNDER AND LIGHTNING

Nature's most spectacular display of static electricity is a flash of lightning. Ancient civilizations once believed that thunder and lightning signified the anger of their gods. During a thunderstorm, raindrops and hailstones hurl up and down inside a thunder cloud, producing charges of static electricity. Positive charges move to the top of the cloud, negative charges to the bottom. The earth under the cloud is positively charged, so the negative charges in the clouds are attracted downward. This is why lightning can occasionally strike the earth. The hottest part of lightning can reach a temperature six times hotter than the surface of the sun. You can make sparks like flashes of lightning that are not dangerous at all!

LIGHTNING FLASHES

1. You will need a large plastic bag, a metal tray, modeling clay, and a metal fork or skewer. It is best to do the experiment on a floor with a vinyl covering.

2. Stand the metal tray centrally on top of the large plastic sheet. Put a piece of modeling clay, large enough to use as a "handle," in the center of the tray. Make sure it is firmly secured to the tray.

3. Grip the clay with one hand. Press down firmly and rotate the tray, vigorously, on the plastic sheet. Do this for at least a minute. Using the clay as a handle, lift the tray off the plastic and keep it suspended in the air.

2

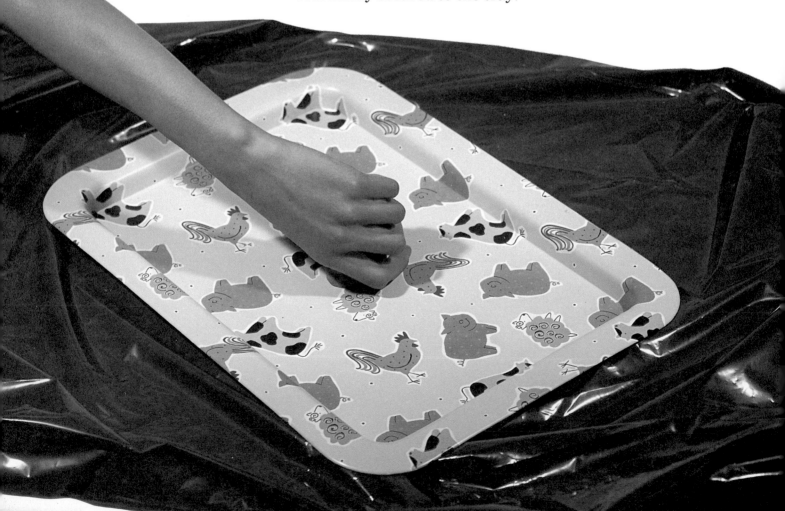

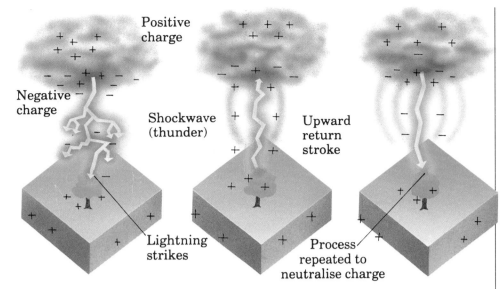

Positive charge

Negative charge

Shockwave (thunder)

Upward return stroke

Lightning strikes

Process repeated to neutralise charge

BRIGHT IDEAS

💡 Rub other materials together. Notice which become positively charged and which negatively charged. See if they repel or attract each other. Try rubbing a strip of paper with a woolen cloth. Then hang it over a ruler. The ends of the paper will repel each other because they are similarly charged. Rub a plastic pen with the cloth, then hold the pen between the ends of the paper. It will attract the paper, pulling the ends together because plastic has a strong negative charge. (A moving plastic conveyor belt in a factory can create severe static, and static eliminators have to be used to neutralize the charge.) Unlike charges attract. Try using other materials. Keep a record of your results.

💡 Make a list of materials and the kind of charge created on them – positive or negative.

WHY IT WORKS

Although electricity can pass through the metal tray, it cannot pass through the plastic. As the tray is rubbed on the plastic, it becomes negatively charged. When the positively charged metal fork is brought close to the tray, the negative charges are attracted to the positive. They pass from the tray to the fork as a blue spark. This is how lightning works.

3

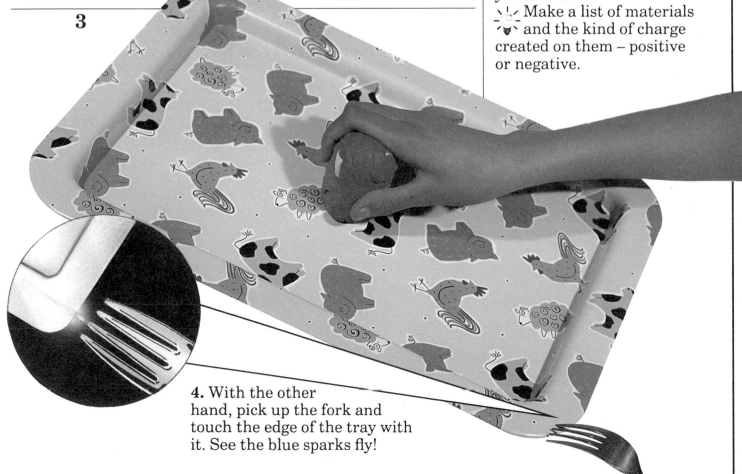

4. With the other hand, pick up the fork and touch the edge of the tray with it. See the blue sparks fly!

A SIMPLE CIRCUIT

Due to the scientific experiments with electricity and magnetism carried out by men like William Faraday, it is now possible to make large amounts of electricity. It can be carried along wires to our homes like water in a pipe, from a power plant. Then it is turned into light, heat, and mechanical energy. Every time you switch on a light you are completing a pathway for the electricity, called a circuit. This allows the current to flow through electrical appliances. It was not until the 1950s that most homes were finally wired up to receive electricity and there are still some areas of the world that have no electricity at all. Our homes are supplied with main-line electricity. Do not try to use main-line electricity for the projects in this book – it is dangerous. Using a battery, you can set up a game that needs only a simple, safe electric circuit.

A GAME OF NERVES!

1.

1. You will need a small 6-volt bulb in a bulb holder. You can buy one of these from a hardware store. Attach two lengths of insulated wire on either side.

2.

2. Form a loop with a piece of thin wire, as shown, and connect it to a long length of insulated wire. Put a plastic straw around the join to form a handle.

3. Now ask an adult to open up a wire coat hanger and bend it into bumps and curves. Attach one side of the bulb holder to the bare wire, taking the other end to two batteries.

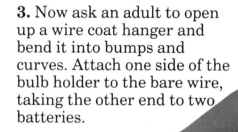

3.

5. Hide the batteries inside a piece of polystyrene and stand the bent wire on the top. Pass the loop along the wire. If the bulb lights up, try again.

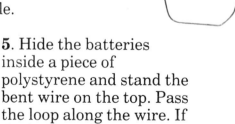

4.

4. Attach the wire loop to the other end of the batteries. You can use modeling clay to hold the wires on the battery terminals.

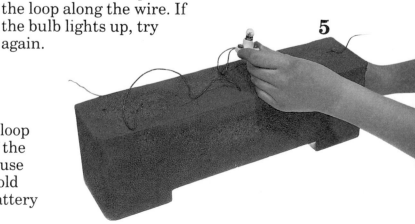

5.

BRIGHT IDEAS

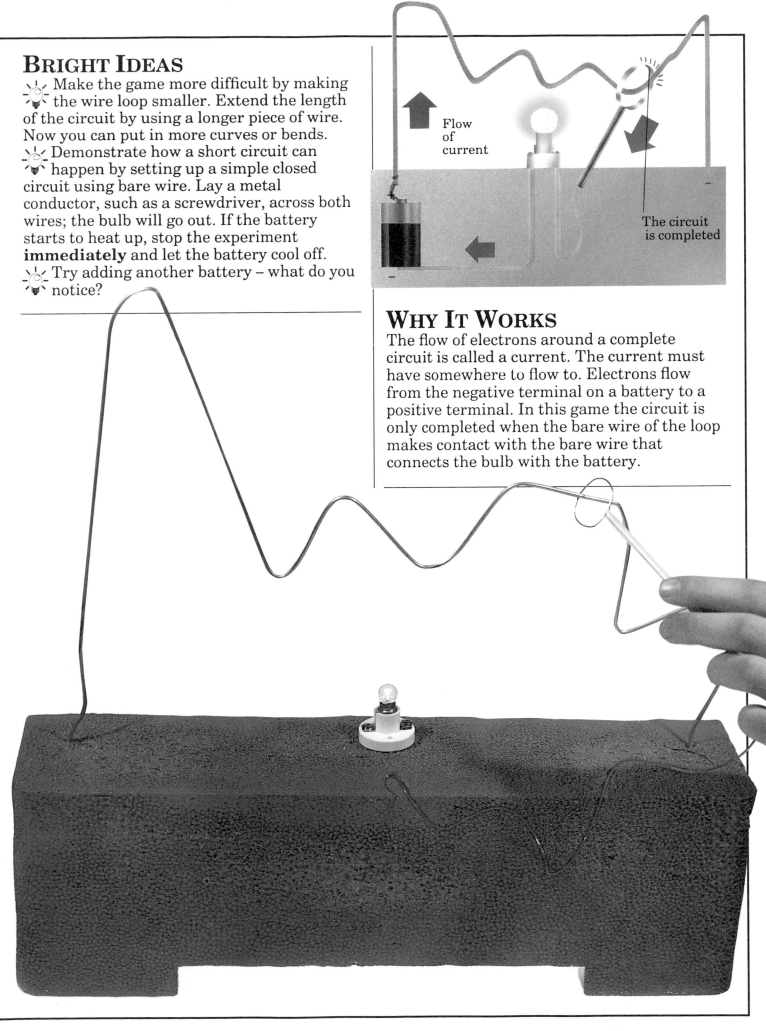

💡 Make the game more difficult by making the wire loop smaller. Extend the length of the circuit by using a longer piece of wire. Now you can put in more curves or bends.

💡 Demonstrate how a short circuit can happen by setting up a simple closed circuit using bare wire. Lay a metal conductor, such as a screwdriver, across both wires; the bulb will go out. If the battery starts to heat up, stop the experiment **immediately** and let the battery cool off.

💡 Try adding another battery – what do you notice?

Flow
of
current

The circuit
is completed

WHY IT WORKS

The flow of electrons around a complete circuit is called a current. The current must have somewhere to flow to. Electrons flow from the negative terminal on a battery to a positive terminal. In this game the circuit is only completed when the bare wire of the loop makes contact with the bare wire that connects the bulb with the battery.

OPEN CIRCUITS

In an open circuit the flow of electricity is controlled by a switch. A switch is the simplest way of controlling the flow of current. When the switch is open, or off, it creates a gap in the circuit. When the switch is closed, or on, the electricity can flow. Telegraphy is the transmission of electric signals. When it was invented in 1838, it allowed people to communicate directly with each other over long distances. In the same year, Samuel Morse introduced his Morse Code – a dot and dash code of short and long electrical signals. These were passed along the wire and decoded at the other end. In 1910, telegraphy was used for the first time to capture a notorious murderer, called Dr. Crippen. The international Morse Code distress signal has always been S.O.S. – three short, three long, three short flashes. Soon ships in distress will transmit a unique identification number via satellite instead.

1. You will need two sheets of polystyrene, modeling clay, two light bulbs and holders, four 1.5v batteries, 6 short lengths of insulated wire, 4 drawing pins, and 2 paper clips.

S.O.S.

2. Place a bulb in each bulb holder and stand them on the polystyrene boards. Connect the two bulb holders and attach wires to the other side of each.

3. Use the drawing pins and paper clips to make a switch for each board. Connect the loose wires to the drawing pins, connecting a paper clip to one of them.

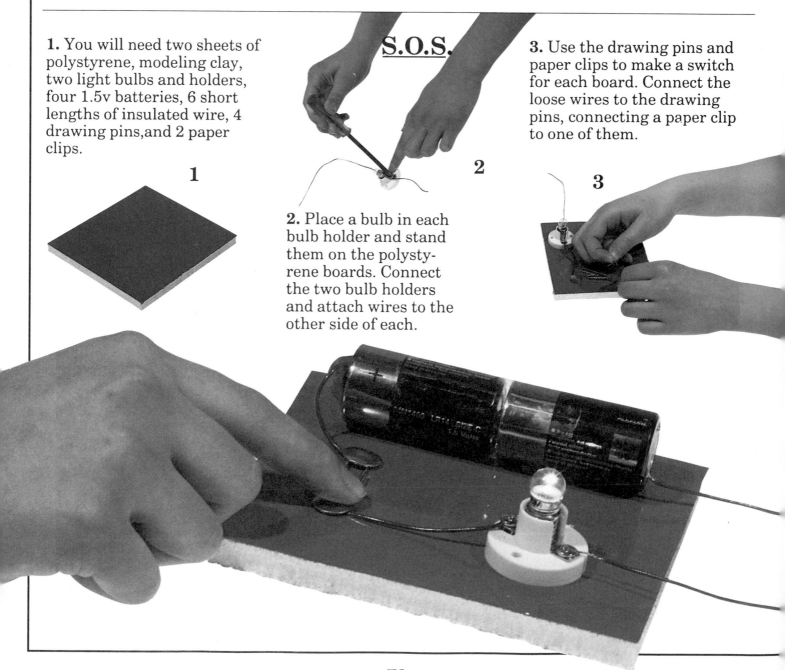

WHY IT WORKS

The paper clips act as switches. Both must be in contact with the drawing pins to allow electrons to flow around the whole circuit, lighting up the bulbs. The sender must raise and lower one paper clip to turn the bulb on and off – the receiver must keep the other down to complete the circuit.

A mechanical switch in the home is slow to work and produces a spark. It joins and separates electrical contacts in the circuit. The spark or arcing produced creates high temperatures. A relay is an electrically controlled switch; it can be operated by various means, but the most common is an electromagnet called a solenoid. The solenoid uses an electromagnet to move a metal rod through a short distance. This opens or closes the relay circuit.

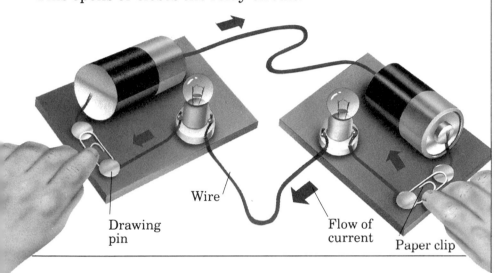

Drawing pin

Wire

Flow of current

Paper clip

4. Rest two batteries end to end on each board and connect them into the circuit using modeling clay. Check to see that the bulbs work by holding down both clips.

5. The bulbs are connected in series. When one bulb lights, both light. A gap in the circuit and the bulbs will not glow.

BRIGHT IDEAS

S.O.S. is 3 short, 3 long, 3 short flashes – now try sending a whole message. Find a copy of the Morse Code. Can you "translate" a reply? Can you build a two-way circuit that will work from another room? If you use bulbs, the wiring must be long enough to link the two. See what happens to the light from the bulb if you use longer wire. How can you tell when each word and sentence ends? Try working out a special code, then you can send secret messages.

Make a burglar alarm system with a pressure switch made out of folded aluminum foil. Hide the switch underneath a rug and connect it into an electrical circuit with a buzzer or bulb. Which kind of alarm do you think is most effective – a bulb or buzzer?

How many switches are there in your home? Where are they? What does each switch operate? Carry out a survey.

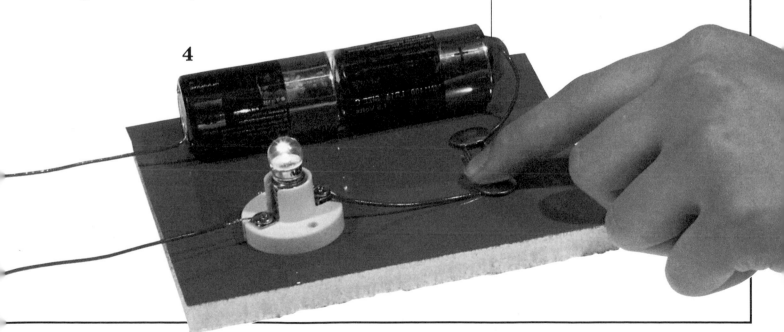

4

73

SWITCHES AND ENERGY

Most modern gadgets, such as hair dryers and toasters, switch off automatically. This is not only important to conserve energy, but is a safety precaution too. Heating appliances, such as stoves and irons, have thermostats so that a selected temperature can be maintained – an internal switch turns the heater on or off as required. Because most of our electricity is generated from sources of energy like coal which will run out, we must be aware of the need to save energy whenever possible. The two-way switch is important today, both as a safety device and as a means of conserving energy. If a light can be switched on or off from the top or the bottom of a staircase, not only is it safer at night, but light energy can be saved. Make your own two-way switch and discover how it works.

SWITCH OFF!

1. Position drawing pins at either end of a board so that two plastic lids can just turn, like knobs, within them.

2. Align four pins as shown and connect them in pairs with two lengths of wire. Make a hole in the top of one plastic knob and insert the two wires connected to a bulb holder.

3. Connect one wire to a paper clip inserted through the lid, as shown, taking the other to the batteries.

4. Form a switch at the other lid in the same way, connecting the wire to the batteries. Modeling clay will hold the wires in place.

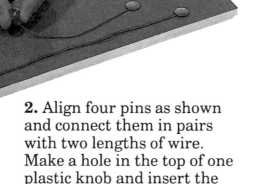

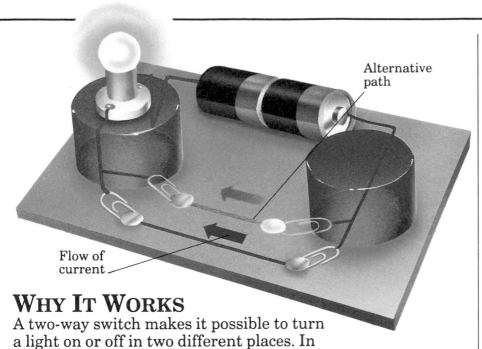

Alternative path

Flow of current

WHY IT WORKS

A two-way switch makes it possible to turn a light on or off in two different places. In order for this to work an alternative pathway for the electricity must be built into the circuit. For the electricity to flow along the blue or red wires, both ends must be connected to the battery at the same time. If the bulb is switched off by moving the paper clip from blue to red at one end, then it can be turned back on by changing from blue to red at the other end.

BRIGHT IDEAS

A person in a wheelchair may need a light switch to be within easy reach. Design a two-way switch circuit to satisfy this need.

Build a two-way switch circuit and incorporate it into a cardboard model staircase. Remember that you must incorporate an alternative circuit so that each switch works in two directions. If you increase the distance between the two switches, does it have any effect on the light produced? Do you need an extra battery? Try shortening the distance. Are there any changes?

Find out how many two-way switches there are in your home or school. Make a record of where they are. Why are they positioned as they are? Identify those places where a two-way switch is needed.

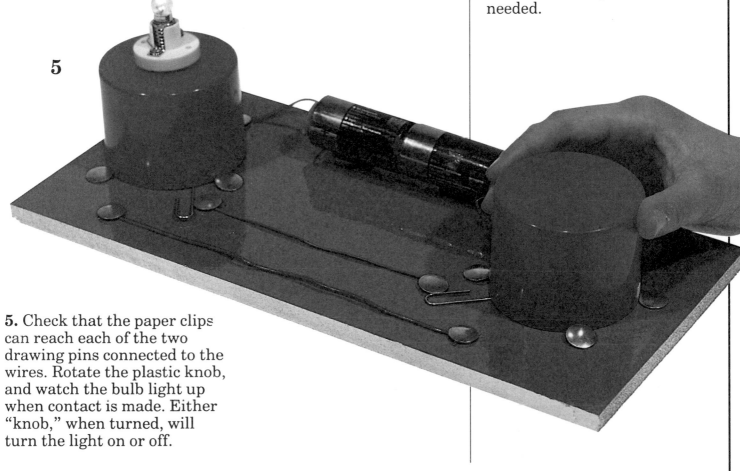

5

5. Check that the paper clips can reach each of the two drawing pins connected to the wires. Rotate the plastic knob, and watch the bulb light up when contact is made. Either "knob," when turned, will turn the light on or off.

BULBS

The warning flashes of lighthouses are vital to the safety of ships around the coastline. It was not until the mid-nineteenth century that lighthouses were equipped with electric light bulbs. Two men were responsible for the invention of the incandescent (white-hot) electric light bulb; Thomas Edison, an American, and Joseph Swan, an Englishman. Edison's light bulbs contained a carbon filament within a vacuum. He first produced this on October 21, 1879. By 1913, the tungsten filament (a type of metal) that is still used today had been introduced. Neon lights, like those pictured here, contain a gas. When electricity is passed through the gas, the tube glows. Electronic bulbs have also been developed. These produce only light – not heat – and so save energy.

DANGER AT SEA!

1

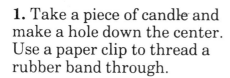

1. Take a piece of candle and make a hole down the center. Use a paper clip to thread a rubber band through.

2

2. Push the candle into a thread spool and attach the band to the top with tape. Also attach a bulb in a holder to the top, passing the wires down through the candle.

3. Use a long cardboard tube for your lighthouse. Cut a piece of polystyrene to fit the end and place the candle through the middle, as shown.

3

6. Line a plastic cup with aluminum foil. Cut out a window to see the bulb. A piece of cardboard with a hole to fit over the bulb will hold it in place.

4. Insert the whole thing into the top of your lighthouse, allowing the wires to hang out of the end.

4

5. Fix the polystyrene, candle, and rubber band in place with two toothpicks. Push them right through the cardboard tube, from one side to the other.

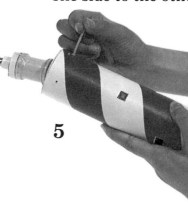

5

WHY IT WORKS

As the bulb puts the electrons to work by making it travel through a very long, thin wire called the filament, electric energy is transferred into light energy. Tungsten is a highly resistant metal that can become white hot without melting. Air is removed from the bulb and replaced by the harmless gas, argon. Electrons flow into the bulb when the circuit is complete and cause the wire to glow. Metal at the base of the bulb makes contact with the circuit. Bulbs can become very hot when switched on.

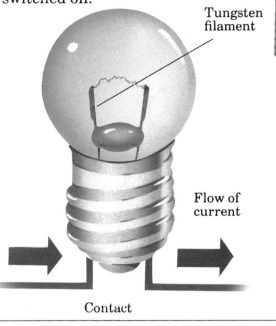

Tungsten filament

Flow of current

Contact

BRIGHT IDEAS

Can you make a different kind of flashing light without switching the current off and on? Adapt the project to make the light revolve and flash in a different way. Try using colored cellophane in the window to make a colored light. Another way to make a flashing light is to use a circle of cardboard, out of which slits like the spokes of a wheel have been cut. Place it in front of the bulb – then revolve the cardboard when the bulb is glowing.

Design and build a traffic light circuit so that the bulbs can be switched on and off in a particular sequence. The sequence of change is different in various countries.

Do you know what causes a fluorescent strip light to flicker? The answer has to do with the fact that main-line electricity uses an alternating current (a current that varies all the time).

Design a poster encouraging people to turn lights off and save energy.

7

7. Connect the wires to a battery and hide it under a papier mâché "rock." Add cotton ball waves. Now twist the thread spool around several times, let go and watch the warning light turn.

INSULATORS AND CONDUCTORS

Our bodies can conduct electricity, especially when they are wet. Never touch plugs, sockets, or light switches with wet hands. A conductor will allow electricity to pass through it. We use conductors to take electricity to where it is needed. We use insulators to prevent it from reaching places where it could be dangerous. Electricians, like the one pictured here, wear rubber boots to protect themselves from electric shocks. Metal wires conducting electricity are insulated with rubber or plastic to make them safe. Conduct your way through a maze, using insulators and conductors as your guides.

AMAZING!

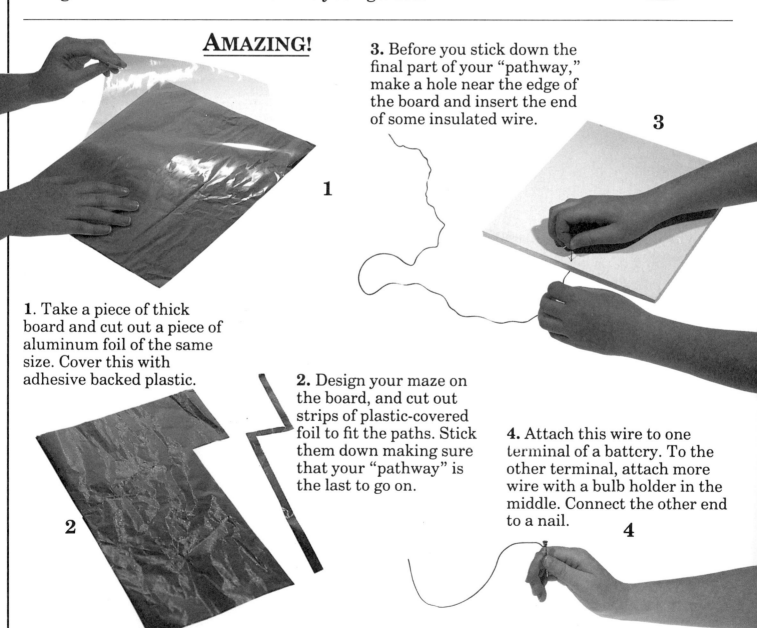

1. Take a piece of thick board and cut out a piece of aluminum foil of the same size. Cover this with adhesive backed plastic.

2. Design your maze on the board, and cut out strips of plastic-covered foil to fit the paths. Stick them down making sure that your "pathway" is the last to go on.

3. Before you stick down the final part of your "pathway," make a hole near the edge of the board and insert the end of some insulated wire.

4. Attach this wire to one terminal of a battery. To the other terminal, attach more wire with a bulb holder in the middle. Connect the other end to a nail.

WHY IT WORKS

The aluminum foil conducts electricity and allows the circuit to be completed. The bulb glows. But when the nail touches the plastic covering in the maze, the bulb goes out. Plastic is an insulator. A substance that conducts electricity must contain charged particles that are free to move around. These free electrons pass on the current. The electrons in the plastic cannot move.

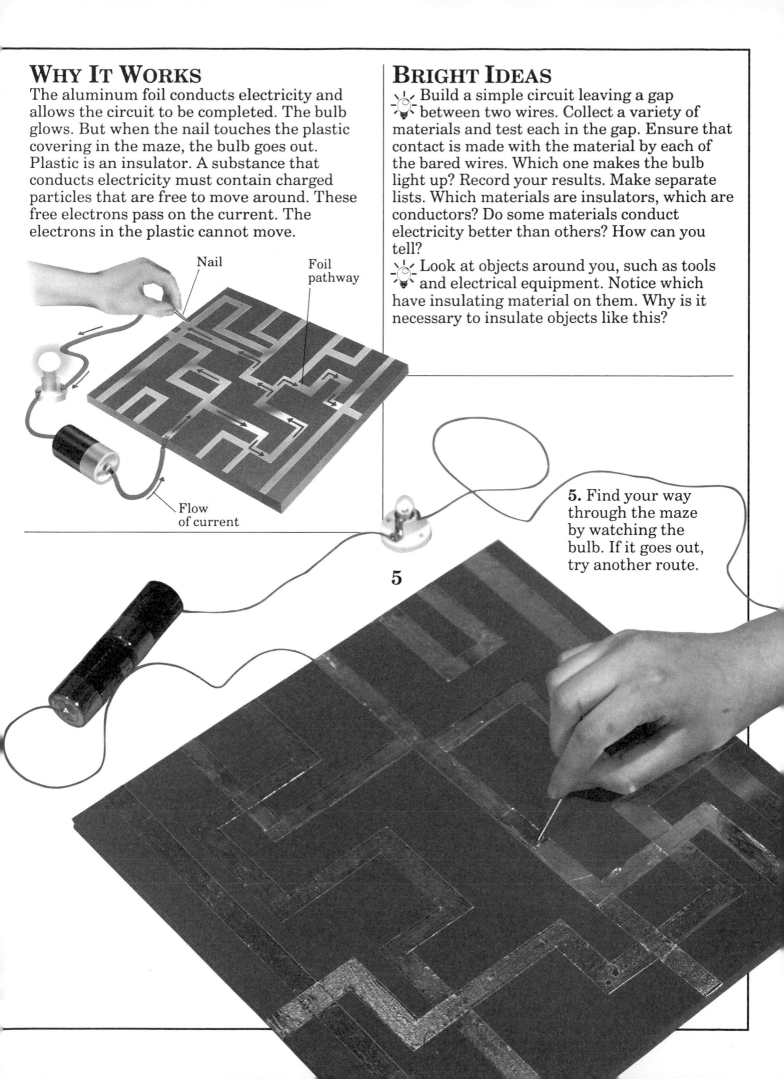

Nail

Foil pathway

Flow of current

BRIGHT IDEAS

Build a simple circuit leaving a gap between two wires. Collect a variety of materials and test each in the gap. Ensure that contact is made with the material by each of the bared wires. Which one makes the bulb light up? Record your results. Make separate lists. Which materials are insulators, which are conductors? Do some materials conduct electricity better than others? How can you tell?

Look at objects around you, such as tools and electrical equipment. Notice which have insulating material on them. Why is it necessary to insulate objects like this?

5. Find your way through the maze by watching the bulb. If it goes out, try another route.

5

ELECTRICAL RESISTANCE

James Watt, inventor of the steam engine, gave his name to the measurement of electrical power, the watt. Electrical resistance is what makes the filament (long, thin piece of wire) in a bulb glow and the element in an electric heater become hot.

Resistance is measured in ohms, after the German scientist, Georg Simon Ohm. Resistors are used in circuits, like the ones pictured here. They are coils of wire, or poor conductors, built into the circuit to reduce the current. A variable resistor, or rheostat, is used to control the speed of a toy car and the volume of a radio or television. By building your own resistor, you can make a night-light with a dimmer switch.

DIM THE LIGHT

1. Set up a circuit using a bulb in a holder, insulated wire, a board, and safety pins. Ask an adult to cut the lead out of a pencil, and cut out two pieces of thick cardboard to rest it on.

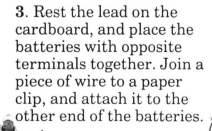

4

4. To reflect the light, make a shade of cardboard and aluminum foil. Cut a slit in the flat disk and glue it into a cone shape.

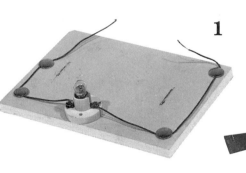

1

5

5. Cut a hole in the center of the cone and place it over the bulb. Slip the paper clip over the pencil lead and watch the bulb light up.

2. Attach one end of the wire to the batteries and the other end to the pencil lead.

3. Rest the lead on the cardboard, and place the batteries with opposite terminals together. Join a piece of wire to a paper clip, and attach it to the other end of the batteries.

2

3

WHY IT WORKS

A pencil lead is made of carbon, which conducts electricity. All conductors have some resistance which becomes higher the farther the electricity has to travel. As the paper clip moves toward the battery, the electricity doesn't have to travel as far. The bulb therefore becomes brighter. As it is moved away from the battery, the light dims.

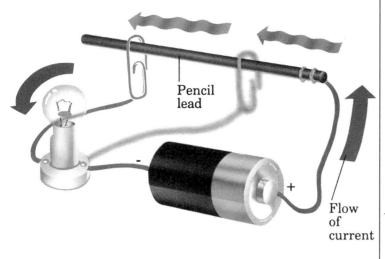

Pencil lead

Flow of current

BRIGHT IDEAS

☀ Repeat the project attaching the paper clip to the wire from the bulb. Attach the pencil lead to the wire from the battery. When is the bulb brightest? Which way must you move the paper clip to dim the light now? Which works best?

☀ Build a model theater set with a circuit of floor lights. Use colored paper to create colored lights. By building a variable resistor into the circuit you can dim or brighten the stage lights.

☀ You can make another kind of dimmer by immersing a length of aluminum foil in salt water while it is connected to a circuit. A second piece of foil, connected to the other end of the circuit, is at the bottom of the container. Watch what happens when you move the top piece of foil up and down in the water.

6. Move the paper clip up and down the pencil lead. The bulb should get brighter or dimmer.

6

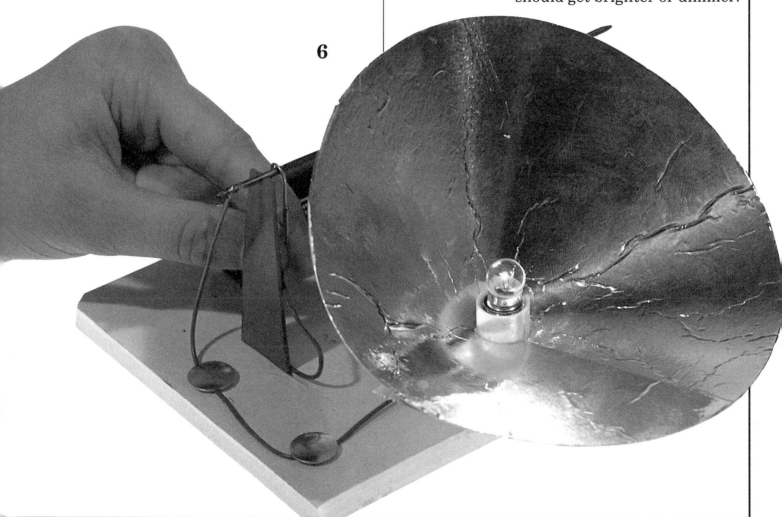

Series And Parallels

As long ago as 1810, many larger cities had street lighting. An electric current was made to jump between two carbon rods – this was called electric arc lighting. First introduced by Sir Humphry Davy, these lamps were connected in series. This meant that all the lamps were connected as a part of one large circuit. It also meant that if one lamp went out, and the circuit was broken, they all went out. This often happens with Christmas tree lights, although they can be arranged in parallel circuits to avoid this problem. It was Thomas Edison who recognized the need to use parallel circuits for street lighting. Each bulb in a parallel circuit has a circuit of its own. If one bulb fails, the others will continue to glow; the current is divided equally between them.

Lots Of Lights

1

1. You will need two large boards, drawing pins, insulated wire, bulbs, bulb holders, and batteries. The drawing pins can act as contacts where your wires join.

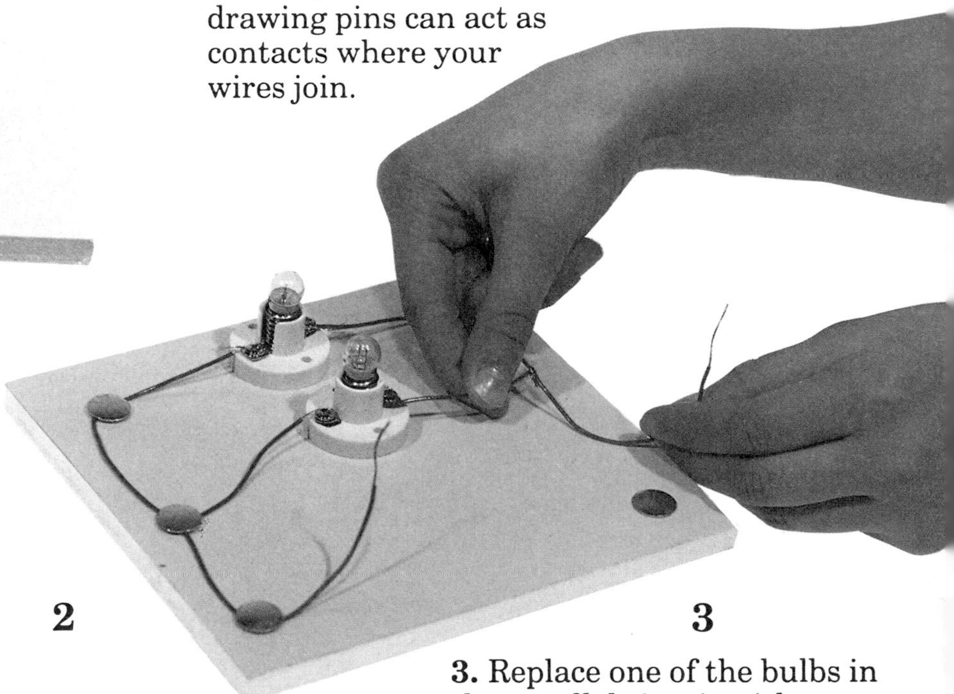

2. Set up your parallel circuit. If one bulb fails the other will remain lit because the circuits are separate. Observe how brightly the bulbs glow.

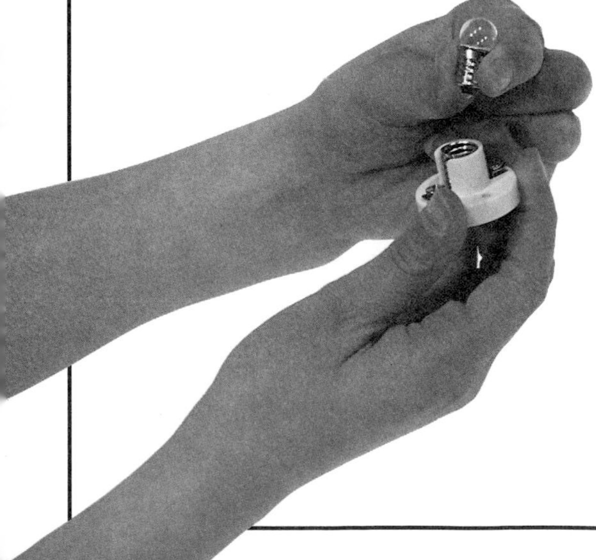

2

3

3. Replace one of the bulbs in the parallel circuit with another battery. Does the light from the bulb change? Now wire up a series circuit like the red one shown here. Include one bulb and two batteries in this circuit. Stop **immediately** if the batteries heat up.

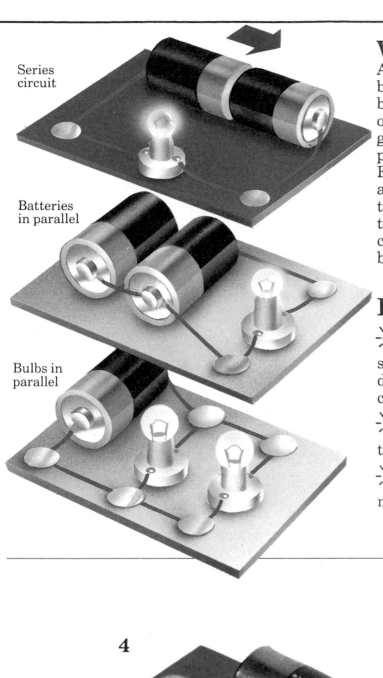

Series circuit

Batteries in parallel

Bulbs in parallel

WHY IT WORKS

A series circuit uses one path to connect the bulb and battery. If two batteries are used, the bulb glows twice as brightly as it would with one. Two bulbs in a series circuit would not glow as brightly as one. A parallel circuit provides more than one path for the current. Each bulb receives the same voltage even if another battery or bulb is added or removed. If two batteries are used in a parallel circuit, their power does not combine as in the series circuit. The bulb receives the voltage of one battery, but glows for double the time

BRIGHT IDEAS

Add another bulb to the series circuit. What do you notice when the current is switched on? Now add another one. What difference does this make? Draw a series circuit diagram.

Wire another bulb into the parallel circuit. What do you notice about the glow from the bulbs? Draw a parallel circuit diagram.

For how long do the bulbs in each kind of circuit stay lit? Which type of circuit is most wasteful of energy?

4. Observe this bulb. Does it shine as brightly as the bulb in the yellow parallel circuit? Try removing one battery. Which bulb is shining the brightest now?

4

ELECTRICITY IN THE HOME

Modern houses contain many electric circuits. Some circuits are for lighting and others power appliances or heaters. Access to the main circuit is made possible through wall sockets. All household lights and appliances are connected in parallel, as this allows all devices to operate on the same voltage. This voltage will not change if a piece of equipment is added or taken away. The current leaves the house through another wire. Faulty wiring may cause a fire in the home. To avoid such a risk, plugs and circuits are fitted with fuses or circuit breakers. A fuse is a piece of wire designed to melt, and so break a circuit, if the current is too high. A complex circuit, like that in a television set, has hundreds or even thousands of circuit parts. They consist of both parallel and series circuits. Make your own game using circuits and switches.

TURN OFF THE LIGHT!

5. Now experiment with your circuit board. Can you light up only one bulb at a time by disconnecting certain switches? Now try lighting up two bulbs simultaneously. You can have hours of fun trying various connections. Observe the bulbs. When do they glow most brightly? When are they dimmest?

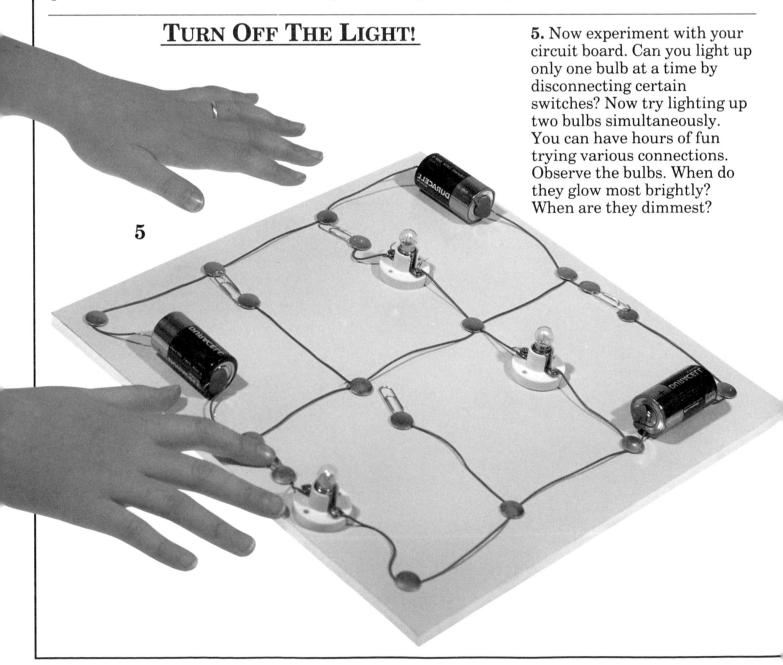

5

1. You will need a large board, three bulbs, three batteries, lengths of insulated wire, drawing pins, modeling clay, and paper clips.

2. Place a battery in three corners of the board. Make sure that unlike terminals are facing. Attach the wires using modeling clay.

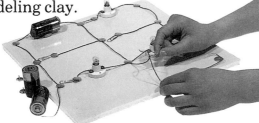

3. Connect the bulbs to the batteries as shown. Leave gaps in the circuits for switches. These can be paper clips and drawing pins.

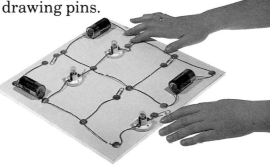

4. Connect each switch by pressing down a paper clip on to a drawing pin. Observe the brightness of the bulbs. If any of the bulbs do not work, check all connections.

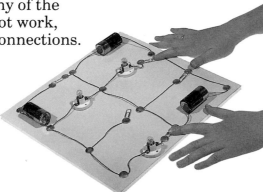

WHY IT WORKS

The flow of electrons is regulated by connecting and disconnecting the switches on the circuit board. When a bulb is isolated by disconnecting a switch, the circuit into which it is wired is broken. When every switch is connected, all the bulbs glow. The high resistance of a fuse restricts the amount of current that can pass through. Each appliance needs a fuse of the correct resistance.

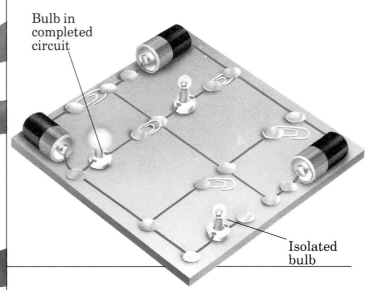

Bulb in completed circuit

Isolated bulb

BRIGHT IDEAS

☀ Position the batteries so that like terminals are facing each other. What effect does this have on your circuit board? Can the bulbs be lit up simultaneously now? Why is this? Remember that electrons travel from negative to positive. Do the bulbs glow just as brightly as before?

☀ If you remove one bulb, how does this affect the circuits?

☀ Ask an adult to show you where the electricity meter is located in your house. Keep a record of meter readings in your home for a week. Figure out how much electricity has been used. Use your figures to make a graph. You could put the information on a computer database if you have one at home or school. Count the number of sockets in your home. Make a list of all the electrical appliances used by your family. Watch the meter dials when each appliance is being used; which uses the most electricity? Figure out some ways in which your family could save electricity.

ELECTRICITY AND MAGNETISM

Hans Oersted, the nineteenth century Danish scientist, first proved the relationship between electricity and magnetism when he noticed that a magnet held near to a compass caused it to turn. When this experiment was repeated, replacing the magnet with a current of electricity, he observed the same effect. This was the beginning of electromagnetism. After Oersted's experiments, it was soon realized that magnets could be made by passing an electric current through coils of wire. The magnetic field (the region around the wire where the force of magnetism is felt) could be switched on and off with the electricity. When a doorbell is pressed, an electromagnet attracts a clapper to strike the bell. Use electromagnetism to hold the clown's nose in place.

RED NOSE DAY

1. Take a piece of thick board and push a nail through the center. Now wind a piece of wire around the nail at least 20 times, leaving two ends of the same length.

2. Cut two triangular pieces of polystyrene to support the board in a sloping position.

3. Attach the triangles, as shown, and pierce a small hole in the side of one of them for a paper clip to fit through.

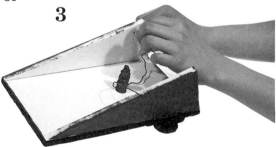

4. On a second sheet of polystyrene draw a clown's face to fit on top of the shape you have made. Do not draw a nose on the face. Color the face, then cut out your clown.

5. Affix a drawing pin to the side of a Ping-Pong ball, colored red. This will be your clown's nose. It will not fit in place yet.

6. Position the batteries inside the shape as shown. Make sure unlike terminals are touching. Now connect a wire from the nail to one end of the batteries using modeling clay. Connect the other to the paper clip. Stop **immediately** if the batteries heat up.

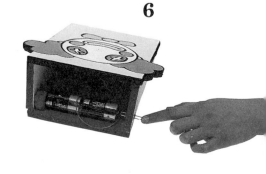

BRIGHT IDEAS

🔆 Reproduce Oersted's experiment. Magnetize a needle by rubbing it in one direction on a strong magnet, and rest it on a piece of folded cardboard that is balancing on a stick. Place it in a jar; this will act as a compass. Now set up a simple circuit, allowing the wire to run above the magnetized needle. Observe the effect on the needle when the current flows. Wind more lengths of wire around your compass. What difference does this make?

🔆 Find out which appliances, such as a telephone, contain electromagnets.

🔆 Can you design a burglar alarm that works because of the effect of an electromagnet?

7. Push the paper clip through the hole until it touches the adjacent battery terminal. Leave half of the paper clip protruding through the hole. Position the red nose on the clown's face.

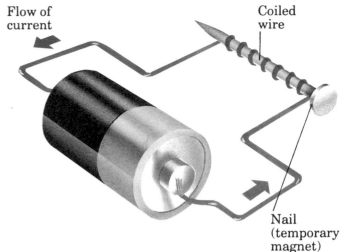

Flow of current

Coiled wire

Nail (temporary magnet)

WHY IT WORKS

When the current is switched on, the nail becomes a temporary magnet. The clown's nose stays in place, held in the magnetic field created by the electricity. When the electric current is turned off, the nose falls off. The nail loses its magnetic properties.

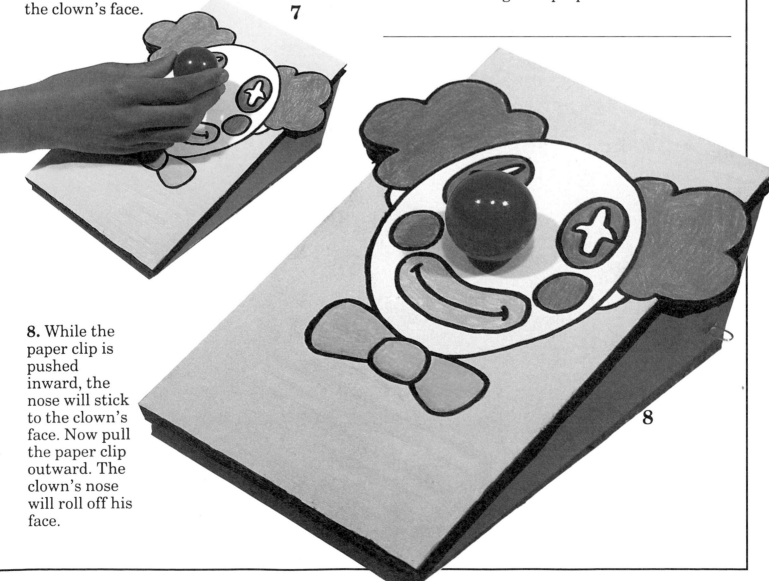

8. While the paper clip is pushed inward, the nose will stick to the clown's face. Now pull the paper clip outward. The clown's nose will roll off his face.

ELECTROMAGNETISM

The English physicist, Michael Faraday, discovered that electrical energy could be turned into mechanical energy (movement) by using magnetism. He used a cylindrical coil of wire, called a solenoid, to create a simple electric motor. He went on to discover that mechanical energy can be converted into electrical energy – the reverse of the principle of the electric motor. His work led to the development of the dynamo, or generator. You can make a powerful electromagnet by passing electricity through a coil of wire wrapped many times around a nail. Electromagnets are found in many everyday machines and gadgets. An MRI scanner (Magnetic Resonance Imaging), like the one pictured here, contains many ring-shaped electromagnets. With a solenoid and a current of electricity, you can close the cage.

CAGED!

1. Take a piece of polystyrene and edge it with cardboard. Stick plastic straws upright around three sides as the bars of the cage.

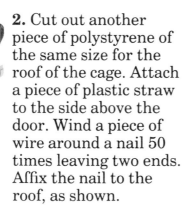

2. Cut out another piece of polystyrene of the same size for the roof of the cage. Attach a piece of plastic straw to the side above the door. Wind a piece of wire around a nail 50 times leaving two ends. Affix the nail to the roof, as shown.

3. Insert a needle into the straw so that it almost touches the nail. Cut out a rectangle of plastic for the door. Make a hole at the bottom of the door for the needle to fit through.

4. Stick a piece of cardboard across the door to help hold it open, and make sure the end of the needle just pokes through the hole. Now attach one of the wires to one terminal on the battery. Leave the other free. Make sure it will reach the other terminal. Put the animal into the cage.

WHY IT WORKS

When the current is switched on, the nail becomes magnetized as the current flows through the wire. The needle in the door of the cage is attracted to the electromagnet. As the needle is pulled toward the nail, the door closes to trap the tiger.

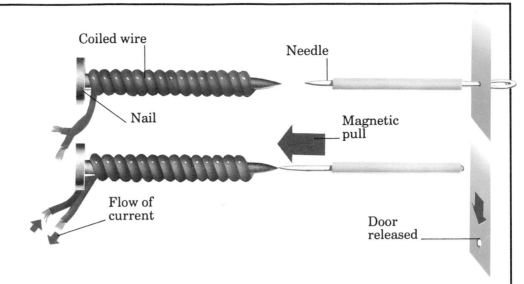

Coiled wire

Nail

Needle

Magnetic pull

Flow of current

Door released

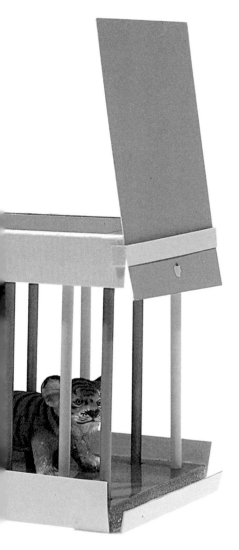

BRIGHT IDEAS

Wind more turns of wire onto the electromagnet. The magnetic effect will increase. What happens if you use a more powerful battery? (Do not let it get too hot.)

Make another electromagnet using a shorter nail. This will also make the magnetic pull stronger.

Make an electromagnetic pickup by winding wire around a nail. What objects can you pick up? What happens when the current is turned off?

Use an electromagnet to make a carousel spin. Attach paper clips around the edge of a circular cardboard lid to be the roof. Make sure it is free to spin, and place an electromagnet close to the paper clips. The carousel should turn as you switch the current on and off quickly.

5. Now pick up the free wire. Allow the free wire to come into contact with the unconnected battery terminal. The needle should be pulled back toward the nail. The door will fall down, trapping the animal in its cage.

ELECTROLYSIS

Electrolysis is a process in which an electric current is passed through a liquid, causing a chemical reaction to take place. The liquid used is called the electrolyte. The wires or plates where the current enters or leaves the liquid are called electrodes. The electrolysis of metallic solutions is useful in putting metal coatings on objects. If you have a look at some car bumpers, you will notice that they may have a nice, smooth, metallic appearance. This is because they are coated with a metal called nickel, in a process called electroplating. This helps to stop the metal underneath from rusting. The same method is used to coat cutlery with silver. This is called silverplating. Michael Faraday discovered the first law of electrolysis. The process is also used to purify metals like aluminum.

COPPER PLATING

1. For this project you will need a glass jar, a copper coin, a paper clip, two batteries, insulated wire, and water. Pour the water into the jar. Place the batteries together with unlike terminals adjacent. Connect wires to the terminals. Attach the copper to the wire from the positive terminal of the battery. The paper clip must be attached to the wire from the negative terminal. Use modeling clay. Do not allow the metal objects to touch in the solution. You could even tape each wire to the side of the jar so that they are suspended.

2. Observe closely what happens. Can you see bubbles? Leave them for a few minutes, then remove. Observe any color changes. Replace them for a while. Are there any further changes?

WHY IT WORKS

The copper coin is connected to the positive terminal of the battery – the current enters here. The other, the paper clip, is joined to the negative terminal – the current leaves here. As the current flows through the water from the positive electrode (anode) to the negative electrode (cathode), the copper is carried from the coin to the clip.

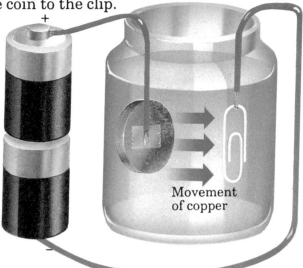

Movement of copper

BRIGHT IDEAS

Repeat the project using salt dissolved in vinegar instead of the water. What difference do you notice – if any? What do you observe about the appearance of the paper clip? Maybe your school has scales that can weigh very small objects? If the coin and the paper clip are weighed before immersion in the liquid and their weight recorded, you can check whether electroplating has really taken place. After carrying out the project weigh them both again. Now replace the battery with a more powerful one, or add a second battery into a parallel circuit, to increase the "push" of the current passing through the liquid. (Remember to stop your experiments if the batteries heat up.) Weigh the coin and paper clip a second time. If the weight of the paper clip has increased further, then you have proved the first law of electrolysis – the size of the charge passed through the liquid determines the amount of copper freed.

2

MAGNETIC ATTRACTION

Archaeologists and beachcombers often make use of metal detectors to locate buried objects or treasure. Materials are either magnetic or nonmagnetic. Most, but not all, metals are magnetic. Iron has the strongest magnetic attraction. Nickel and cobalt are also magnetic, as are the alloys, or mixtures, of these metals. Aluminum, copper, and gold are nonmagnetic. Magnetic ferrites (metals containing iron) can be used to make hard magnets, like the refrigerator magnets pictured here. These are known as permanent magnets. Soft magnets are temporary and are easy to magnetize and demagnetize. Magnetic materials can be easily separated from other materials. When aluminum cans are recycled, they are sorted from other metals by using a magnet. You can make your own metal detector with an ordinary magnet. See if you can find any buried treasure!

SECRETS IN THE SAND

2 Hold the cone in place by attaching small strips of paper to it and winding them tightly around the stick. Now decorate the cone with paint or colored paper.

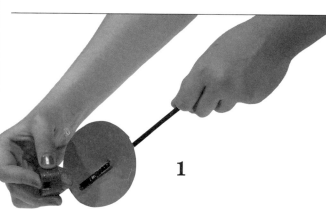

1

1 Make a circle, 4 inches across out of colored cardboard and cut a slit from the edge to the center. Overlap the two ends and glue, to create a flat cone. Push one end of a stick through the center and attach a button magnet to the stick with clay.

2

3 Half fill a shallow container with clean sand. Bury a variety of objects in the sand, metals and nonmetals.

4 Move your metal detector slowly above the surface of the sand. Try it at various heights. You will soon discover how low you must hold it to attract objects.

3

WHY IT WORKS

A magnet exerts a force on a nearby piece of magnetic material by turning it into a weak magnet – this is magnetic induction. A magnet is made up of many tiny parts called domains. Each one is like a mini-magnet, and they all point in the same direction. The domains in a metal are jumbled up. When a magnet comes into contact with the metal, the domains line up and the metal becomes magnetized. A strong magnet can act over quite a distance. Each object picked up from the sand is a temporary magnet because the domains inside become aligned.

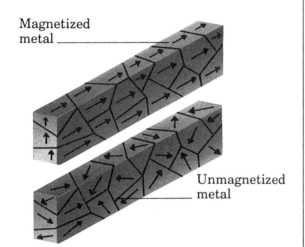

Magnetized metal

Unmagnetized metal

BRIGHT IDEAS

🔆 Predict which objects you expect your magnet to pick up - you may be surprised! See how near to the sand the magnet must be held before it picks anything up. At what height does it fail to attract any of the hidden objects? Keep a record of your results.

🔆 Which objects does your magnet pick up? Which are left buried in the sand? What does this tell you about them? (Hint: the answer is on this page.) Notice whether any of the magnetic objects keep their magnetism and attract other objects.

🔆 Try a different kind of magnet. See if you can pick up any more objects with it. See what happens if you add more sand to the container.

🔆 Find out which other metals are non-magnetic. Collect some empty drink cans and sort them with a magnet. Remember, aluminum is nonmagnetic. Save the cans for recycling.

4

WHERE IS MAGNETISM?

Magnetite, or lodestone, is a naturally occurring magnetic ferrite. The first magnets were made by stroking magnetic materials with a lodestone. You will find magnets of many shapes and sizes – bar, horseshoe, and button are only a few. Every magnet is surrounded by something called a magnetic field, wherever magnetism is found. The areas of the magnet where magnetism is at its strongest are called the poles. Every magnet has at least two poles. Poles are named after the direction they point in. These are North and South.

Iron filings

FLAT FIELDS

1 Place two bar magnets beneath a large sheet of paper, resting each end of the paper on a thin book. Position the magnets with unlike poles facing each other.

2

2 Ask a grown-up to make some iron filings by filing down an iron nail. Now scatter them over the surface of the paper, around the positions of both magnets. Tap the paper gently and watch the magnetic fields form.

WHY IT WORKS

Magnetic lines of force run from north to south and they are strongest where the lines are closest together. This indicates where the poles of the magnet are located. Because like poles repel, for example two south poles, the magnetic fields of the magnets also repel each other. As the iron filings are magnetized they are drawn into the magnetic field, showing the lines of force around the magnet.

BRIGHT IDEAS

Move the two magnets so that like poles are facing each other. Notice that the shape of the magnetic field has changed.

Repeat the experiment with magnets of different shapes and observe the pattern of the magnetic field of each.

Hit a magnet with a hammer – notice what effect this has on the magnet. See if you can still show its magnetic field with the iron filings.

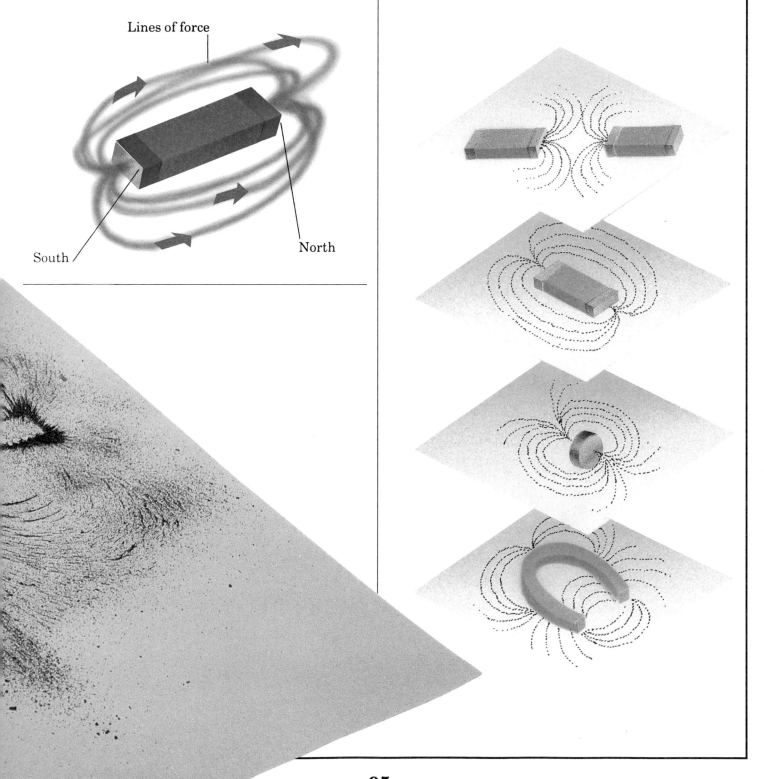

Lines of force

South

North

95

MAGNETIC FIELDS

The space around a permanent magnet in which its effects can be felt is called its magnetic field. A permanent magnet exerts a force that extends some distance from it in every direction. These invisible lines are like closed loops, with part of the loop inside the magnet and part forming the field outside. The lines of force never touch or cross. You have already seen how iron filings give a flat picture of a magnetic field. A magnetic field can cause a compass needle, which is itself a bar magnet, to move. The presence of a magnet near electrical equipment can create havoc, in the same way as the magnetic needle in a compass is made to move. Magnetic shields are designed to avoid such problems. Using iron filings and oil you can demonstrate the three-dimensional nature of a magnetic field.

OIL FIELDS

1. Fill a see-through container almost to the top with a clear, thick liquid like cooking oil or glycerine. Scatter iron filings into the liquid and gently stir the mixture with a stick to disperse the filings evenly.

2. Now place a bar magnet underneath the jar and allow the filings to settle. View them from above. You will see the magnetic field of the magnet as a three-dimensional pattern formed by the iron filings.

1

BRIGHT IDEAS

Try holding a horseshoe magnet against the outside of the jar. See what effect this has on the iron filings in the oil. Notice where the lines of force are closest together.

Jar

Oil

Iron filings

WHY IT WORKS

The iron filings become temporary magnets while inside the magnetic field of the bar magnet, bunching together where the field is strongest. The oil supports the filings in the shape they form around the magnet. The lines of force in a magnetic field move from north to south. Every magnet has a North and South pole at each end, like the Earth. As you can see from the shape appearing in the oil, magnetic lines of force are closest at the poles – this is where the magnet is strongest. The weakest part of a magnet is at its center.

2

ATTRACTION AND REPULSION

Within its magnetic field a magnet will either attract or repel another magnet. If two metal objects attract each other, it is difficult to tell which one is the magnet. The only true test of a magnet is to see if it is repelled by another magnet. A bar magnet has two poles, one North and one South. If a bar magnet is broken in the middle, new poles will appear at the broken ends. As we know that like poles repel and unlike poles attract, it is wrong to describe the North-seeking point of a compass needle as "North." In fact, it is the South pole of the magnetic needle that is attracted to the earth's magnetic North Pole. Always use the term "North-seeking" to avoid confusion. Using the laws of magnetic attraction and repulsion, see if you can move a toy car around the track. The attraction and repulsion between the two magnets should be strong enough to push and pull the car. Maybe you can win a race!

TRACK EVENT

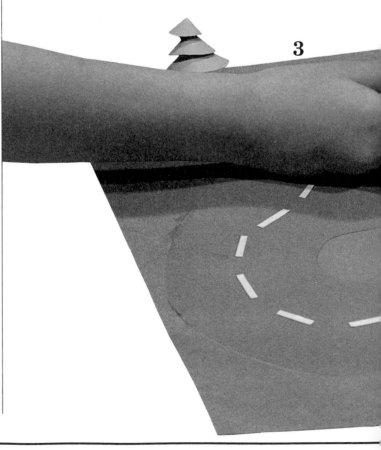

1

1 Firmly attach a bar magnet to the roof of a toy car. Use some strong tape. Make sure that the magnet is well balanced.

2 Cut out a racetrack from gray cardboard and attach it with glue to a sheet of green cardboard – make sure there are no bumps. Add some trees.

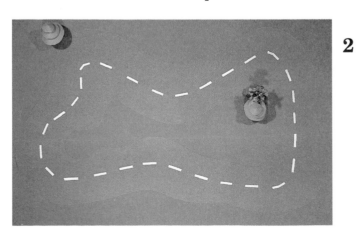

2

3 Place the car on the track. Hold one end of a bar magnet close to the end of the magnet at the rear of the car. If the car moves backward turn the magnet you are holding around the other way. You can push or pull the car around the track by holding the magnet in different places.

3

WHY IT WORKS

Magnets can push or pull because like poles repel but unlike poles attract. This attraction and repulsion is strong enough to push and pull the car around the track.

When two north poles face each other the opposing magnetic fields cancel each other out – this is called the neutral point. The repulsion between two like poles can be so strong that it is impossible to push them together. This magnetic force can be used to push the toy car around the track. In the same way, the attraction between opposite poles can be used to drag the car along.

BRIGHT IDEAS

Suspend a small magnet above a needle attached by thread to a flat surface. Watch the needle rise up into the air.

Suspend a bar magnet freely. Close to it suspend a second magnet. Watch them move as the like poles pull away from each other.

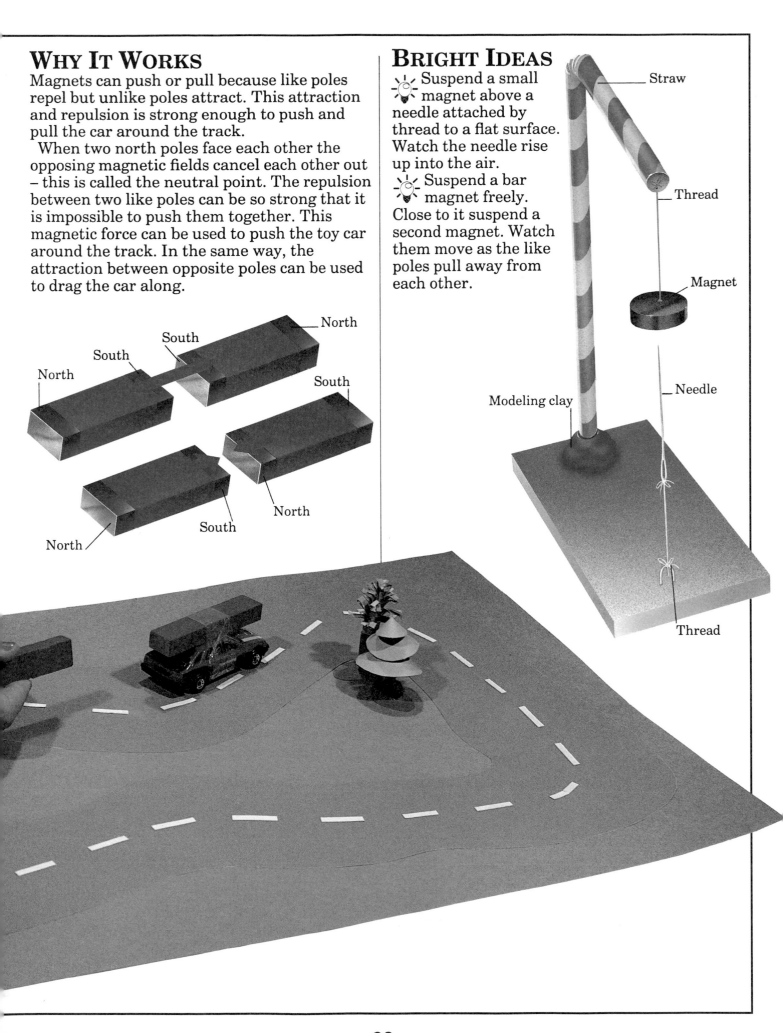

North

South

South

North

North

South

South

North

Straw

Thread

Magnet

Modeling clay

Needle

Thread

MAGNETISM TRAVELS

A magnetic force can travel through many substances. It can even travel through water. Treasure on the seabed can be detected by a diver carrying an instrument called a magnetometer. The same is true of other nonmagnetic materials – you have already seen how magnetic lines of force can travel through paper to the iron filings. What other materials do you think magnetism could travel through? Because tiny magnets as fine as powder are used to store images and sounds on tapes and computer disks, a magnetic field can interfere with the quality. The effect can only be lessened by placing another magnetic object within the magnetic field. This is a shield that cancels out the effect. Make this hockey game and prove that magnetism can travel through nonmagnetic materials.

1 Cut out two figures holding hockey sticks from cardboard. Color them so that they are wearing different shirts. Behind each hockey stick attach a small magnet with modeling clay.

FACE-OFF!

2 Attach a bar magnet firmly to one end of two long sticks. These sticks can then be held underneath the "rink" and used to move the players.

3 The hockey rink can be made from a painted cardboard lid raised up on four wooden legs. Fold two strips of cardboard to be the goalposts. Mark the center line and circles with colored tape. Put the "players" in position, facing each other. You can score goals using a Ping-Pong ball.

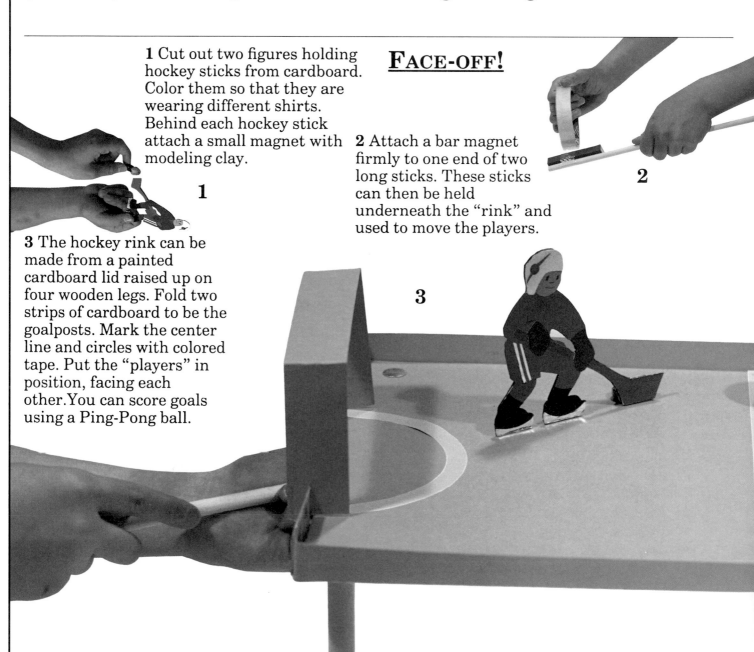

WHY IT WORKS

Nonmagnetic materials allow a magnetic field to pass through them. A magnetic material will pick up the magnetic force and weaken it. Cardboard is not magnetic. It allows a magnetic force to pass through it. Distance is important. If the magnet is too far away or if the nonmagnetic material is too thick, the effect of the magnet will not be felt. Some magnets are stronger than others. The weaker the magnet, the closer it must be held to the magnetic material. A strong magnet can be held further away because its magnetic field is larger.

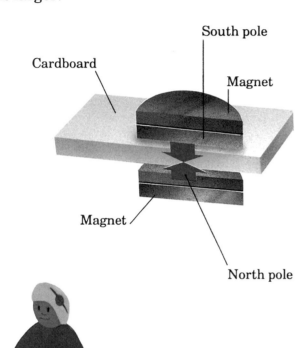

Cardboard
South pole
Magnet
Magnet
North pole

BRIGHT IDEAS

Fill a plastic see-through container with water and attach a paper clip to the bottom with modeling clay, as shown. Now take a cork and insert another paper clip to make a hook. Using a bar magnet on the outside of the container, see if you can drag the cork to the bottom and anchor it to the clip. See what other materials magnetism will work through. Try plastic, wood, and china.

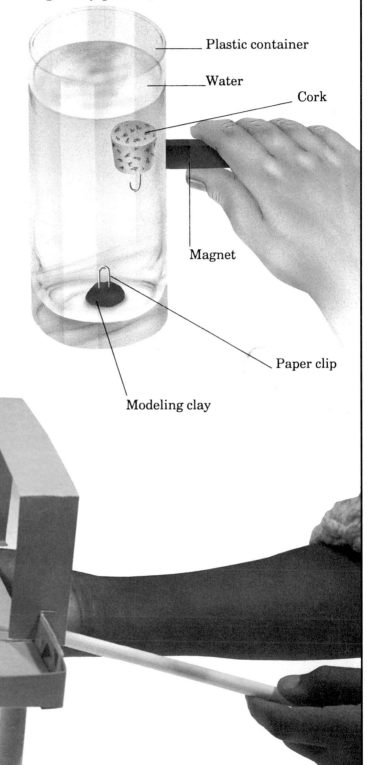

Plastic container
Water
Cork
Magnet
Paper clip
Modeling clay

101

THE EARTH IS A MAGNET

As long ago as 1600, William Gilbert noted that a round lodestone showed all the magnetic properties of the earth in miniature. He called it a "terella," meaning "little earth." The inside of the earth behaves like a massive magnet. Imagine a giant bar magnet at its center. A compass needle points to the magnetic North Pole, not true north. When orienteering (mapreading), always allow for the difference between the two by lining up north on the map with north on the compass. Migrating birds are thought to use the earth's magnetic field to navigate. Racing pigeons are known to fly off course during a magnetic storm, when changes occur in the earth's magnetic field. The Northern and Southern lights are an impressive sight at the Poles. They are caused by the collision of solar winds with the earth's magnetic field.

SEEKING NORTH!

1
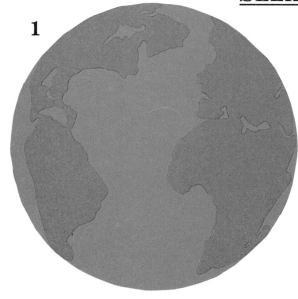

1. Cut out a circle of blue card-board and trace the map of the world onto cardboard of another color. Now stick this down to represent the earth.

2. You will need five compasses to lay around the outside of your map.

2

3

3. Lay the bar magnet under your map, with the North pole at the top and South pole at the bottom.

WHY IT WORKS

The north-seeking poles of the compasses follow the magnetic lines of force of the bar magnet, not those of the real Earth. A similar field, however, lies around the earth. At the top half of your map, the north-seeking pole of the compasses points to the north pole of the magnet and the miniature Earth. At the bottom half of the map, the south-seeking pole points to the south pole of the map. Lines of force span the earth from pole to pole.

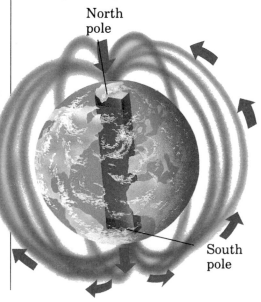

North pole

South pole

BRIGHT IDEAS

💡 Place a compass on top of a map of your locality. Establish where magnetic north is, then rotate the map until north on the map is lined up with the north-seeking point of the compass needle. This is called orienting a map. In which direction are east, south, and west in relation to north?

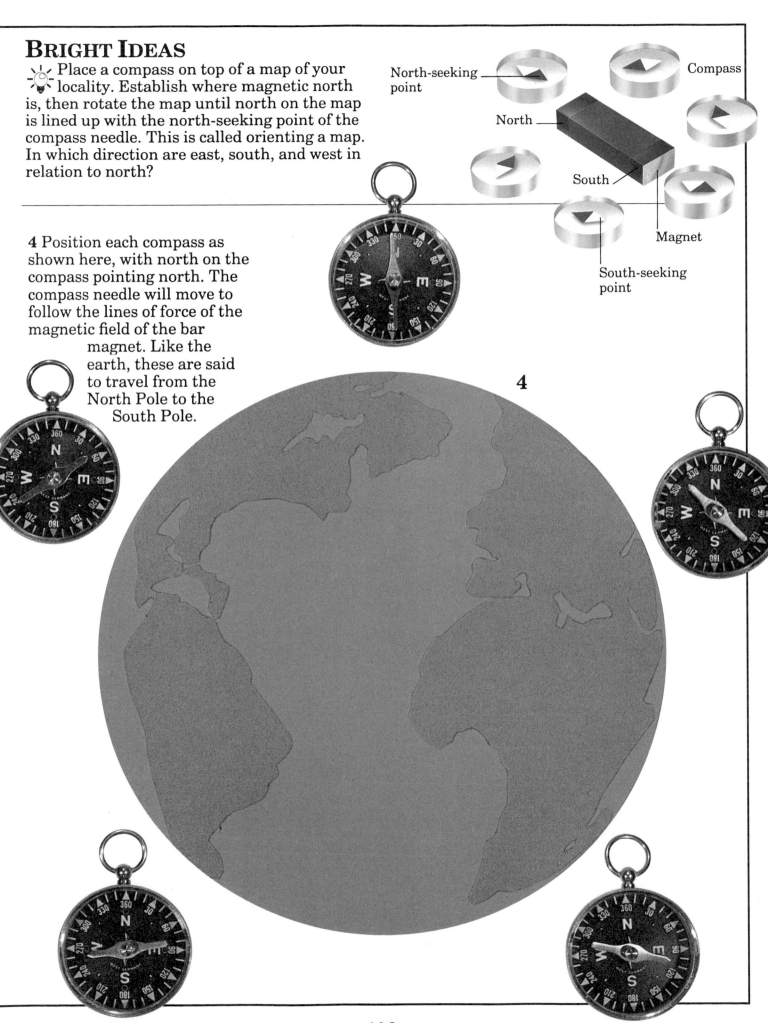

North-seeking point

Compass

North

South

Magnet

South-seeking point

4 Position each compass as shown here, with north on the compass pointing north. The compass needle will move to follow the lines of force of the magnetic field of the bar magnet. Like the earth, these are said to travel from the North Pole to the South Pole.

4

FOLLOWING MAGNETS

Almost 2,000 years ago, the Chinese knew how to make a simple compass by suspending a long, thin piece of magnetite or lodestone. Later, sailors used a lodestone to magnetize the needle for a ship's compass. Compasses were being used in China in the eleventh century. The Italian explorer, Amerigo Vespucci, whose name was mistakenly given to America, understood the concept of a magnetic North Pole. It was not until the sixteenth century, however, that it was fully accepted. Christopher Columbus was unable to navigate with total accuracy, because his compass readings were inaccurate – probably due to magnetic interference. Today, many large ships have a gyrocompass. This gives a bearing (compass direction) in relation to true north. Make your own simple compass by magnetizing a needle.

CRAFT A COMPASS

1 You will need a waterproof plate, a cork, a magnet, and a steel needle. Half fill the plate with clean water. Holding the magnet the same way all the time, stroke the needle with it at least 50 times. Always stroke in the same direction and lift the magnet off the needle each time you want to begin another stroke.

2 The needle has now been magnetized permanently, because it is steel. Push it through the cork so that the cork balances on the water evenly. Allow the water to become absolutely still. The needle will seek out the earth's magnetic North Pole to point north. Make sure there are no magnetic materials nearby.

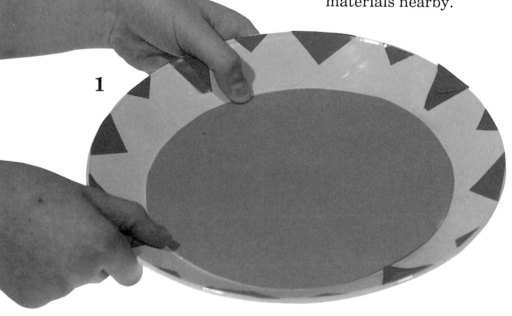

WHY IT WORKS

By stroking a permanent magnet along the needle, the domains inside become aligned. This turns the needle into a magnet, too. Any magnet free to turn horizontally will settle pointing north/south, as the north-seeking pole is attracted to the earth's magnetic North Pole.

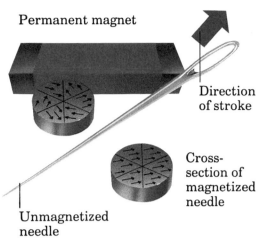

Permanent magnet

Direction of stroke

Unmagnetized needle

Cross-section of magnetized needle

BRIGHT IDEAS

🔆 Find a way to mark your compass clearly with the four compass directions. You could even design a compass rose.

🔆 Make a different kind of compass by pivoting a magnetized needle on folded cardboard on top of a stick. The stick is kept upright inside a container using modeling clay.

🔆 Place a paper clip underneath a metal lid made from a magnetic metal. Try to move the paper clip from beneath the lid with a magnet. You will find it difficult. Why is this?

🔆 Using a bar magnet you can show how a compass needle seeks out north. Suspend the magnet freely - make sure there are no magnets nearby - the magnet will rotate until it points north-south. The north-seeking pole (which is the south pole of the magnet) will face north.

🔆 Try floating a bar magnet on wood or cork in a bowl of water. What do you expect to happen?

🔆 Draw an eight-point compass. What is the size of the angle between each compass point?

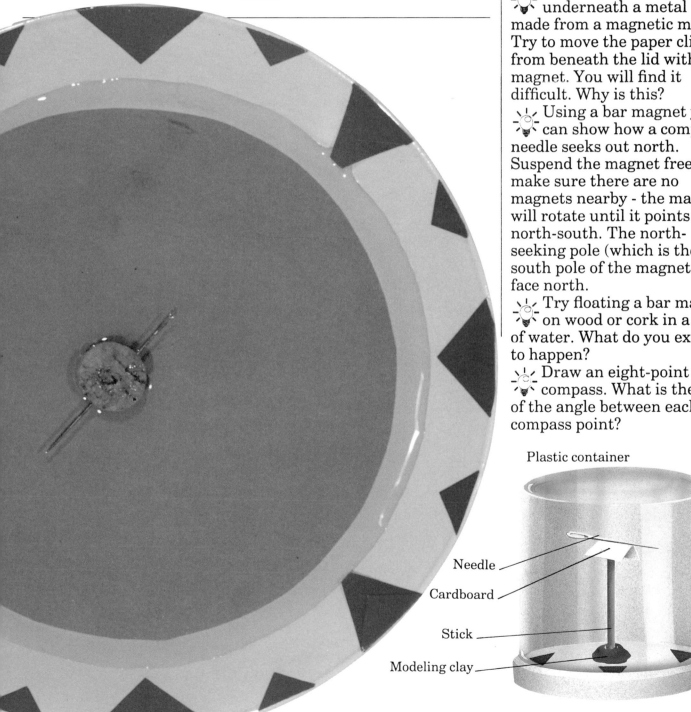

Plastic container

Needle

Cardboard

Stick

Modeling clay

ELECTROMAGNETS

The discovery of electromagnets in the 1800s was the first step in investigating the relationship between electricity and magnetism. In 1820, a Danish physicist, Hans Christian Oersted, discovered that a wire conducting an electric current produces a surrounding magnetic field. We now know that when electricity flows through a coil of wire wrapped around a soft iron core it creates a strong magnet, called an electromagnet. Electromagnets are used in many appliances and machines. Doorbells, telephones, and burglar alarms are only a few. The most powerful electromagnets are those used in scrapyards to lift heavy pieces of metal. You can build your own pickup using an electromagnet.

A MAGNETIC PICKUP

1 Use two boxes to make the crane. Make the arm from cardboard, using a thread spool and pencil to create a lever. Wind insulated wire (blue) around an iron nail 50 times.

1

2 Take one end of the blue wire to the battery in the base and the other to a drawing pin in the side of the body. Attach a paper clip to this pin to create a switch (as shown), and insert another pin within reach of the clip.

2

3 To this second pin attach the red wire, taking the other end to the battery. When the paper clip joins both drawing pins, electricity flows through the wires causing the nail to become magnetized.

3

106

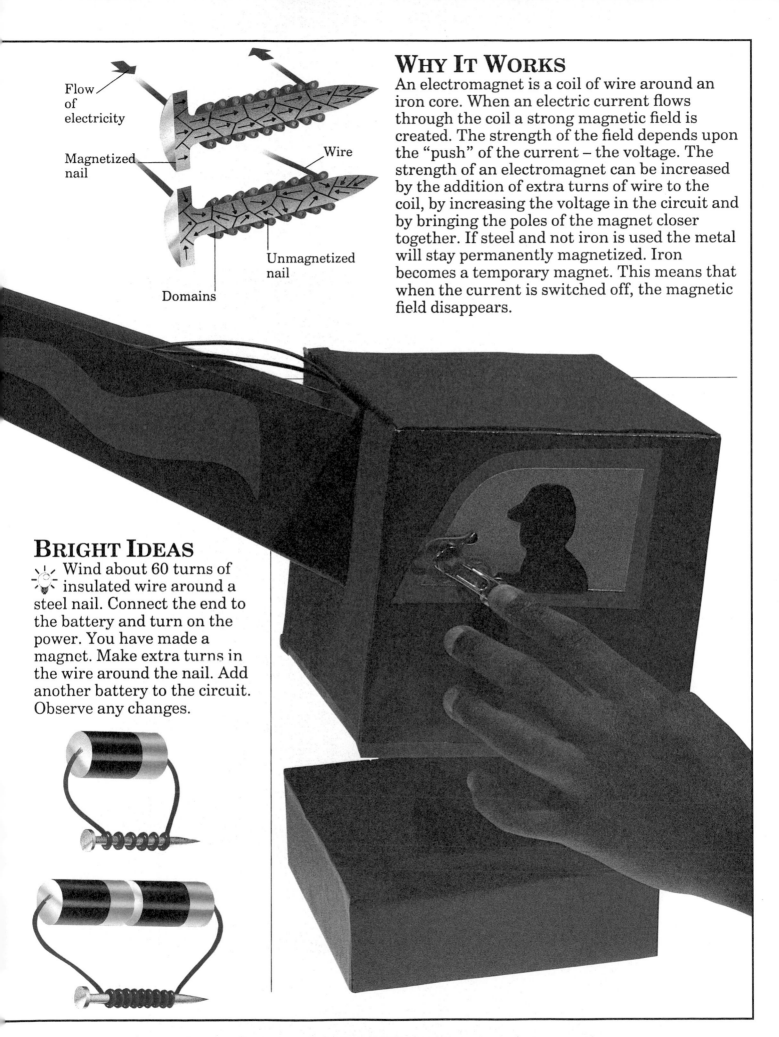

Flow
of
electricity

Magnetized
nail

Wire

Unmagnetized
nail

Domains

WHY IT WORKS

An electromagnet is a coil of wire around an iron core. When an electric current flows through the coil a strong magnetic field is created. The strength of the field depends upon the "push" of the current – the voltage. The strength of an electromagnet can be increased by the addition of extra turns of wire to the coil, by increasing the voltage in the circuit and by bringing the poles of the magnet closer together. If steel and not iron is used the metal will stay permanently magnetized. Iron becomes a temporary magnet. This means that when the current is switched off, the magnetic field disappears.

BRIGHT IDEAS

Wind about 60 turns of insulated wire around a steel nail. Connect the end to the battery and turn on the power. You have made a magnet. Make extra turns in the wire around the nail. Add another battery to the circuit. Observe any changes.

ELECTRICITY & MAGNETISM

During the 1800s, many people believed that magnetism could cure the sick. Franz Mesmer, a doctor, practiced conveying "animal magnetism" to his patients by gazing into their faces. The American scientist, Joseph Henry, discovered a more practical use for magnetism when he developed an even more powerful electromagnet. It was also discovered that electrical energy could be converted to mechanical energy by using a cylindrical coil of wire called a solenoid. This principle was later employed by Michael Faraday (pictured right) when he built his simple electric motor. Make your own solenoid and watch the mouse hide in the cheese.

HIDE AND PEEP

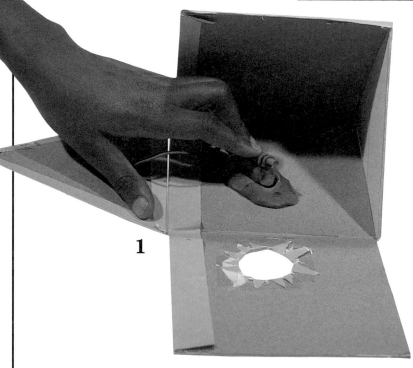

1

1. Make a "wedge of cheese" with three square pieces of cardboard and two triangular sides. Color it yellow and hinge the sides to give access to the inside.

3

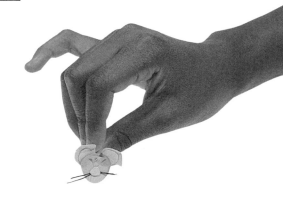

2. Through the triangular door insert wires connected to a battery. Coil the wire around a straw at least twenty times. Secure the straw on modeling clay inside the trap, making a hole in the side

2

3. Attach a cardboard mouse's head to a needle. Make sure the head of the mouse will fit through the hole next to the straw.

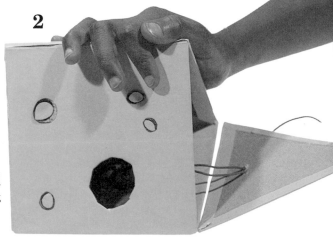

WHY IT WORKS

An electric currrent is made up of tiny invisible particles, called electrons. When an electric current is passed through a wire it creates a magnetic field. This magnetic field becomes very strong when the wire is coiled many times around the straw. This solenoid acts as an electromagnet, pulling the needle inside the straw when the electric current is switched on.

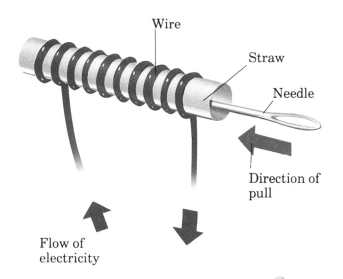

Wire

Straw

Needle

Direction of pull

Flow of electricity

BRIGHT IDEAS

Make the solenoid even stronger by winding more turns of wire on to the coil. See what happens when the current is turned off. Can your mouse peep out of the cheese again?

Remove the needle from the solenoid and test it for magnetization. See if it can pick up paper clips. Is it a temporary or permanent magnet?

Reconstruct Oersted's first experiment to show how a compass needle is deflected by the magnetic field produced by an electric current. Magnetize a needle and rest it on top of a piece of paper balanced on a stick (see page 19). Pass a wire carrying an electric current over the "compass," making sure there are no magnets nearby. Now repeat the experiment, winding coils of wire around a real compass.

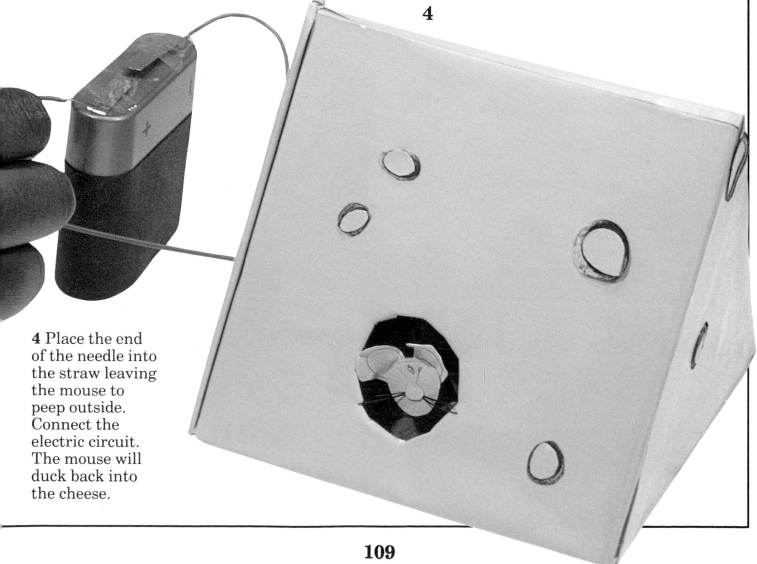

4

4 Place the end of the needle into the straw leaving the mouse to peep outside. Connect the electric circuit. The mouse will duck back into the cheese.

MAGNETS & MOVEMENT

Electric motors use magnets to turn electricity into movement. In 1821 Michael Faraday developed the electric motor. He discovered that continuous motion could be produced by passing an electric current through a conductor in a strong magnetic field. Electrical appliances like washing machines and vacuum cleaners have electric motors. The TGV, one of France's most powerful trains, is powered by electric motors. An electric motor is a coil turning between the two poles of a permanent magnet. When current flows through the coil, a magnetic field is produced that turns the rotor. This movement is converted into electricity. A generator that powers bicycle lights (right) works on this principle.

SPIN THE COMPASS

1 Position two batteries with opposite terminals touching and hold them in place with paper and tape.

2 Wind a long length of insulated wire around a cardboard core at least 50 times – this could be a slice of cardboard tube. Leave two ends free to connect to the battery.

3 Attach the coil of wire to the base with tape. You have made a solenoid. Also attach the batteries.

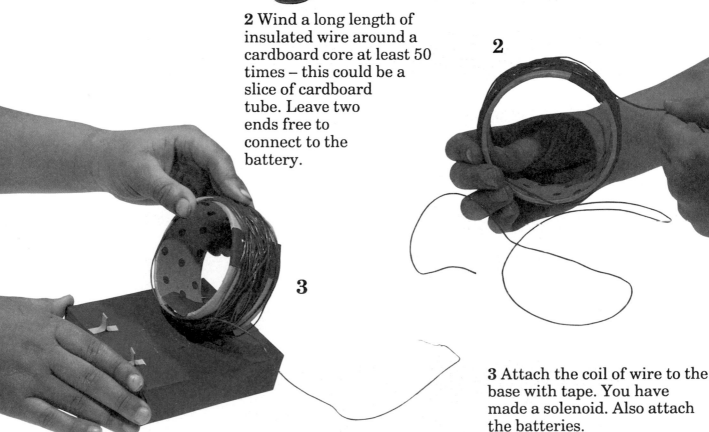

WHY IT WORKS

The magnetic field created by the electric current through the coil is strong enough to move the compass needle. When the current is turned on and off rapidly, the compass needle spins around continuously. The wire is copper. It is not magnetic and it does not affect the compass. When the electricity is turned on, each turn of wire has its own magnetic field. It is called a solenoid. A simple electric motor is a coil of wire mounted on a rod, so that it can rotate in a magnetic field. A current is passed into and out of the coil. An electric motor is clean and quiet.

BRIGHT IDEAS

💡 A simple electric motor like the one pictured here can be found in toy cars, hair dryers, and power drills. Maybe you could open up a broken toy and have a look?

💡 Recreate Faraday's experiment to illustrate the reverse principle - how a magnet can induce an electric current. You will need a small compass, placed inside a box. Wind at least 20 turns of wire around the box; at the other end of the wire you need a coil of at least 50 turns. Slowly pass a bar magnet through the coil and observe the compass.

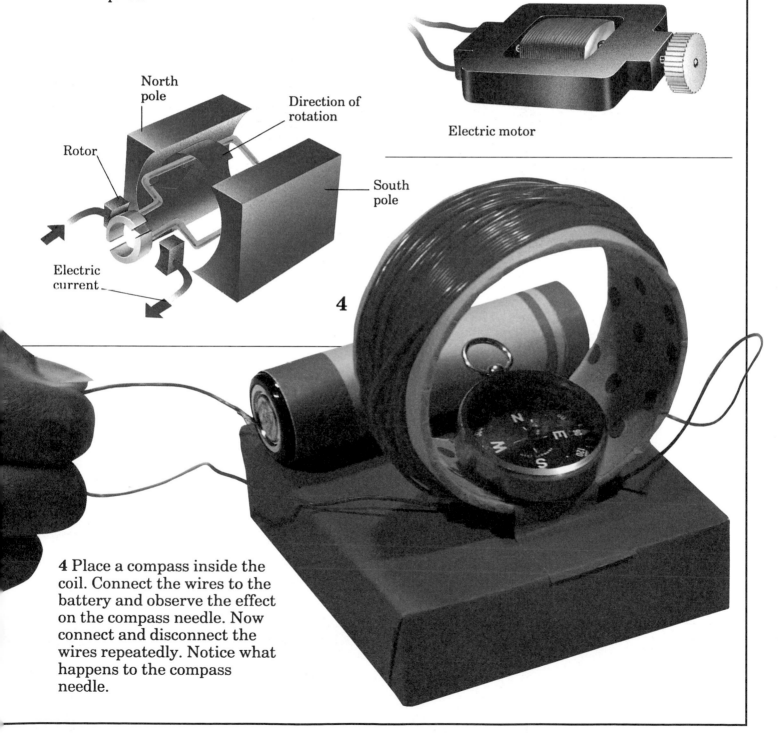

Electric motor

North pole

Direction of rotation

Rotor

South pole

Electric current

4

4 Place a compass inside the coil. Connect the wires to the battery and observe the effect on the compass needle. Now connect and disconnect the wires repeatedly. Notice what happens to the compass needle.

USING MAGNETISM

The magnets used by scientists vary in size, shape, and strength. With the development of electricity, the electromagnet is now part of much modern equipment, both scientific and domestic. Numerous gadgets and machines work for us because of magnetism. They range from a lid-holding can opener to an atom-smashing machine, called a particle accelerator. In our homes, weak magnets help to hold refrigerator doors firmly shut. In factories, magnetic conveyor belts transport iron and steel cans. Precision instruments may have lightweight moving parts suspended inside them with a magnet. We all make use of machines like the ticket machines pictured here. They can sort coins into their different values. You can also sort coins using your own magnetic slot machine.

A MAGNETIC SLOT MACHINE

2 Now fit the cardboard diagonally inside a tall box as shown. Hinge one side of the box to allow access.

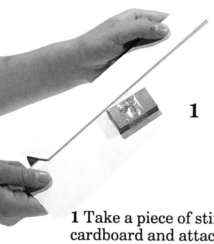

1

1 Take a piece of stiff cardboard and attach a strong magnet underneath with tape. Attach it to the left side of the piece of cardboard.

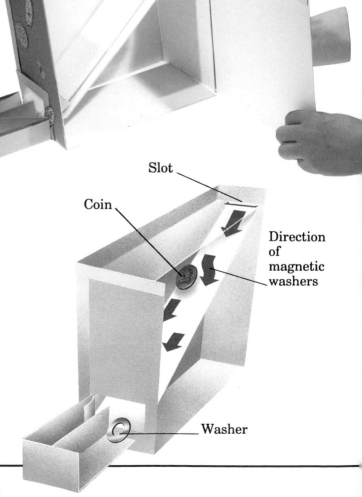

2

Slot

Coin

Direction of magnetic washers

Washer

WHY IT WORKS

When you drop the coins and washers into the slot, they travel down the shute, passing over the magnet. The metal washers, which are magnetic, are diverted by the magnetic field and fall into the left-hand compartment. The coins, which are not magnetic, carry on straight down the chute landing in the right-hand compartment. A real vending machine tests the coins with an electric current. It can sort the coins by testing the amount of electricity conducted.

BRIGHT IDEAS

☀ If you push the "coins" through the slot with greater force does it make any difference? Examine your results and draw conclusions from them.

☀ With small button magnets you can make some magnetic stickers. Cut out letters or shapes and color them in. Use them to make a board game.

☀ Draw your own weather map on magnetic material and design some weather symbols that can be mounted on small magnets.

3 Cut an opening at the bottom of the box, the same width as the stiff cardboard. Attach a cardboard tray divided into sections, as shown. Enclose the top of the box, cutting a slit adjacent to the top of the stiff, sloping cardboard. Make the slit long enough to allow coins to be pushed through.

3

4 Finish off your machine by decorating the outside. Collect as many different coins and metal washers as you can and roll each through the machine.

FLOATING MAGNETS

You have already learned that like poles repel and unlike poles attract. This principle has been adapted and used in industry and the world of transportation. In factories and other places where steel sheets need to be lifted, magnetic floaters, which are large permanent magnets, are placed on either side of steel sheets. They magnetize the steel and cause poles to form in adjacent parts of the sheets. As the like poles repel one another they cause the top sheet to lift off the pile. Electromagnets can create a moving magnetic field. The Maglev train (pictured above) works on this principle. The Maglev has no wheels – it is levitated along the track as two magnetic fields repel each other.

LEVITATION

1

3

2 The cutout magician is secured to a cardboard window that is the same size as the back of the box. Slide the magician inside the box so that he stands behind the magnet, touching it.

1 You will need a cardboard box wide enough to hold a bar magnet, two strong bar magnets, cardboard, and tape. Cut away one side of the box and fold back a second side to give access to the "stage." Attach two strips of cardboard to the floor wide enough to hold one of the bar magnets in place. Position the North pole of the magnet to the left side of the stage when you are facing it.

2

3 Cover the sides with fabric to look like curtains. To the second magnet attach a cardboard cutout "assistant," as shown. Ensure that the head of the figure is positioned at the North pole of the magnet.

WHY IT WORKS

Magnets can push as well as pull. The strongest part of a magnetic field is at the poles and like poles repel. As both ends of the magnets repel each other, the top magnet is able to float above the other. It is important to support the top magnet at the sides so it cannot be pushed off in one direction.

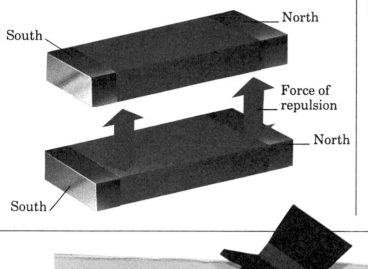

South
North
Force of repulsion
North
South

BRIGHT IDEAS

💡 Place some balsa wood between two magnets with opposite poles facing each other. Tape them together at each end and remove the wood. Press down on the top magnet. You will feel the "spring" of repulsion. This is how the Maglev train works.

💡 Get some small ring magnets and arrange them along a pencil. Place them so that they repel each other and see them float.

Maglev train

4

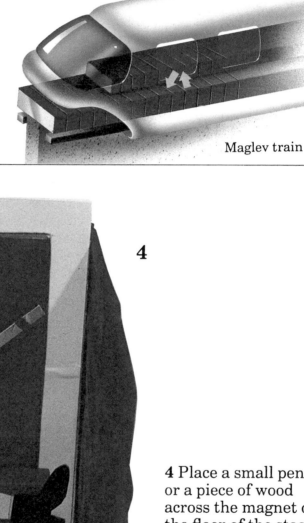

4 Place a small pencil or a piece of wood across the magnet on the floor of the stage. Gently position the "assistant" on top of it, parallel with the first magnet. Her head should be on the left. You may need to tape the ends of the two magnets together. Carefully remove the pencil and watch the lady levitate.

FUN WITH MAGNETS

Now that you know more about magnets, how many do you think you could find around your home and school? Maybe you have refrigerator magnets or a magnetic notice board. Somebody you know may have a magnetic catch on their bag or maybe you own a magnetic travel game like chess or checkers. If you want them to be, magnets can be lots of fun. But you must take care of them! All magnets become weaker over time and should be stored carefully, in pairs, with unlike poles together. Every magnet should have a piece of soft iron, called a keeper, across each end. Be careful not to drop your magnets, as this can result in them losing their magnetic powers. Magnetic sculptures can be bought in stores, but you can make your own with paper clips. Gather together your magnets and have some fun!

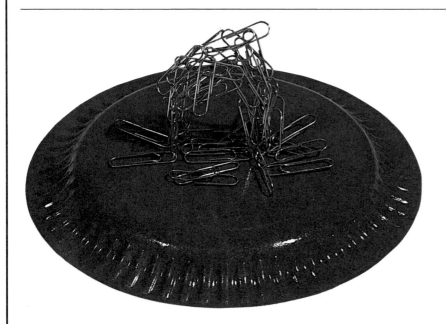

MAGNETIC SCULPTURE

Place a bar magnet beneath an upturned paper plate. Gather together some paper clips and scatter them on top of the plate. The magnetic field of the magnet travels through the plate, magnetizing the paper clips. Now you can build up a sculpture, making all kinds of different shapes. How high can you build? See what happens when you take the magnet away.

BEARDED FACE

Draw and color in a man's face on a paper plate. Leave out his hair, eyebrows, and moustache. Now place some iron filings on the plate. Keeping the plate level, lift it in one hand and hold a magnet underneath with the other. By moving the magnet around under the plate, you can make hair grow. You could even create a hair-raising monster! To make another picture, just remove the magnet and shake.

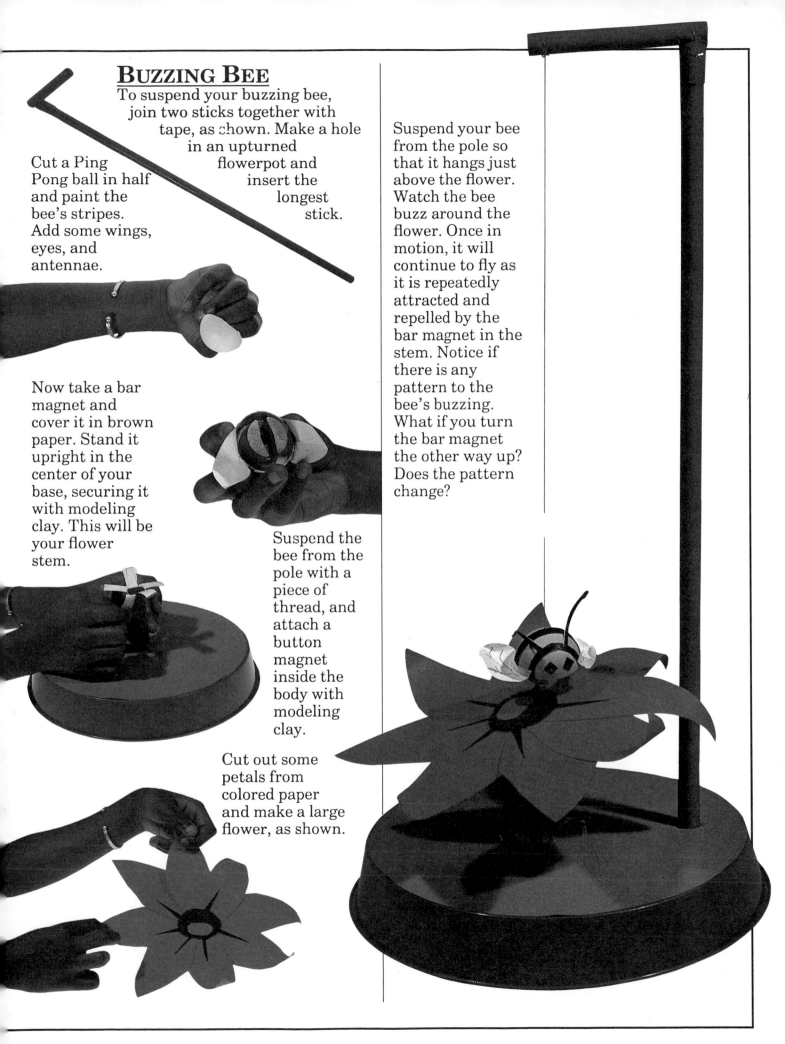

BUZZING BEE

To suspend your buzzing bee, join two sticks together with tape, as shown. Make a hole in an upturned flowerpot and insert the longest stick.

Cut a Ping Pong ball in half and paint the bee's stripes. Add some wings, eyes, and antennae.

Now take a bar magnet and cover it in brown paper. Stand it upright in the center of your base, securing it with modeling clay. This will be your flower stem.

Suspend the bee from the pole with a piece of thread, and attach a button magnet inside the body with modeling clay.

Cut out some petals from colored paper and make a large flower, as shown.

Suspend your bee from the pole so that it hangs just above the flower. Watch the bee buzz around the flower. Once in motion, it will continue to fly as it is repeatedly attracted and repelled by the bar magnet in the stem. Notice if there is any pattern to the bee's buzzing. What if you turn the bar magnet the other way up? Does the pattern change?

117

SOUND AND LIGHT

CONTENTS

INTRODUCTION

The sun is our most important source of natural light. Without this there would be no life on earth, no crops for us to eat or to release oxygen for us to breathe. Fire was the first man-made light source followed later by candles, oil lamps, gas light and electric light. Today, because of advanced technology, we can use sunlight directly to heat and light our homes. Light is color and it is light which makes it possible for us to see.

Sound is also a form of energy, like light or heat. It may be a baby crying, the drone of traffic, an alarm clock or our favorite music. Sound can travel through liquid, gas or a solid. Sound can be "bounced" – or reflected off a solid object. This is called an echo. Sounds are produced by vibrating objects which cause sound waves to travel at a speed of 1,115 feet per second to reach our ears. There are even sounds which we can't hear because they are too high but which can be heard by some animals like dogs or bats. Other sounds are too low but we may apppreciate them as vibrations.

Safety Tips

Take care when experimenting with light – don't look directly at the sun for a long time and never through a lens. In experiments that require artificial light, use a torch with two batteries of 1.5 volts. Never use mains electricity. If you are using sharp scissors to cut up a plastic bottle ask an adult to help you. Always take care with balloons and plastic bags – don't put them over your face.

VIBRATIONS

Have you ever thrown a pebble into a pond and watched the ripples spread? The impact of the pebble in the water creates waves – and in a similar way all sounds cause waves in the air. Unlike water waves, sound waves do not move up and down, but travel forward in regions of high and low pressure. Sounds are produced by very fast back and forth movements called vibrations. If you hold your throat lightly a few inches below your chin and talk, you will feel the vibrations. These vibrations produce sound waves in the air by pushing and pulling it to produce pressure changes. We hear the sound when these waves reach our ears. There is no sound on the moon because there is no air to carry the waves.

BEAT THE DRUM

1

1. Stretch a piece of thick polyethylene or plastic over the open top of a pail or large can. A metal pail will be more effective than a plastic one.

2. Keep the plastic in place with string, or with rubber bands. Pull the polyethylene down to make a tight skin and trim the spare polyethylene away.

3

3. To give your drum a professional finished look, make a cardboard cover to decorate the outside of it. Make the cover 0.5in taller than your drum and leave 5 in overlap for attaching it on when it is finished.

4. A rectangle of white cardboard is ideal for the cover. Work out a pattern using other colors of cardboard, or you could use scraps of material, paints, felt tip pens, wax crayons etc. The green strips shown above provide a border that gives a neat look to the whole thing.

4

5

5. Wooden drumsticks are best. Make sure they have rounded ends and finish them off with a touch of paint. Now your drum is ready to play. Remember – don't hit your drum too hard or you will quickly damage the skin.

Compressions

Vibrations

WHY IT WORKS

When you bang the top of the drum, the plastic skin vibrates. As the skin moves up, it pushes against the air and causes a compression, or squashing, of the air above the drum. As it moves down, it compresses the air below the skin, while just above it the air expands to fill the space. As the skin vibrates and moves up again, an expansion is caused below the skin and a new compression takes place above it. One compression and one expansion together is called one cycle. A series of cycles makes a sound wave.

BRIGHT IDEAS

Put sand or grains of rice onto your drum and bang it. Watch the vibrations of the drum's skin make the sand or rice vibrate, too. Does a loud bang make bigger vibrations?

Watch the loudspeakers in a radio or stereo. Can you see them vibrate? Is there a difference when the sound is turned louder?

SOUND WAVES

Sound waves are similar to light waves in some ways. Like a beam of light can be reflected from a mirror, so a sound can be reflected from a surface like a wall. If you shout loudly in your school hall, the sound waves travel to the wall and are bounced back, reaching your ears a split second later – this is an echo. Bats make use of echoes when finding their way, or hunting. They give out a very high pitched sound that bounces back from objects or insects, telling them how far away things are. We can also use this method to find objects that we cannot see. Sonar uses sound to locate objects at the bottom of the sea, such as shipwrecks and shoals of fish.

FIRING WAVES

1. This cannon will send a narrow "beam" of sound waves. Begin by making a pair of wheels for your cannon using circles of cardboard, paper plates, thread spools, and a wooden stick.

1

2. Make a large tube of stiff cardboard for the cannon itself, 18-20 inches in diameter, and four feet long. Make the back of the cannon by covering a circle of cardboard with plastic wrap. Fix it with tape. **2**

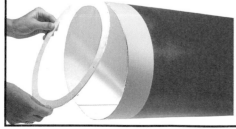

3

3. The front of the cannon is a disk of stiff cardboard with a 1 in hole in the center. You could decorate this with a disk of colored paper.

4

4. Tape the ends of the cannon firmly with double sided tape – this will enable you to fix the ends onto the tube and not into it.

5. Fix the tube to the wheels with tape, and weight the back end of the cannon so that it does not tip forward. Aim the cannon at a wall and tap the plastic wrap quite firmly – from a distance you should get an echo. Make a curtain from 0.5 in strips of foil. Fire your cannon at the curtain. You should see the sound waves making the foil vibrate.

5

WHY IT WORKS

When you strike the piece of plastic wrap (diaphragm) on the cannon, the vibrations lead to sound waves being formed. The waves travel outward from the diaphragm, making the air particles around move back and forth in the same direction. When the waves leaving the front of the cannon meet a solid object, some of them are reflected while some continue traveling through the object, making it move slightly like the air particles. A bat uses sound to find objects in the dark. It produces sounds and then listens for the echoes to be reflected. This is called echolocation.

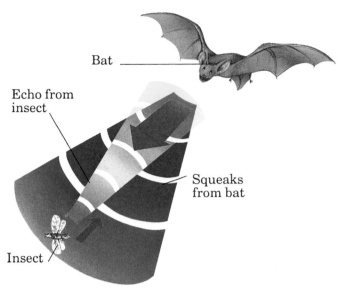

Bat

Echo from insect

Squeaks from bat

Insect

BRIGHT IDEAS

☀ Which surfaces are best for echoing? Can you make an echo in a bathroom, a kitchen, a cafeteria, a hall, a subway? Try other places, too. Do you think hard surfaces are better than soft surfaces for giving echoes? Which sounds echo the best?

☀ Try shouting, knocking two stones together, banging two blocks of wood together, whistling, and talking. Do short, sharp sounds echo better than long soft ones?

☀ The cannon channels the sound waves in one direction. Make a megaphone to channel your voice. Make a narrow cone, and then a wide cone. Shout to a friend through each cone. Shout again, aiming the megaphone 30 feet to their side. What happens? Which cone makes your voice sound louder, and which can you hear best from the side? Can you figure out why?

123

HOW SOUNDS ARE HEARD

When sound waves enter our ears, they strike the eardrum which vibrates back and forth. This in turn causes tiny bones called ossicles to vibrate. These vibrations are turned by our "inner ear" into electrical signals that pass along nerves to the brain. When the signals reach the brain, we hear sounds. People cannot hear some sounds because they are too high or too low – not everyone can hear the high-pitched squeak of a bat. Dogs can hear higher pitched sounds than people, and a scientist called Sir Francis Galton (1822–1911) invented a whistle for calling dogs which was too high for people to hear. This kind of sound is called ultrasonic sound, or ultrasound.

WHY IT WORKS

The sound waves from your friend's voice make the plastic wrap vibrate. These vibrations are transmitted into your cardboard "ossicles" and can be seen by watching the mirror for movements. This is a simple model of how a real ear works.

Vibrations in the air (sound waves) enter the outer ear and make the eardrum itself vibrate. The three bones, the malleus, the incus, and the stapes, together known as the ossicles, transmit the vibrations through the middle ear

to the oval window, or vestibular fenestra. The force of the vibrations on the oval window is over 20 times greater than that of the original vibrations on the eardrum. The oscillations (or vibrations) of the stapes makes the fluid in the part of the inner ear called the cochlea vibrate. The cochlea also contains fibers that pick up the vibrations and send messages along nerves to the brain. Other parts of the ear control our balance – these are called semicircular canals.

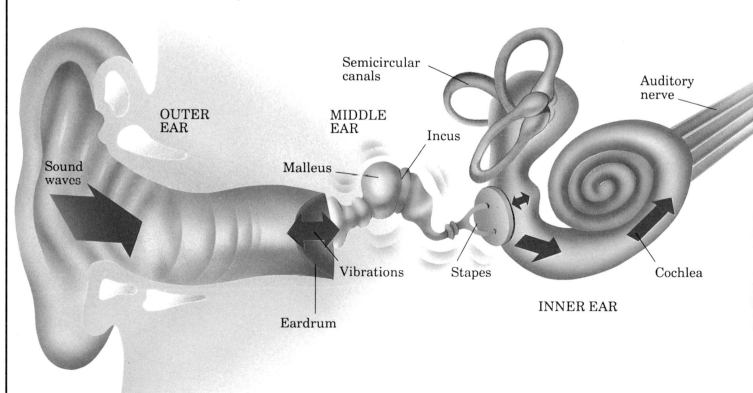

HEAR THIS?

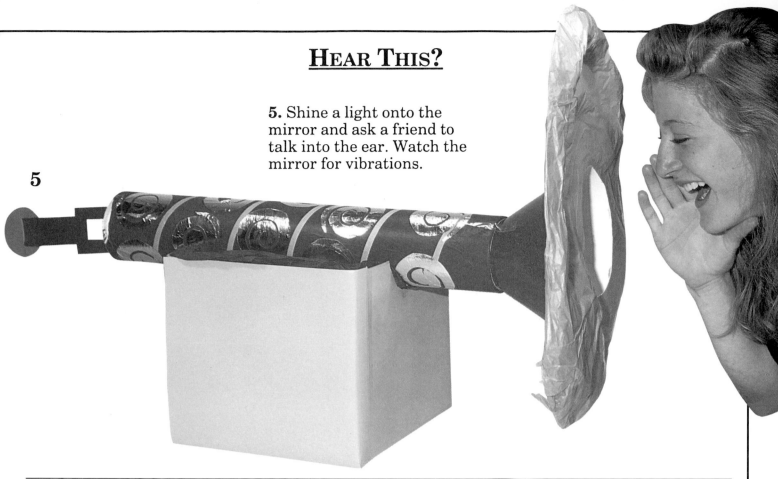

5. Shine a light onto the mirror and ask a friend to talk into the ear. Watch the mirror for vibrations.

5

1

1. To make an eardrum, stretch a piece of plastic wrap or a piece of an old balloon across the end of a tube. Fix in place with a rubber band.

2. Make a set of "ossicles" with two disks and a fork shape of thin cardboard held together with double sided tape.

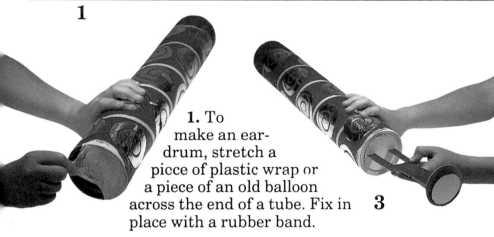

2

4. Make an outer ear from a cone of cardboard with a hole at its end. With careful use of pink tissue paper you can achieve quite a realistic look!

3. Attach a small mirror or a disk of shiny foil to one end, and attach the other to the plastic wrap "eardrum" on the tube. Your middle ear is complete.

3

4

BRIGHT IDEAS

- Watch the oval window of your ear again. How does it respond to shouting, whispering, whistling etc? The vibrations of your oval window could be a result of blowing on the eardrum, rather than the vibrations of sound waves. Use a radio to create sound without blowing.

- A hundred years ago, people who suffered from hearing loss used ear trumpets. Find out about these devices! Can you make your own?

- Listen to sounds blindfolded. Put your hand over one ear and try to tell which direction a sound is coming from. Listen to the same sound with both ears. Can you hear a difference? It is easier to hear the direction of sound with both ears.

TRAVELING SOUNDS

It is not only air that can transmit sound waves. North American Indians knew that the ground itself could carry sound waves, and would listen to the noises of approaching animals and enemies by putting their ears to the ground. Swimmers can hear sound through the water. Whales and dolphins can communicate underwater. Some substances are better transmitters of sound than others, and sound travels faster through some materials, for example steel, than others, like air.

BUILD A TELEPHONE

1. You can make a simple "string telephone" and see how a piece of string transmits sounds. Pierce a small hole in the bottom of a plastic cup with a sharp pencil. Repeat with a second cup.

2. Thread a piece of thin string through the cups and tie several knots in each end of the string. You can decorate your cups by painting them if you want to.

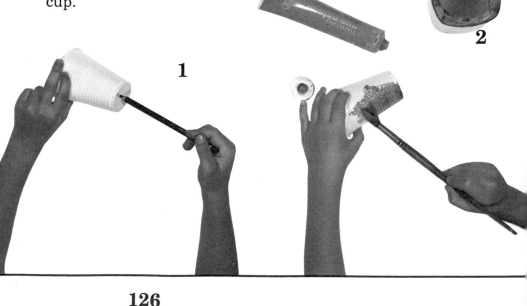

1

2

WHY IT WORKS

When you talk into the plastic cup, your voice makes sound waves that travel through the air. When the vibrations of the air reach the cup, the plastic begins to vibrate in response. Substances that carry sound are called the sound medium. When the string vibrates, it acts as a sound medium, carrying the sound waves to the other cup. Here, the vibrations cause the air inside and around the cup to oscillate, too – carrying the sound to the receiver's ear.

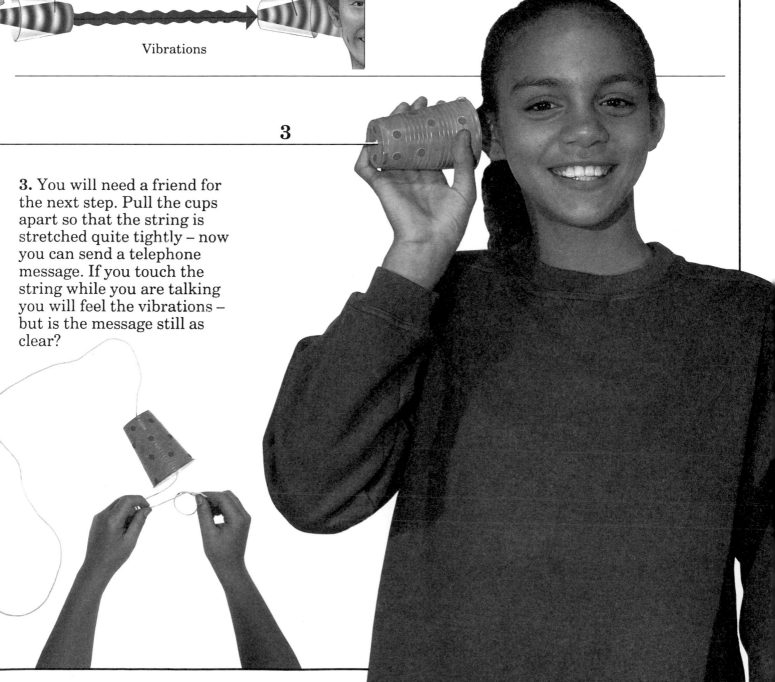

Sound waves

Sound waves

Vibrations

BRIGHT IDEAS

- Suspend a long, loose spring, such as a Slinky, on pieces of cotton so that it is hanging horizontally. Tap one end with a spoon. Can you see the vibrations travel along the spring? It is carrying the sound waves and acting as a sound medium.
- Put a glass to the wall. Put your ear to the glass. Can you hear noises in the next room? The wall and the glass are acting as sound media.
- Ask a friend to bang two stones together in a bucket of water. Listen to the sound through a piece of hose pipe which has one end in the water.

3

3. You will need a friend for the next step. Pull the cups apart so that the string is stretched quite tightly – now you can send a telephone message. If you touch the string while you are talking you will feel the vibrations – but is the message still as clear?

AMPLITUDE AND LOUDNESS

This is an oscilloscope – a machine that can measure sound waves. The louder a sound is, the higher the wave patterns will be from top to bottom. When an object vibrates, the air surrounding it moves back and forth as well. The distance each particle of air moves from its starting position is called the amplitude of the wave. As loudness depends on a person's ability to hear a sound, scientists cannot really measure loudness. Instead, they measure the energy, or "intensity," of a sound wave. The units they use are decibels.

WHY IT WORKS

When you plucked it gently, the string of the guitar only vibrated a little. During compression, particles of air will move a little way from where they started, and during expansion, they will move back to their original position and a little beyond. On the graph below, imagine that the green line shows where the string or particle of air started, the top of the red line shows how far it moved on compression, and the bottom of the red line shows the same for expansion. The distance from one peak to the next (the red line) is called the wavelength. The distance from the green line to the top of the peak is called the amplitude; the greater the amplitude, the larger the wave.

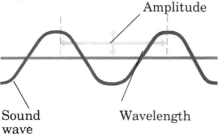

Amplitude

Sound wave

Wavelength

STRUMMING AWAY

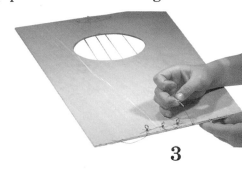

1. You can make your own guitar, but you will need a little help from an adult. Cut a piece of plywood 24 in by 16 in and make a wide hole 6 in from one end. Use sandpaper to remove the rough edges.

2. Ask an adult to cut two pieces of copper pipe or wood dowels, 12 in long. For the strings you can use thin wire or string, but fishing line gives the best results. Cut four or five lengths.

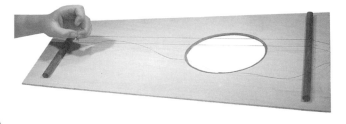

3. Fix the strings to metal eyes screwed into the plywood. If the ends come out on the other side, cover them with a little tape. To give a range of notes, tighten the top strings more than the bottom ones. Note where the copper pipes or wood dowels go.

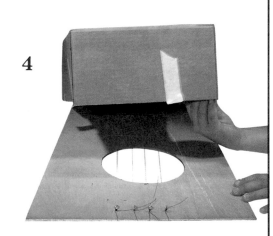

4. A soundbox made of cardboard can now be fixed to the back of your guitar. A wooden box, however, gives a better sound quality. Now you are ready to play your guitar!

BRIGHT IDEAS

Remove the soundbox and listen – is the guitar as loud? Inside the soundbox, the sound waves bounce around (reverberate) before escaping through the hole.

Try a larger or a smaller sound box. Does this make any difference?

Ask a friend to play your guitar and listen to it first from in front, and then from behind. Is there a difference in loudness?

See if you can borrow a tuning fork. Tap the tuning fork on a wooden block (not metal or stone as this will damage it). Listen to the tuning fork. Now tap the tuning fork again and gently hold its base onto different objects, for example, a cookie jar, a table, a cushion, your guitar. The hard objects reverberate more and make the sounds louder than the soft objects.

STOPPING SOUND

Do you like singing in the bath? Somehow your voice can sound more powerful, can't it? This is because the sound waves are reflected off the hard, flat surface of the bathroom walls; the sound "reverberates." In a room like your living room, your voice will sound weaker because the sound is soaked up by the drapes and the furniture. In a recording studio, the engineers have to be very careful not to have too much reverberation, but not to have too dead a sound either. They also soundproof the walls to keep the sounds in!

SOUNDPROOFING

1

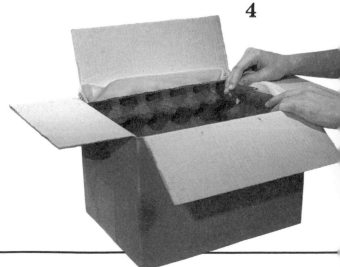

1. You can make a soundproof box to give the same effect as an insulated recording studio. Begin by collecting five or six old cardboard cartons used for storing eggs.

2. Find an old cardboard box that is in good condition with its lid intact. Line the four walls and the bottom of the box with a thick soft material, for example, old dish towels.

4. When you have done this, make sure all your linings are held in securely. Next, prepare the top insulation of egg carton and cloth.

3

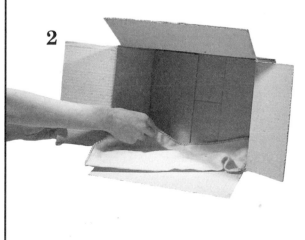

3. Cut the egg cartons carefully to size so that they fit neatly and exactly into the inside of the box. Line the bottom and all four walls with the boxes, saving one for the top.

2

4

5. To test the soundproof qualities of your box you need a portable radio, or perhaps a portable alarm clock, a music box, or a toy that buzzes. Turn on your "noise-maker" and place it carefully into the box. Make sure it is something really noisy that you would normally be able to hear through the walls of a box.

5

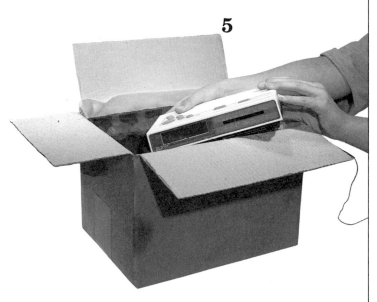

6. Insert your final layer of insulation and close the lid of the box. Notice what has happened to the level of the noise. The intensity of sound is measured in decibels. The quietest sound people can hear is about 20 decibels, and the loudest they can stand is 120 decibels. How many decibels do you think your soundproof box has cut out?

6

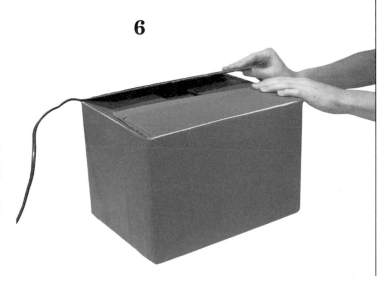

WHY IT WORKS
Your box stops the sounds of the radio in two ways. First of all, the soft materials that the egg carton and the towel are made from, are poor transmitters of sound. They do not vibrate and do not cause reverberation. Second, there are no solid, flat surfaces inside the box for sounds to echo or bounce off. Instead, the uneven surface of the egg cartons absorbs the sound, weakening it. The acoustic qualities of the box prevent the energy of the sound from escaping.

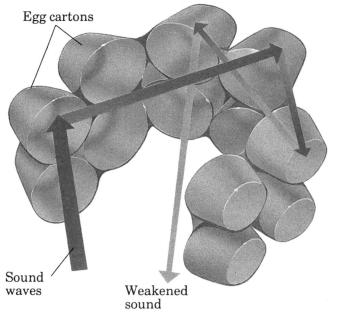

Egg cartons

Sound waves

Weakened sound

BRIGHT IDEAS
☀ Materials that stop sounds from traveling are called insulators. Experiment with different materials to find good and bad insulators. You could try styrofoam tiles, carpet squares, newspaper, wood, and so on.
☀ Call to someone through a window. Can they hear you? Try this again through a double glazed window – is it easy to hear? The space, or cavity, between the two panes of double glazing helps to insulate and keep out noise.
☀ Can you make yourself some noiseproof earmuffs?
☀ Do you have a toy that buzzes, like a wind-up train? Wind it up and let it go on a table (lay it on its side so it doesn't roll away). Listen to the noise. Now insulate it by standing it on a soft cloth or dish towel. Has the noise been lessened?

ORCHESTRAL SOUNDS

How many of the instruments in an orchestra can you name? Each one you can think of produces a different sound. Violins, cellos, and double basses have only four strings that vibrate when the musician moves a "bow" over them. Inside a piano there are many wires of different thickness that produce their sound when struck by small "hammer." The wires respond by vibrating, although the loud sound does not come from them directly. The vibrations spread to the body of the piano which makes the sound louder. In wind instruments, such as the flute or clarinet, the air inside the instrument vibrates and produces the music. There are three groups of instruments: percussion, which make a sound when struck, strings which are bowed or plucked, and wind which are blown.

SHAKE YOUR MARACA!

1. A popular percussion instrument is the maraca. Originally, maracas were made from hollowed out gourds, but you can make one of your own from papier mâché.

3. Make sure that you overlap plenty of papier mâché onto the cone handle. When the whole thing is well covered, leave in a warm, dry place. After a couple of days, burst the balloon and remove it before painting.

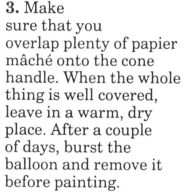

4. For a lasting finish you could varnish your shaker. When dry, drop a handful of beans into it and seal the end with a cork or a piece of tape. Now you are ready to make your own music! (You can change the sound by using sand and rice instead of beans.)

2. Smear a balloon lightly with cooking oil, then cover it with five or six layers of newspaper and paste. At the base of the balloon place a cone of cardboard with an open end.

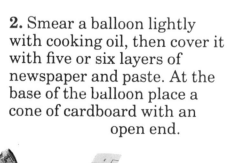

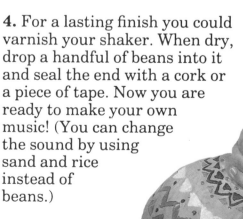

WHY IT WORKS

Whether plucking, striking, blowing, bowing, or shaking, a musician is using the same scientific principle to make the sound. When struck, the piano string and drumskin both vibrate, sending sound waves through the air. When bowed, the violin strings produce sound waves that reverberate around the sound-box and then reach our ears as music. And when you shake your maraca, the beans striking the papier mâché case cause vibrations that create sound waves again. The skillful musician knows how to produce the right notes.

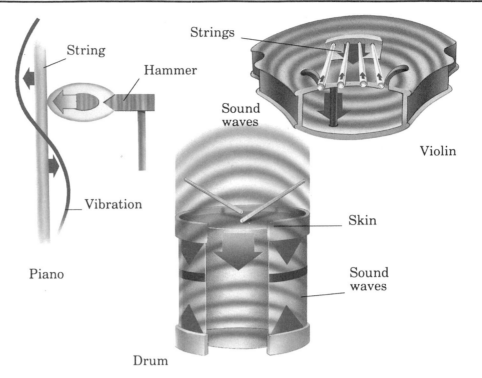

String

Hammer

Vibration

Piano

Strings

Sound waves

Violin

Skin

Sound waves

Drum

BRIGHT IDEAS

You can make a "comb kazoo" by folding a small piece of wax paper over a comb. Put the comb and paper to your lips and blow. You should be able to feel the comb begin to vibrate.

Ask an adult if you can put some water into a wine glass. Wet your finger and slowly rub it around the rim of the glass. You can produce a note.

Comb

Paper

Air

FREQUENCY

Have you ever heard an organ playing? The notes that come from the larger pipes can be very low, while the notes from the smaller pipes are much higher. The higher pitched sounds have a higher frequency. Do you remember how a sound wave is made of expansions and compressions of air? One compression and one expansion is called a cycle. An object vibrating very quickly would have more cycles in one second. Scientists measure frequency in cycles per second, or hertz. One cycle per second is one hertz. A piano string that gives a high note vibrates at about 4,000 hertz. The lowest frequency that a good human ear can hear is about 20 hertz, the highest is 20,000 hertz. Radio and other frequencies are also measured in hertz.

BOTTLE XYLOPHONE

1. You can make a simple bottle xylophone. Find five bottles that are all the same and wash them well. Color some water with a little food coloring – this will make it easier for you to see what you are doing. Put different amounts of water into the bottles, as shown below.

1

WHY IT WORKS

The air inside the organ pipe vibrates and produces the musical note. In a large pipe there is more air, which vibrates slowly, making a low frequency sound. The small pipes contain less air, which vibrates more quickly, and the higher frequency of the sound waves sounds higher pitched to us. Your bottle xylophone works in the same way – where there is more water and less air to vibrate, the sound waves have a higher frequency.

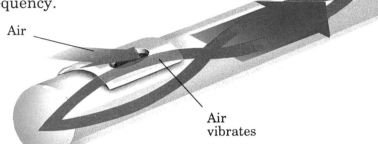

Air

Air vibrates

Flute

2. Stand the bottles on a piece of styrofoam or wool and make your musical sounds by tapping gently with a spoon or a wooden stick above the water line. To get a good range of notes you can alter the amount of water in each bottle. As an alternative, you can blow across the top of the bottle to make a sound. Can you play a tune?

BRIGHT IDEAS

☀ Make some flowerpot chimes. Hang pots of different sizes and gently strike them with a wooden stick. (The pots must be clay ones, not plastic.)

☀ Make your own set of tubular bells. You will need help from an adult here. Cut 6 lengths of copper pipe at 1.5 in, 3 in, 4.5 in and so on to 6 in. Tape a 12 in loop of string onto each one and hang them over a pole or stick. You can play the "bells" by hitting them with a spoon or stick.

☀ Make notes with very high frequencies on your bottle xylophone. Find the highest note you can make. Do the same for low frequencies.

HIGH AND LOW PITCH

Notes with a high frequency have a high pitch, and it is the pitch of the sound, rather than the frequency, that we hear. The notes on the left-hand side of a piano have a low pitch – they are deeper sounds; those on the right are higher pitched. In a band, like a jazz band, different instruments tend to produce different ranges of pitch. A trumpet is higher pitched than a bass drum or a double bass. Notes with the same pitch can sound quite different though – a middle C from a violin is quite distinct from the same note of a piano. They do not have the same "tone quality."

PLUCK THAT BASS!

1

1. You can have a lot of fun playing your own version of a double bass. Here is how to make one. Start by finding a wooden pole about five feet long – an old broom handle would do. You can paint it with gloss paint.

2. Knot the end of a piece of strong string and attach it to the end of the wooden pole with a thumbtack or a small nail. Next you will need a large cardboard box – the bigger the better. Secure the lid down tightly and cut a hole 10 inches in diameter into the top.

2

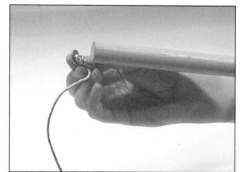

4. Attach your string securely to the loop, and now you can play your double bass. Hold the pole and pull it away from the box to produce notes with a higher pitch. Relax your hold and slacken the string to make lower pitched sounds. Next, write your own jazz song!

3. Paint the box and then make a small hole in the top. Push the pole through so that the base rests on the bottom of the box. Carefully push a sharp stick or nail across the corner and loop a second piece of string around the ends, as shown on the far right.

3

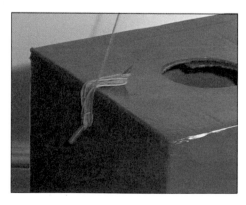

136

4

WHY IT WORKS

When you pluck the string in a slack state, it vibrates more slowly and therefore its frequency is lower. The top blue line shows a slow vibration with only two cycles. The note produced would be of a low pitch. When you pull the string tight and pluck it again, it vibrates more quickly and its frequency is raised. The bottom blue line shows four cycles in the same amount of time it took the top one to complete two. This would produce a higher pitched note. In actual fact, the high-pitched note of your double bass is probably vibrating at about 250 cycles per second. Therefore it has a frequency of 250 hertz.

Slow vibration

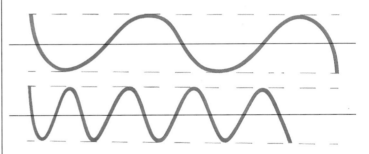

Faster vibration

BRIGHT IDEAS

💡 Try changing your double bass string for a thicker string, or fishing line, or wire. You will notice that the tone of the sound is different, although the pitch may stay the same.

💡 Turn on an electric fan and listen. At first the blades turn slowly and produce a low-pitched sound. As they speed up, the pitch gets higher. This is because the fast spinning blades vibrate at a higher frequency.

💡 Make a cookie tin guitar by stretching rubber bands around a tin that has its lid removed. You can loosen and tighten the bands to change the pitch of the sounds you make.

💡 If you have a guitar, pluck a string and then tighten and loosen the tuning keys at the same time. The pitch of the note will change as the tension of the string changes. Don't tighten the strings too much or they may break.

SPEED OF SOUND

Have you ever watched a thunderstorm? You see the flash of lightning, then wait to hear how loud the clap of thunder will be. In fact, both happen at the same time. You see the flash first, however, because light travels at 186,000 miles per second, a lot faster than sound's 1,000 feet per second. The sound of thunder travels one mile through the air in about 5 seconds – so a 10 second gap between the lightning and the thunder would mean the storm is 2 miles away. A very loud sound, like thunder, travels through air at the same speed as a soft sound, like a whisper. If the thing making the sound, like a fire engine's siren, is moving, however, the pitch of the sound appears to change. This is the Doppler effect.

WHY IT WORKS

By observing the time gap between seeing the balloon burst and hearing the bang, you have proved that sound travels more slowly than light. The Doppler effect happens because sound waves travel quite slowly through the air. As a fire engine comes toward you, the siren has a high pitch. The pitch will appear to fall as it moves past you and away. This is because the sound waves in front of the vehicle become compressed together as the fire engine follows behind. This causes a high-pitched sound. As the vehicle moves away, the sound waves become more spread out, leading to a lower pitched sound.

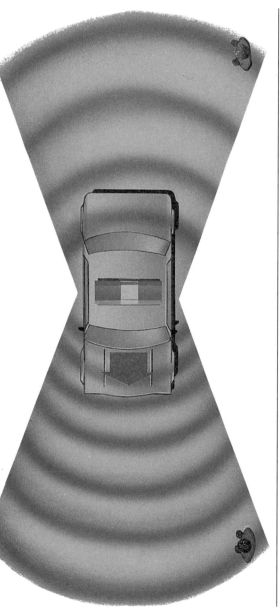

FLOUR BURST

1. Cut off the top end of a plastic bottle and fix a balloon over the spout. Secure the balloon with a rubber band.

1

2. Use the bottle as a funnel, and pour flour through it into the balloon. When the balloon is full, tie the end securely.

2

3. Hold the balloon of flour in front of you, and ask a friend to watch from about 150 feet away. The distance needs to be quite large, to distinguish between the bang and the flour burst.

3

4. Now take a pin and burst the balloon in one motion. Your friend should be able to see the cloud of flour before they hear the bang of the balloon bursting. This is because light travels to your eyes more quickly than sound reaches your ears.

4

BRIGHT IDEAS

Ask your friend to stand 300 feet away from you when you burst the balloon. The time gap between the bang and the flour burst should be longer. At 150 feet it should have taken 1/7 of a second for the banging sound to arrive. At 300 ft, the sound should take 2/7 of a second to reach your friend's ears.

Find out about the sound barrier. Supersonic airplanes like the Concorde break the sound barrier, causing a "sonic boom." This happens when the plane travels so fast it overtakes its own sound waves.

Next time you are in a big cave or a deep valley, shout loudly and listen for your echo. Time how long it takes to return. Do you think it would take longer to come back across the valley or the cave?

CHANGING WAVELENGTHS

Have you wondered how it is that an instrument, like a flute, can produce such a large range of different notes? The flute, like a clarinet or an oboe, is made basically of one tube. By blowing across the flute, the musician sets the column of air inside the tube vibrating. By pressing the keys, the size of the air column is changed – when it is shortened it vibrates more quickly, and so has a higher frequency. Because of this, the length of the sound wave (or wavelength) is shorter and the note has a higher pitch. Do you remember the organ pipes and bottle xylophone? Can you see how those work in a similar way, as the amount of air is altered by adding water?

PANPIPES

1. For the pipes, use plastic drinking straws – the wider straws are much better than the thin ones. As an alternative, you could use plastic tubing or even hollowed out bamboo canes. You can buy these from gardening stores, as they are often used to support plants.

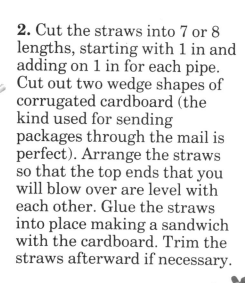

2

2. Cut the straws into 7 or 8 lengths, starting with 1 in and adding on 1 in for each pipe. Cut out two wedge shapes of corrugated cardboard (the kind used for sending packages through the mail is perfect). Arrange the straws so that the top ends that you will blow over are level with each other. Glue the straws into place making a sandwich with the cardboard. Trim the straws afterward if necessary.

3. Your panpipes will look very effective if you decorate them with paint. Glue two extra strips of cardboard along the top and bottom of the cardboard sandwich for extra strength. When you play the pipes, keep your head still and move the pipes, as you would with a harmonica.

1

3

WHY IT WORKS

When you blow over the pipes, you will notice how the longer ones create a lower pitch. The longer column of air vibrates more slowly when you blow across it. For a slow vibration, the gap between each compression or each expansion is longer. Look at the wave pattern at the top – the wave is a longer pattern because there are fewer cycles in a second. A shorter pipe will create a higher pitched sound, with a higher frequency and shorter waves. Wavelength is usually measured in inches from one compression (the top of the wave) to the next.

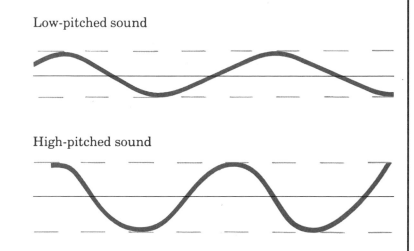

Low-pitched sound

High-pitched sound

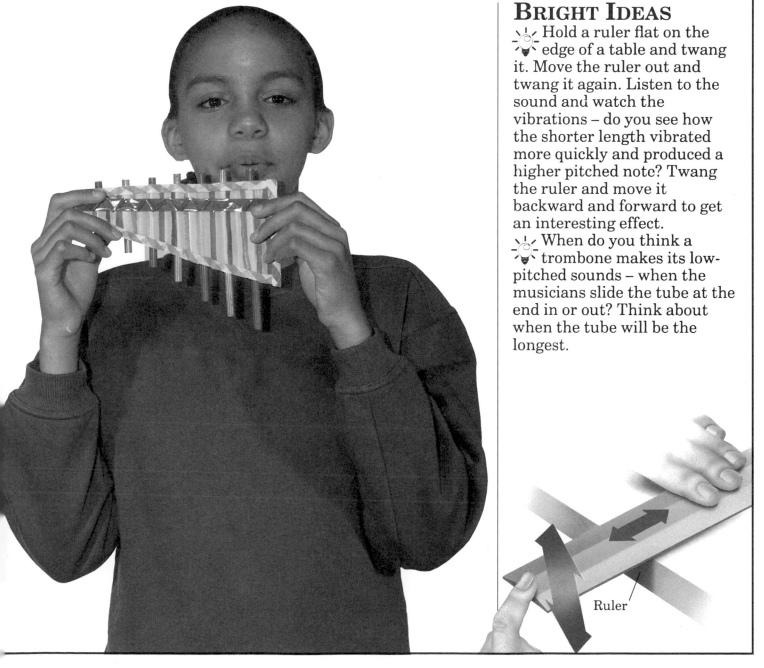

BRIGHT IDEAS

🔆 Hold a ruler flat on the edge of a table and twang it. Move the ruler out and twang it again. Listen to the sound and watch the vibrations – do you see how the shorter length vibrated more quickly and produced a higher pitched note? Twang the ruler and move it backward and forward to get an interesting effect.

🔆 When do you think a trombone makes its low-pitched sounds – when the musicians slide the tube at the end in or out? Think about when the tube will be the longest.

Ruler

141

Fun with Sound

Some of the most difficult instruments to play in the orchestra are the reed instruments, for example an oboe or a bassoon. The reed is held to the musician's mouth and blown to make the reed vibrate. An inexperienced player, though, can blow and blow without getting a sound from the reed! Organs, too, create their sounds by blowing through reeds, though in this case, the air is pumped through by bellows. Originally, reeds were made from the reeds that commonly grow by the edge of water.

Why It Works

When you blow, the tips of the reed vibrate. This sets the air inside the straw vibrating too, which transmits sound waves to our ears. Inside the tube there is a column of air that also vibrated in response to the vibrating of the reed. You can vary the length of the column of air depending on where you place your fingers. The larger the column of air, the slower the vibrations and the lower the pitch of the note becomes.

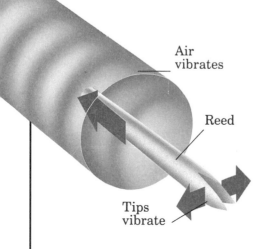

Air vibrates

Reed

Tips vibrate

REED SOUNDS

1. Begin by finding (or making) a tube of cardboard or oak tag. It needs to be about 20 in long and 1 inch in diameter. Paint your tube and leave it to dry.

2. When dry, carefully mark out the position of the finger holes of your reed instrument. Start with the first hole about 6 inches from one end and continue along the length of the tube. Make the hole with a sharp pencil.

3. Next, make the reed – you will need a 4 inch length of plastic drinking straw or art straw for this. Squash the straw flat at one end and cut a 0.5 inch piece from the center outward toward the edge. Repeat on the other side.

4. Place a cork or stopper in the end of the tube that has the finger holes. Next, practice blowing the reed. Place the squashed end into your mouth so that the cut parts are just inside your lips. Hold it lightly and blow gently.

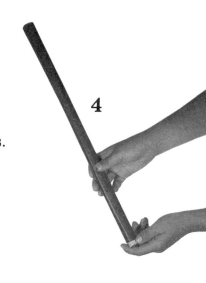

5. If at first your reed makes no sound, carefully open out the cut flaps so that they are just about 0.07 in apart. Try again. By making very fine adjustments to this gap, your reed will eventually work. When it does, put the end of the reed into the tube and change notes by covering different holes.

BRIGHT IDEAS

☀ Make more reeds. Change the length of the reeds and find out whether longer reeds played on their own make notes with a lower pitch. Make a cone of oak tag and place it on the end of your reed. It will act as an amplifier, making the sound louder.

☀ Put the end of a hollow tube into a bowl of water and blow across the top. Move the tube up and down, so changing the amount of air inside it; what do you notice about the pitch of the sound?

☀ You can turn your reed pipe into a flute! Make another, larger hole 4 in from the end. Make the first finger hole, 2 in from this, larger too. Now hold the pipe sideways underneath your mouth and blow across the first hole to create a flutelike sound.

STORING SOUNDS

Storing sounds so that we can play them back is very big business today. It is possible to buy musical recordings on compact disks read by laser beams, on magnetic or digital audio tapes, and on vinyl records. The very first "record players" played back music recorded on wax drums, but the sounds were rather faint and very crackly by today's standards. Old-fashioned "gramophones" are easy to recognize – they have a large cone that is designed to amplify the sounds from the records. When a record is made, electrical signals cause vibrations and cut a groove in a plastic disk. When this is played back, vibrations in the stylus are converted back into the original signals, producing a sound. You can make your own simple gramophone.

SPIN A DISK

3. Make a turntable from cardboard. Once it is in the right position, push a sharpened piece of a stick into the boxtop. As you see here, the box can be decorated.

5

3

5. Stick the cone down to a cardboard disk and then carefully push a sharp stick through the cone and the center of the cardboard. Next push a dressmaking pin or fine needle through the end of the cone so that it faces down from the disk.

1

1. Turn three identical bottle tops upside down and stick them to the top of a cardboard box as shown.

2

2. Inside the bottle tops place a small piece of plastic straw. Make sure your "bearing" sticks up and out of the top and turns freely. Position the tops carefully so that a thread spool can be attached to the corner of the box when the record is in place.

4. To amplify the vibrations of the needle, make a large cone from a sheet of thin cardboard or stiff paper. Start off with a semicircle shape to give a neat finished cone. Glue it securely.

4

6

6. Now firmly push the stick through the spool on the corner of your box and through the top of the box. The disk should rest on the top of the spool.

BRIGHT IDEAS

💡 Do the cone and the needle move across as you turn the record? If not, grease the top of the thread spool to reduce friction. Spin the record fast to create faster vibrations – do you notice how the pitch of the music goes higher?

💡 Experiment with larger and smaller cones.

💡 Draw the needle over other rough surfaces – what sounds do you make? WARNING!!!!!! Do not use any records that you want to play on a record player again as your home made gramophone will damage them! Use only old records.

WHY IT WORKS

Inside the grooves of the record the surface is not perfectly flat. It is designed with a special rough surface which makes the needle vibrate as it travels along the groove. The vibrations of the needle alone would produce sound waves almost too quiet to hear, but the cardboard cone and the air inside it are made to vibrate too, and this makes the sound louder – it amplifies it. The acoustic qualities of the cone would be changed if you used plastic instead of cardboard, or substituted the whole thing with a cookie tin. This is because different materials have different resonant qualities.

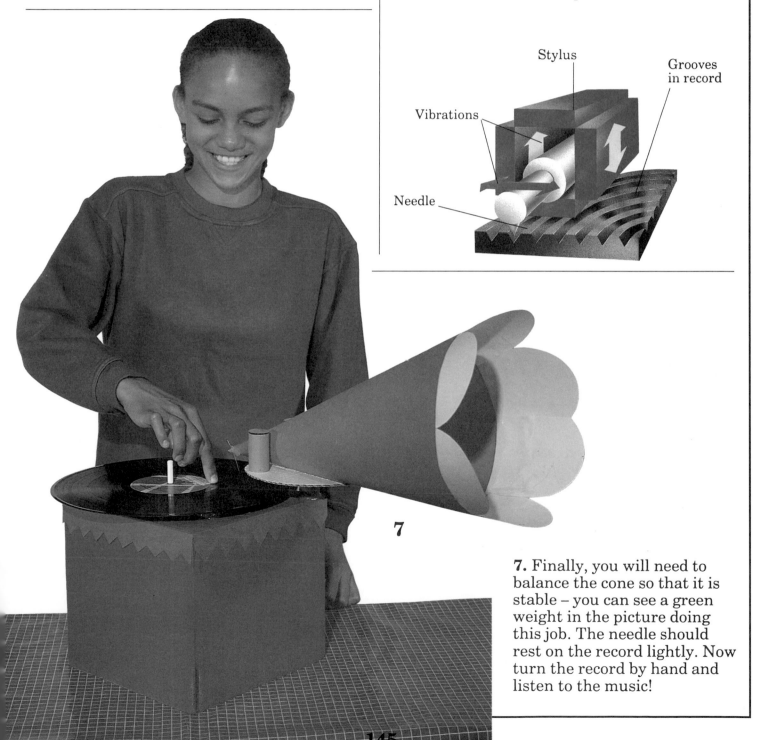

Stylus

Grooves in record

Vibrations

Needle

7

7. Finally, you will need to balance the cone so that it is stable – you can see a green weight in the picture doing this job. The needle should rest on the record lightly. Now turn the record by hand and listen to the music!

LIGHT AND SHADOW

On the morning of July 11, 1991, the shadow of the moon stretched for 100 miles across Hawaii and the mainland of the United States during a solar eclipse. A solar eclipse happens when the moon lies directly between the earth and the sun, preventing light from reaching the earth. Light radiates (spreads out) in all directions from its source. Light is made up of tiny particles of energy, called photons. These travel in small waves and move in straight lines, called rays. Because light cannot bend around objects, shadows form behind objects. For centuries, time has been calculated using shadows. A sundial is a clock that uses shadows to tell the time.

SHADOW SCENE

1. You will need sheets of stiff, dark-colored oak tag, paper fasteners, tracing paper, glue, and straws. Your light source may be a flashlight or a penlight. Draw the characters on the oak tag, as shown, leaving the body separate from the limbs. The weapons are cut out attached to the hands, the shield is cut out separately.

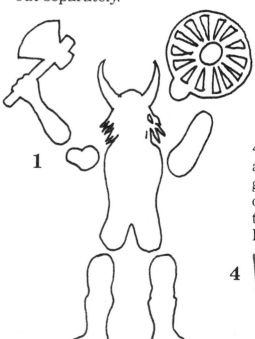

2. Join the limbs to the body with the paper fasteners to make them movable. Attach the shield in the same way.

3. Attach two plastic straws to the feet, as shown here. This allows you to control the puppet's movements.

4. Cut a semicircle out of another sheet of oak tag, and glue a piece of tracing paper over the hole. Make supports to keep the screen upright. Decorate the front.

BRIGHT IDEAS

☀ Make a sundial like the one shown here. Use a watch to check the time each hour and mark where the shadows fall. The shadows will not be the same length all year around.

☀ Substitute the light for your shadow theater for a more powerful one. What do you notice about the silhouettes now?

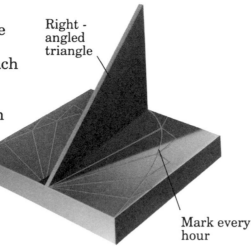

Right-angled triangle

Mark every hour

5. Cut out scenery to stand behind the screen. Someone behind the screen must manipulate the puppets while someone else directs the light source on to them.

WHY IT WORKS

Shadow is the absence of light. A shadow forms on a surface when light rays are obstructed by an opaque object. The cardboard shadow puppets are opaque. This means light cannot pass through them. The nature of the shadow depends upon the size and position of both the light source and the object. The closer the light to the object, the larger the shadow.

Because light travels in a straight line, it cannot turn corners. A very small source of light – a point source like a pinhole – creates a sharp shadow that is equally dark all over. The presence of an opaque object – like the moon in the path of the sun – creates the dark shadow that we call an eclipse. A large or extended source of light creates a larger shadow with a central dark region. The darker part of the shadow with a sharp edge is called the umbra. The paler, fuzzy part of the shadow encircling it is the penumbra.

147

WHAT IS LIGHT?

Natural sunlight contains lots of different types of light, including infrared rays and ultraviolet rays. These are invisible to our eyes. Light travels very fast, much faster than anything else in the universe. It can travel through air and other transparent substances. Visible light cannot travel through opaque materials like cardboard. Glass is opaque to ultraviolet light, which is invisible. Visible and invisible light have different wavelengths. White light is made up of all the colors you can see in a rainbow. Colored glass or paper filters white light to create stunning effects. A famous stained-glass window is the rose window in the Notre Dame Cathedral in Paris.

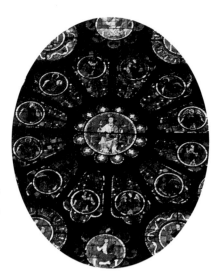

WHY IT WORKS

We see an object only if light from it enters our eyes. A totally transparent object is invisible. Clean air is transparent because light passes through it. It does not bounce off it. A translucent object allows some light to pass through it and it scatters the rest – a cloud is translucent. An opaque object scatters all light – a book is opaque. Luminous objects like the sun, make their own light. Nonluminous objects scatter light from a luminous source. For example, the moon is illuminated by the sun. Pieces of colored plastic or glass that only allow one color of light to pass through them are called filters. Clear, red glass or plastic allows all the red light to pass through. Translucent red glass does not produce such an intense color.

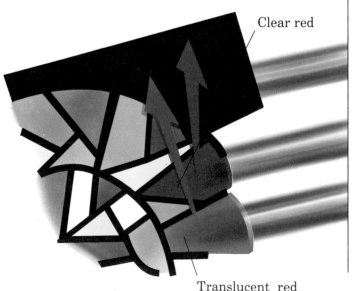

Clear red

Translucent red

COLORFUL WINDOWS

1. You will need black oak tag, colored tissue paper, glue, and felt-tip pens.

2. On the sheet of black oak tag, design your stained-glass window and cut out each section as shown. Cut pieces of colored tissue for your window, and use felt-tip pens to color in white tissue. Glue them in place as shown.

BRIGHT IDEAS

☀ Suspend a sheet of bubble wrap so that you can walk around it. Darken the room and project a picture onto it using a slide projector. Bubble wrap is translucent – you can view the picture from both sides.

☀ Collect a variety of materials. Shine a light from behind each and ask someone to observe whether they are opaque, transparent, or translucent. See what kind of shadow is created.

3

3. Finally, secure the whole window, and place it inside a real window. When sunlight filters through, you will notice the different amounts and colors of light that pass through.

SUNLIGHT

The sun is a star that gives us light and heat energy. The sun is about 93 million miles from the earth. All plants grow toward the sun. If you see a field of sunflowers, like the one pictured here, you will notice that they all face the same way, toward the sun. Plants use the sun's energy to make their own food. This energy is trapped by the green chlorophyll in a plant's leaves. During a process called photosynthesis, oxygen is released into the air as the sunlight is used to convert nutrients from the soil into food. The Greek word "photo" means light. Bioethanol is a fuel made by fermenting the food produced by plants like wheat. One day it could replace gasoline.

LEAVES

1. Half fill a shallow container with soil and scatter cress seeds on the top. Keep the soil moist and place the tray in a sunny position. Leave it until the seeds sprout.

3. Leave the tray in its sunny position. You may have to wait as long as two weeks. Keep the soil moist while the cress is growing.

3

1

2. Cut out your initials from some cardboard, and place it over the seedlings. Make sure the sunlight cannot reach the plants beneath.

4

2

4. During this growing time do not remove the cardboard. You may want to turn the tray occasionally to allow an equal amount of light to reach every part of the tray.

5. When you observe that the cress is fully grown, remove the cardboard. You should be able to see your initials in the seedlings. They will be a much darker green than the rest of the cress, where the light could not reach.

WHY IT WORKS

Sunlight is used by plants to convert nutrients from the soil into chemical energy for growth. When the leaves are covered, sunlight cannot be absorbed. No food can be manufactured inside the plant. Plants absorb carbon dioxide and water. These are converted by the green chlorophyll in the leaves into oxygen and simple sugars. The sugars are converted into food for the plant while the remaining oxygen and water is released into the air through small holes called stomata. These are located on the underside of the leaves. This process is called photosynthesis.

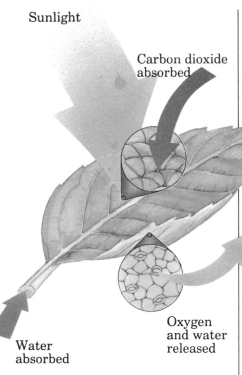

Sunlight

Carbon dioxide absorbed

Water absorbed

Oxygen and water released

BRIGHT IDEAS

Starch is produced when leaves photosynthesize. You can test for starch. Ask an adult to help you. Remove some cress from different parts of the tray and soak them in rubbing alcohol to remove any green chlorophyll. Then place them on a clean surface and put drops of dilute iodine on the surface of each. Where starch is present, the leaves will turn blue, where there is no starch they will turn brown.

Plants always grow toward the sun. This is called phototropism. Plant a seedling in a pot and place it in a shoe box. Place a hole at one end of the box for the light to enter. The shoot will appear through the hole.

5

THE EYE

You see an object when light is reflected from it into your eyes. The eye is like a very small, but accurate, camera. The lens that is inside the eye and the cornea, which covers the colored iris, act together as the focusing apparatus. Light bounces off the object in view and travels in straight lines to the eye. An upside-down image is formed on the retina at the back of the eye. A nerve called the optic nerve carries a message to the brain, where the image is seen right-side up. In the dark, the pupil widens to allow more light to enter the eye. This is why nocturnal animals often have large eyes. A blind person may use other senses, such as touch, for "seeing."

5

PINHOLE CAMERA

1

1. You will need a rectangular cardboard box, a cardboard tube, tracing paper, oak tag and a large rubber band. Position the cardboard tube at one end of the box and draw a circle around it. Cut out the circle. At the other end of the box, make a small viewing hole.

2. Cover one end of the cardboard tube with tracing paper and secure it in place with a rubber band. Cover the other end with an oak tag circle, making sure that no light can enter. Make one small pinhole in the center.

2

3. Insert the tube inside the box with the tracing paper – covered end going in first. Leave the other end sticking out to look like the lens of your camera. Secure it in place with masking tape.

4. Add a decorative button for the top of the camera, as shown, and paint it brightly. Make sure that the only way light can enter the camera is through the pinhole in the front. Your eye will cover the viewing hole at the back.

3

4

5. Hold the finished camera up to your eye, and direct it toward an object near a window. As light rays from the object enter through the pinhole in the front of the camera, you can view an image of it on the circle of tracing paper.

WHY IT WORKS

There is a lens, made of a soft, jellolike substance, in each of your eyes. In the pinhole camera, the pinhole acts as the lens. The inverted (upside-down) image it creates is produced when one ray of light from each point of the object passes through the pinhole and falls onto the screen. A two-dimensional image is formed. The pinhole camera works only because light travels in straight lines. The size of the image depends on the distance of the object from the pinhole and the distance of the pinhole from the screen.

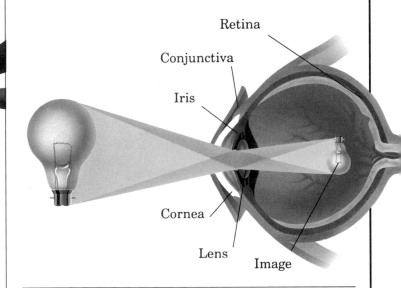

Retina

Conjunctiva

Iris

Cornea

Lens

Image

BRIGHT IDEAS

Move the pinhole camera closer to the object. What can you see now?

As both eyes see a slightly different picture of an object, it is possible to create optical illusions. See if the two bars are the same distance apart all the way along. What about the two lines? Are they the same length? Are the yellow circles the same size?

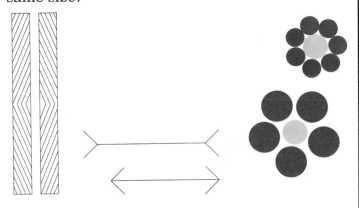

REFLECTION

When light rays hit a surface, they bounce off again, like a ball bouncing off a wall. This is called reflection. The way light behaves when it hits a reflective surface is used by people and animals to see more clearly. Cats have eyes designed to reflect as much light as possible, because they need to see in the dark. Inside high-quality periscopes on board submarines, prisms (blocks of glass) are used to bend beams of light around corners, making objects at the surface visible. Light can be made to reflect off a surface. Mirrors can also be used inside a periscope. Make your own periscope and let nothing spoil your view!

UP PERISCOPE!

1

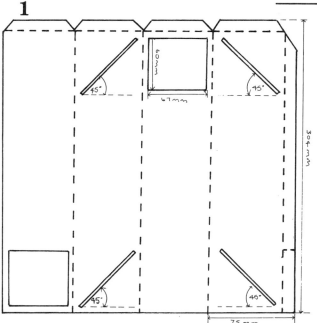

2

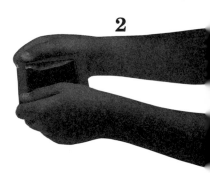

1. Use a ruler and pencil to measure and draw a plan of your periscope like the one shown here. Cut out the two windows and the four slits. Fold along the dotted lines.

2. Take two flat mirrors of the same size and put masking tape around the edges. These should be slightly wider than the periscope.

4. Slide the mirrors into the slits so that the reflecting faces are opposite each other. The edges of the mirrors will protrude from the periscope case. Make sure that they are secure. If they are not, they may slide out and break.

3. Use glue or colored masking tape to stick down the folded sides and flaps. Paint the outside of your periscope.

4

3

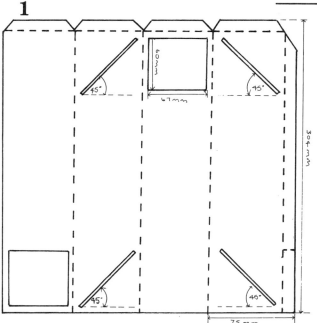

WHY IT WORKS

Light is reflected at the same angle as it hits an object, but in the opposite direction. The top mirror of the periscope is positioned to reflect light from the object downward to the other mirror. The bottom mirror is at the same angle as the top one and reflects the beam out of the periscope and into the eye.

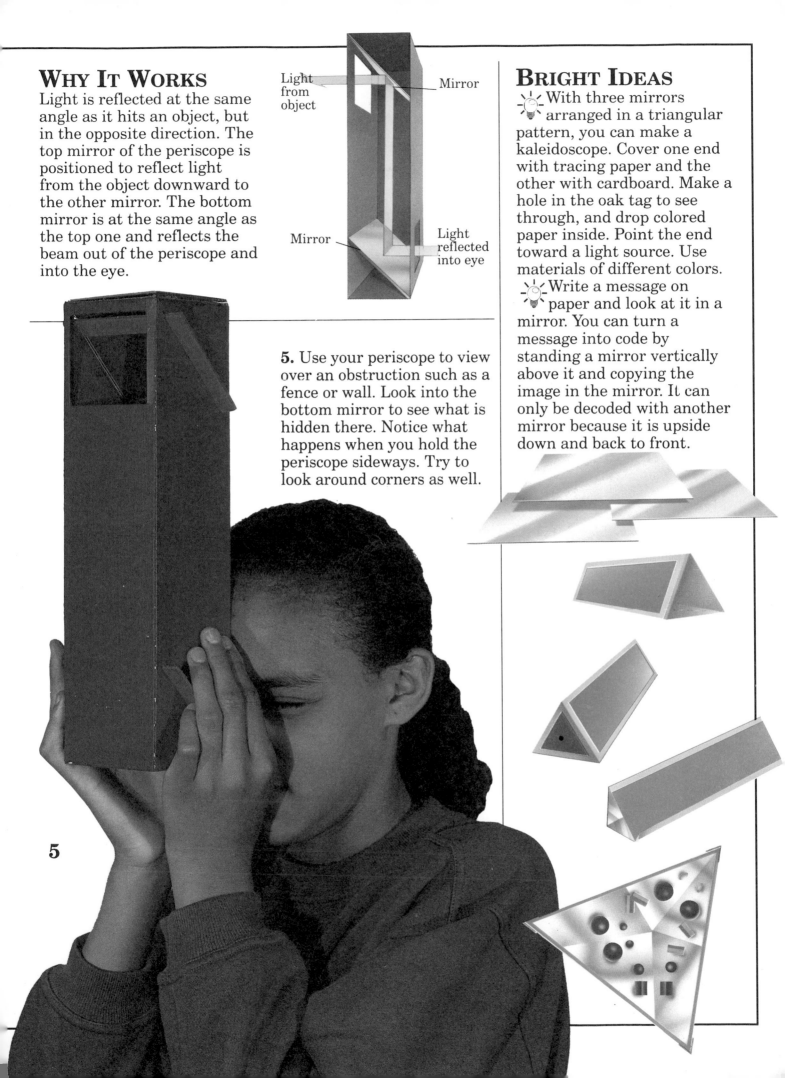

Light from object

Mirror

Mirror

Light reflected into eye

BRIGHT IDEAS

☀ With three mirrors arranged in a triangular pattern, you can make a kaleidoscope. Cover one end with tracing paper and the other with cardboard. Make a hole in the oak tag to see through, and drop colored paper inside. Point the end toward a light source. Use materials of different colors.

☀ Write a message on paper and look at it in a mirror. You can turn a message into code by standing a mirror vertically above it and copying the image in the mirror. It can only be decoded with another mirror because it is upside down and back to front.

5. Use your periscope to view over an obstruction such as a fence or wall. Look into the bottom mirror to see what is hidden there. Notice what happens when you hold the periscope sideways. Try to look around corners as well.

5

CURVED MIRRORS

The reflecting telescope, developed by Sir Isaac Newton (1642 –1727), uses two mirrors to reflect light through a small lens. In 1781, William Herschel became the first scientist to see the planet Uranus using a reflecting telescope. Today, large telescopes like the one pictured here, use huge, curved mirrors to produce real images of distant stars. In an amusement park, the house of mirrors uses curved mirrors to create weird distortions. Build your own simple reflector telescope and have a closer look at the moon.

MAN IN THE MOON

1. To make a reflecting "telescope" you will need a concave mirror on a stand, a convex lens or a magnifying glass, and a flat mirror.

2. Mount the flat mirror on stiff cardboard so that it can be held without covering the image formed in it. Polish both mirrors to ensure a sharp, well-defined image in each.

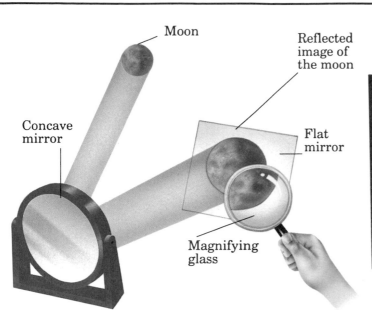

Moon

Concave mirror

Reflected image of the moon

Flat mirror

Magnifying glass

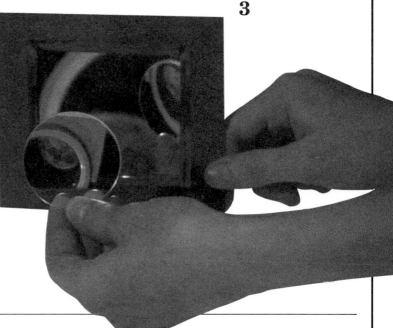

3

3. This project is best attempted on a clear night when there is a full moon. Place the concave mirror in a window so that it points toward the moon. Position the flat mirror so that the image of the moon in the concave mirror is reflected into it.

4. Now look at the moon's image in the flat mirror through the convex lens. It will look much brighter. A magnifying glass can be used instead of a convex lens. Never look at the sun through a telescope; you may cause damage to your eyes. This project must only be attempted at night. Try to focus on a particular constellation of stars with your "telescope."

BRIGHT IDEAS

A simple way to see the difference between the images produced in concave and convex mirrors is to look into both sides of the bowl of a shiny, metal spoon. Look around you to find other examples of curved mirrors used in everyday life. Remember that any shiny surface behaves like a mirror. Make two lists, one for concave and one for convex. Look in the side of a cool shiny kettle. Notice how a light from a car's headlights is reflected. Find a safe place to stand beside a stationary car and observe your reflection in the curved walls of the lights.

WHY IT WORKS

A concave mirror (left) curves inward. When light hits the mirror, the light rays converge (move closer together). A convex mirror (right) curves outward, causing the light rays to diverge (move farther apart).

In this simple reflecting telescope, the concave mirror reflects the light and brings it in focus. The beam then reflects onto a small, flat mirror where the image can be magnified with a lens or magnifying glass.

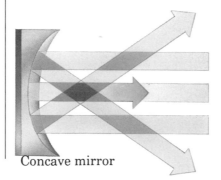

Concave mirror

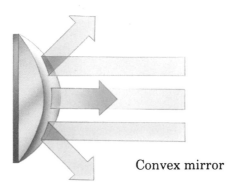

Convex mirror

REFRACTION

A mirror reflects light, a lens refracts (bends) light. Light waves are refracted as they pass through a transparent substance like a glass lens. Light also refracts as it passes from one substance to another, such as from air to water. When light rays are refracted, objects may appear closer or farther away than they really are. Lenses can be used to make things look bigger. The microscope was invented by Robert Hooke in about 1665. One of the first things he viewed through it was a hair louse clinging to a human hair. Today, microscopes range from a small pocket version, to a powerful electron microscope, like the one pictured here. This one can magnify objects by 1 million times their size.

WHY IT WORKS

There are two types of lens – convex and concave. A convex lens bulges out at the center, a concave lens is thinner. In a concave lens the light rays diverge (move apart) – the image appears smaller. In a convex lens, light rays converge (move closer) – the image seen may appear larger. The water drop in the simple microscope acts as a convex lens. The light is reflected from the mirror, through the object. The light is then magnified as it passes through the drop of water and into the eye.

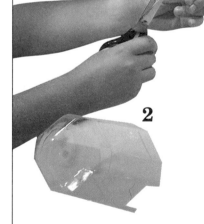

Concave lens

Convex lens

MAKE A MICROSCOPE

1. To make a microscope you will need a see-through plastic bottle, a small, flat mirror, scissors and a drop of water. First cut the top off the bottle and cut a strip 1-2 in wide and 5-6 in long from each side.

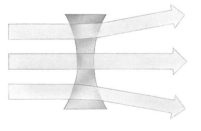

2. Use one of these strips as a slide on which the object to be viewed will be positioned. The second strip will act as a lens holder for the drop of water. The object will be viewed here, through the drop of water.

3. Insert the ends of one strip through the slits in the sides. Leave room for the slide holding the object to be held underneath. A drop of water will be balanced on the top strip.

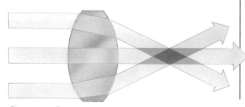

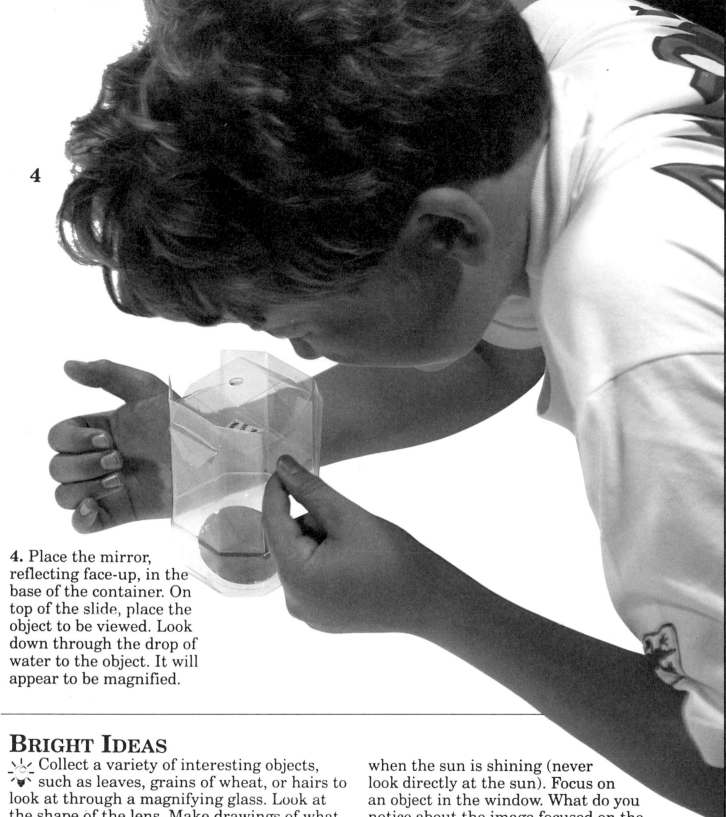

4. Place the mirror, reflecting face-up, in the base of the container. On top of the slide, place the object to be viewed. Look down through the drop of water to the object. It will appear to be magnified.

BRIGHT IDEAS

☀ Collect a variety of interesting objects, such as leaves, grains of wheat, or hairs to look at through a magnifying glass. Look at the shape of the lens. Make drawings of what you see through the lens. Hold a convex lens between the magnifying glass and an object. You have made a simple microscope.

☀ Look through a plain glass marble at a small object of interest – what do you notice? Now hold a magnifying glass vertically between a sheet of white paper and a window when the sun is shining (never look directly at the sun). Focus on an object in the window. What do you notice about the image focused on the paper?

☀ Water also refracts light. Half fill a transparent beaker with salt solution. Carefully pour pure water on to the top, using the back of a spoon so that the two do not mix. Place a pencil upright in the beaker. It will appear to be broken in two places.

LENSES

It is generally accepted that the refracting telescope, invented in 1608 by a Dutch eyeglass-maker, Hans Lippersahey, was the first telescope to be invented. By 1610, Galileo Galilei was able to make a scientific study of the known universe using a refracting telescope. His observations challenged the popular belief that the earth was the center of the universe. Lenses are used in microscopes and telescopes. A telescope gives a close-up view of a distant object by producing an image of the object inside the telescope tube. The eye piece then magnifies the image. A refracting telescope uses a lens to form the image, not a mirror.

WHY IT WORKS

The large convex lens at the end of the telescope is called the object lens. It gathers light from the object being viewed. When light from the object strikes the lens, the rays are refracted and brought together to form a focal point. A small image is formed here. As light enters the eyepiece, the image is enlarged and appears closer. The image is also upside down. The telescope is focused by changing the distance between the object lens and the lens in the eyepiece.

In focus

Out of focus

IN FOCUS

1. Take a large cardboard tube and fit a convex lens into one end. This tube should be wide enough for another tube to fit inside.

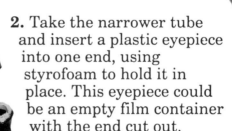

2. Take the narrower tube and insert a plastic eyepiece into one end, using styrofoam to hold it in place. This eyepiece could be an empty film container with the end cut out.

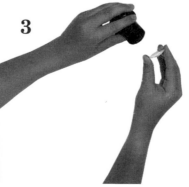

3. Insert a small convex lens into one end of the eyepiece. This will be the end that you look through.

4. Push the narrow tube inside the wider tube, making sure that it slides smoothly in and out. Your telescope is now ready to use. Hold it up to your eye and point it at a distant object.

BRIGHT IDEAS

💡 Adjust the telescope to focus on objects at various distances. Make another kind of refracting telescope using one convex and one concave lens instead of two convex lenses. Attach a thick concave lens upright with modeling clay at the end of a length of wood or plastic, marked off in inch divisions. Line it up with a distant object and ask a friend to position a thin convex lens along the wood until the object is in focus. Hold it in position with clay. How far apart are the lenses? Does the object appear upside down? Is it magnified? Repeat the exercise, looking at other distant objects. Place a second convex lens between the other two. Notice what effect this has on the image seen.

💡 Ask an adult to concentrate sunlight onto a sheet of paper using a magnifying glass – do this outside. The convex lens concentrates the light rays at the center sufficiently to set the paper on fire. This can also happen using a concave mirror.

THE SPECTRUM

In 1666, Sir Isaac Newton used a prism (a triangular block of glass) to demonstrate how white light can be split up into lots of different colors. These colors are called the spectrum. With a second prism, he showed how white light could be re-formed by mixing the colors. Prisms can be used to make beams of light turn corners inside periscopes. The Frenchman, Augustin Fresnel, introduced the use of glass prisms to collect the light rays from a lighthouse into one powerful beam. When a light ray strikes a prism, light is refracted. Raindrops act as prisms under certain conditions, creating a rainbow across the sky. Try making your own rainbow.

BRIGHT IDEAS

Look all around you for examples of white light being split up – take particular notice of glass objects. You can learn the correct order of the colors in the spectrum and in a rainbow by using the initials of each color in a name like ROY G. BIV.

WHY IT WORKS

Water acts like a prism, splitting light into its different wavelengths and producing a spectrum of seven colors: red, orange, yellow, green, blue, indigo, and violet. The spectrum occurs because as the light is refracted (bent) by the water, each color is bent at different angles, splitting the white light into colors. Raindrops falling while the sun is shining can cause refraction and reflection of white light. Colored rays of light spread out across the sky to create the curved band of a rainbow.

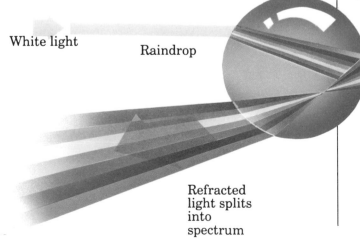

White light

Raindrop

Refracted light splits into spectrum

COLORS OF THE RAINBOW

1. Seal the edges of a mirror with tape. You will need two clips that are joined together like the ones shown here.

2. Half fill a glass container with water, and use the clips to hold it in the water at an angle. You may have to alter the angle later.

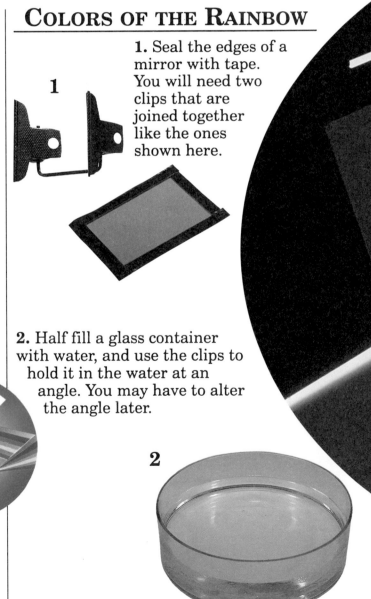

3. Find a piece of black oak tag, large enough to block out the light source completely. With sharp scissors, cut out one long, narrow strip as shown here. This will allow the passage of light from the light source to the mirror.

4. Rest the flat mirror at an angle in the container of water so that the light entering through the slit will strike it. Place a smaller piece of white oak tag beneath the slit in the black oak tag. Adjust the mirror's position until a rainbow appears.

3

4

COLORED LIGHT

Color and light are inseparable. The eye perceives color because of three sets of receptors called cones, one for each of the primary colors. All the colors seen on a television screen are made up from colored dots of the three primary colors. The color of an object will depend on which colors of the spectrum it absorbs, and which it reflects. An object looks yellow because the yellow light rays are reflected into the eye, while the rest are absorbed. A black object absorbs all the colors of the spectrum, while a white object reflects them all.

BRIGHT IDEAS

 Reconstitute white light by spinning a wheel like the one shown here. Color the wheel with colors of the spectrum and then spin it.

 Make a hole in one end of a shoe box. Remove the lid and fill the box with objects of different colors. Make 2 or 3 cellophane covers, each a different color. Cover it with one of them, then shine a flashlight through the hole. Look through the cellophane. What color are the objects?

Colors of the spectrum

The colors disappear

SPOTLIGHTS

2. Attach these filters to three long, cardboard tubes. Make sure the filters cover the end of each tube completely.

2

WHY IT WORKS

We have discovered by splitting light that each color has a different wavelength. Mixing colored lights produces new colors by adding light of different wavelengths. Colored light mixtures are sometimes called additive color mixtures or color by addition. Luminous sources of light, like color televisions, combine colors by mixing very small dots of light. Black means the absence of light because there are no colors to mix together. When red, green, and blue lights are combined, white light is the result. A secondary color is an equal mixture of two primary colors. Red and green lights shining onto a white object will make it appear to be yellow. Any two colors of light that form white light when mixed are called complementary. Other colors are formed by mixing the primary colors in different proportions.

3. Place a large sheet of white card on the floor in a darkened room. Three people need to hold the tubes at right angles to the floor while shining a flashlight into the top of each. The beams of light should be directed onto the white card.

1. To mix colored light you will need cellophane filters in the three primary colors – green, red, and blue.

4. Find out how to make new colors by positioning the three lights in such a way as to produce a variety of combinations. Where the three combine, white light is produced.

PIGMENTS

Thousands of years ago, natural pigments from the earth were being used by Stone Age artists to create cave paintings. Later, plants were to provide dyes for cloth. Color in painting is not made by splitting white light. The primary colors of paint are magenta, cyan, and yellow (red, blue, and yellow). If you look closely at color on a printed page, you will see that it is made up of tiny dots of these colors. The primary colors of paint mix together to make black, not white like light. Pigments combine to create other colors inside the eye and brain without being mixed themselves. Pigments can be separated using chromatography.

CHROMATOGRAPHY

1. For this project, use water-based felt-tip pens or inks. You will also need blotting paper and a deep container, one-quarter full of clean water. Cut the blotting paper into long strips about 2 in wide. On each strip make a blot of color. Mark some strips with different shapes, using a different color on each.

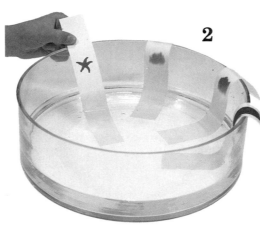

2. Lay the strips over the edge of the container of water, with the colored mark nearest to the water. The end of each should just touch the water. Leave the bowl undisturbed for some time. The water will soak upward, due to capillary action, spreading the pigments up each strip.

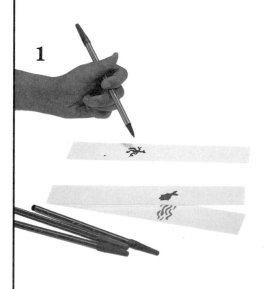

3. As the water travels up the blotting paper, the pigments in the inks begin to move also. When the pigments can travel no further, remove the strips and allow them to dry.

WHY IT WORKS

The pigments in inks travel at different speeds. As the water rises up the paper the pigments separate out in bands of color.

The primary pigments make other colors because they absorb color. Each primary color of paint absorbs one of the primary colors of light and reflects the other two. The colors are formed by subtractive mixing and are different to those created by the additive mixing of light. Pigments in paint reflect light from other sources. A white sheet of paper reflects all the light that falls on it – no subtraction takes place. A black sheet absorbs all of the light – all three primary colors are subtracted.

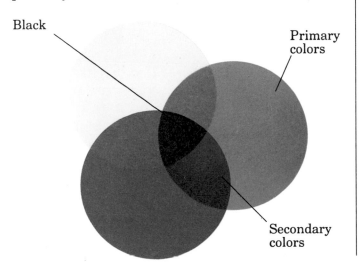

Black

Primary colors

Secondary colors

BRIGHT IDEAS

☀ Paint an Impressionist picture using dots of paint in primary colors. Stand back and look at your picture from a distance. See if the dots merge to form new colors.

☀ Adapt your main project to make a color wheel. Cut out a circle of white blotting paper, large enough to rest on top of a transparent beaker. At the center make a large dot with water-based ink or felt tip. Fill the beaker almost to the top with water and rest the circle on top. Cut a strip from the edge to the center and fold it so it hangs in the water. As the ink dissolves it will separate into its various colors to form rings.

4. Study the strips carefully. Which pigments seem to travel fastest? These colors will have traveled further up the strips. What has happened to your shapes?

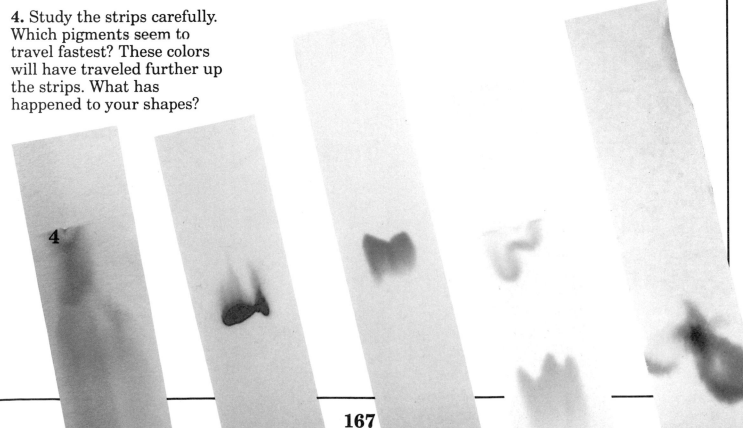

MOVING PICTURES

Eadweard Muybridge was the first person to photograph a horse in full gallop, using 12 cameras in sequence. Moving pictures are only possible because of the nature of the human eye. In fact, they deceive the eye because each picture is really a "still" photograph. If these photographs pass in front of the eyes fast enough, there seems to be continuous movement. Cartoon films (animation) use the same technique. "Snow White and the Seven Dwarfs," pictured left, is a famous animated film by Walt Disney. A popular forerunner of the movies was the praxinoscope. You can make your own praxinoscope and watch your drawings come to life.

You can trace this design to make your own praxinoscope.

Use bright colors to illustrate your praxinoscope.

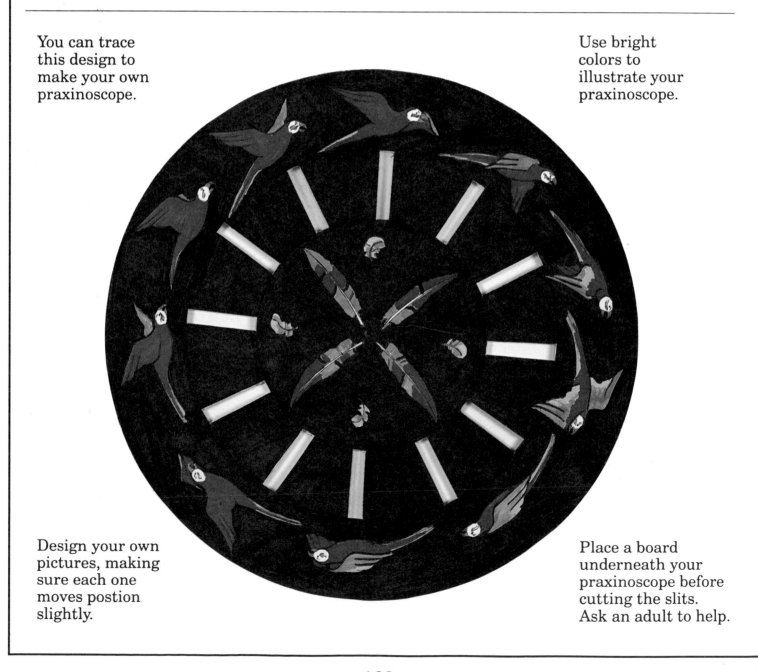

Design your own pictures, making sure each one moves postion slightly.

Place a board underneath your praxinoscope before cutting the slits. Ask an adult to help.

WHY IT WORKS

Moving pictures depend upon illusion. A moving film is a series of still pictures seen one after the other at high speed. Every image remains in the eye of the viewer for 1/10 of a second after it has left the screen. As the next image appears, it merges with the picture before it, producing the illusion of continuous movement. Usually, 24 pictures or frames are taken every second by a movie camera. As light enters the movie camera, a lens focuses an image onto one frame of the unexposed film. After it has been exposed, the film is drawn through the camera, exposing the next frame. The light entering the camera is also bent into the eyepiece using a prism, where the image can be viewed by the operator.

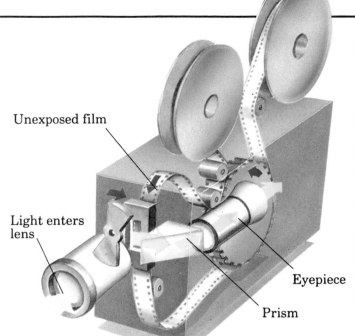

Unexposed film

Light enters lens

Eyepiece

Prism

A PARROT PRAXINOSCOPE

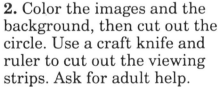

1. Draw a circle of 6 inches in diameter. On the outside draw a series of images at different stages of movement. Mark out where the slits should be cut as shown.

2. Color the images and the background, then cut out the circle. Use a craft knife and ruler to cut out the viewing strips. Ask for adult help.

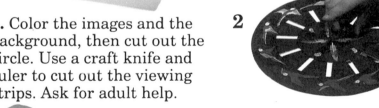

3. Pierce the center of the cardboard with a nail and push it through to the back. Slide a washer and then a cork onto the nail. This will be your handle.

4. Ask a friend to hold a flat mirror in front of you so that the praxinoscope is reflected back to your eyes. Hold the cork and rotate the cardboard. View the parrots in flight through the viewing slits. Make sure that you rotate the circle in the right direction or the parrots will fly backward.

BRIGHT IDEAS

Make your own cartoon movie with a tin lid and a bamboo stick. Make a spinning top with the lid and stick, then attach a paper strip of about 20 drawings to the outside edge. To create a sense of movement, draw the same figure in a slightly different position each time. Ask a friend to spin the lid while you view the "movie" through a pinhole in a sheet of cardboard.

Make a flip book. A different moving picture can be made by drawing a face onto two sides of a folded sheet of paper. The face on the top "page" should not be smiling. The same face on the bottom "page" should be smiling. Hold the paper at the fold and roll the top page around a pencil. Now move the pencil quickly back and forth over the smiling face underneath to make the smile "move."

CONCENTRATED LIGHT

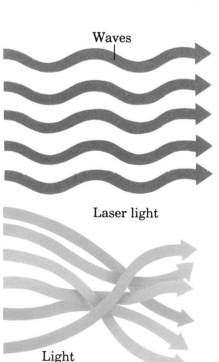

Lasers produce a beam of pure light in which the waves are all identical. The light is very concentrated and can be used in many ways. You may have a compact disc player. These contain a laser beam which reads the disc. Surgical lasers are used in hospitals, for example, to carry out delicate eye operations. You may have seen a hologram on a credit card. These are 3-D photographs produced using laser light. Light can also travel along fibers of glass to carry images or sounds. This is known as fiber optics. Optical fibers can carry telephone messages long distances. A fiber-optic endoscope enables a doctor to look inside a patient's body.

WHY IT WORKS

The light produced by a laser is all of the same wavelength. Each color of white light has a different wavelength. In ordinary light, the waves travel in different directions. In laser light, the waves are all in step. A laser can be concentrated onto a tiny point. It can be used for eye surgery and it can cut metal.

Waves

Laser light

Light

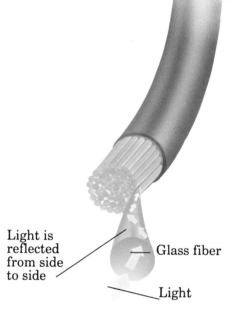

Light is reflected from side to side

Glass fiber

Light

Fiber optic devices depend upon internal reflection that allows laser light to pass along a narrow glass fiber. Light bounces from side to side within the fiber and cannot escape. The light can travel long distances without fading. A fiber-optic cable can carry thousands of signals at the same time at high speed.

BRIGHT IDEAS

Holograms are often seen today – keep a record of those you see. Why are they used on credit cards?

Next time you are in a supermarket, at the checkout, observe how each item is checked off. Some shops use lasers that produce infrared rays similar to light rays. The laser reads the bar code on each item, so that a beam reflects from it, sending a signal to a computer. The computer sends the price back to the checkout and records the item sold.

Find out about the many uses of lasers – they are used by dentists and surgeons. Laser light is often used to create special effects to entertain. You may have seen a laser show.

A Stream of Light

1. First paint a transparent plastic bottle black and then cut off the top. With a drawing pin, make one pinhole near the bottom of the bottle. On the other side of the bottle, opposite the pinhole, scrape away a small area of paint, sufficient to allow light to pass through. Now stand the bottle in a large flat glass dish, with the pinhole facing inward.

2. Place the dish in a darkened room and half fill the bottle with water. Shine a flashlight through the bottle as shown and place your finger in the stream of water that will emerge from the pinhole. You should be able to see a spot of light on your finger. The jet of water acts like the glass fiber of an optic cable. The light from the flashlight is bounced back and forth along the stream of water, and concentrated into a small spot on your finger.

CLOCKS AND WHEELS

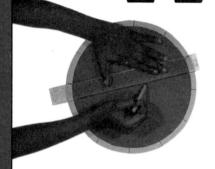

CONTENTS

INTRODUCTION

Moving ourselves and objects from place to place has always been important. Early man struggled to find ways of doing this and produced wheels, levers, pulleys and screws. These are all simple, basic machines but nonetheless make our lives much easier. They represented the beginning of the modern mechanical world. When experimenting with these simple moving devices we must also consider the effort or force needed to move something and ways in which this could be done with less effort and a smoother movement.

We ask questions such as "How many ?" and "How long?" all the time. The answer to both questions involves numbers but for the first question we need to count to get an answer, and for the second we need to measure. Each time we look at a clock we are using measurement; we are reading a measurement of time. We constantly ask "How long is the journey ?" "What time do we arrive ?" There are also many other kinds of measurement – for example, clothes size, shoe size, and weight.

Safety Tips
Get an adult to help when cutting with sharp scissors. NEVER cover your nose and mouth with plastic and take care not to inhale balloons. If your work surface becomes wet and slippery always remember to clean it up.

CALENDARS

Before the invention of the clock, people had to rely on nature's timekeepers - the Sun, the Moon and the stars. The daily movement of the Sun across the sky provided the simplest unit, the solar day. The time period of a year was estimated by watching the seasons, and the constancy of the lunar cycle led to the division of each year into months. Traditionally, calendars were controlled by priests. They were devised either by counting days or by following the phases of the Moon. Nowadays, the Gregorian calendar is most common. This was worked out by Pope Gregory XIII in the 1580s.

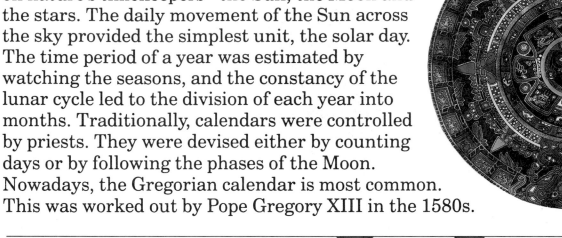

DAY BY DAY

1. Cut out two circles of cardboard. The largest should be 12 in across, the other 11in across. Stick one on top of another and divide into 12 equal pieces to indicate the months.

2. Cut out 12 paper circles of 0.5in across. Find out the number of days for each month and write them around the edge of each small circle. Now stick them in order around the large circle. The first day of the month should be nearest the edge as shown.

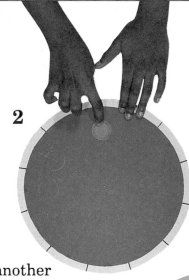

3. Cut another cardboard circle 10.5in across. Cut a hole, radius 0.5in, to correspond with the position of the paper circles. Cover the hole with stiff, transparent plastic. Attach a red arrow marker, as shown.

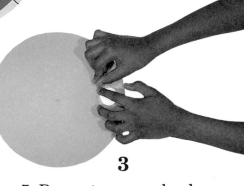

4. Cut out a cardboard circle, radius 0.5in. Carefully make a tiny "window," to view the date through. Position it over the 0.5in hole, and fix it to the plastic with a paper fastener, so it turns.

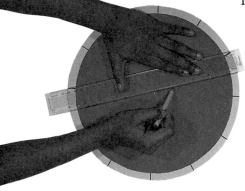

5. Decorate your calendar before joining the separate sections together. Position the smaller circle centrally over the larger circle and join them together with a paper fastener. Rotate your calendar until it is set on the correct day for the current month.

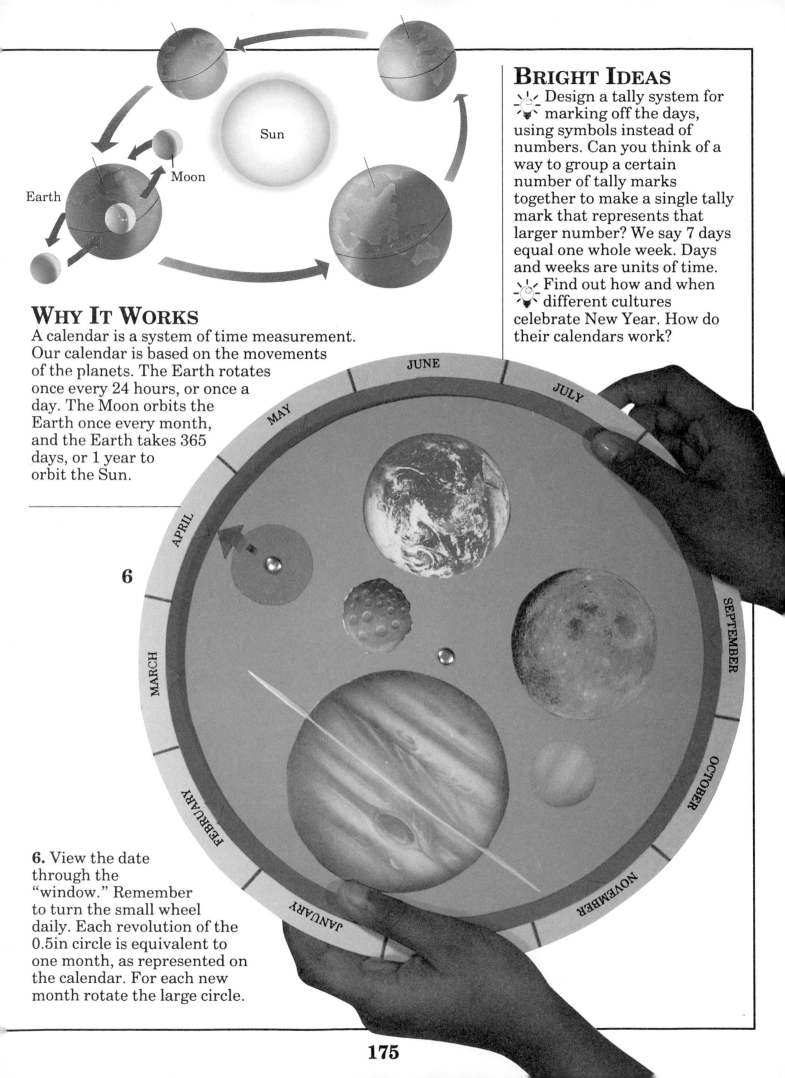

BRIGHT IDEAS

Design a tally system for marking off the days, using symbols instead of numbers. Can you think of a way to group a certain number of tally marks together to make a single tally mark that represents that larger number? We say 7 days equal one whole week. Days and weeks are units of time.

Find out how and when different cultures celebrate New Year. How do their calendars work?

WHY IT WORKS

A calendar is a system of time measurement. Our calendar is based on the movements of the planets. The Earth rotates once every 24 hours, or once a day. The Moon orbits the Earth once every month, and the Earth takes 365 days, or 1 year to orbit the Sun.

6. View the date through the "window." Remember to turn the small wheel daily. Each revolution of the 0.5in circle is equivalent to one month, as represented on the calendar. For each new month rotate the large circle.

175

PLOTTING THE STARS

Astronomy is the study of the stars, planets and other objects in the universe. For centuries, astronomers have striven to learn more about our Universe. Through observation and careful measurement, using scientific tools like the telescope, we now know that the Sun is the center of our solar system. Accurate measurement of star distance is a science developed over the centuries by astronomers like Tycho Brahe (1546-1601). Centuries ago, sailors calculated time at night by observing the movements of star clusters near the fixed Pole Star. Watches aboard ship were timed from the position of these constellations in the sky.

STAR TIME

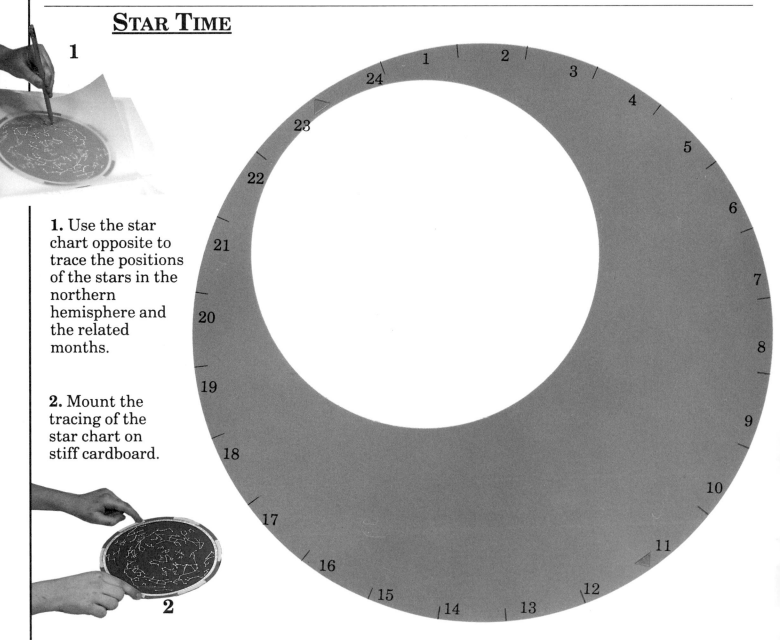

1. Use the star chart opposite to trace the positions of the stars in the northern hemisphere and the related months.

2. Mount the tracing of the star chart on stiff cardboard.

3. Trace the shape on the opposite page onto cardboard. Mark the 24 hours of the day, starting with Noon at the bottom.

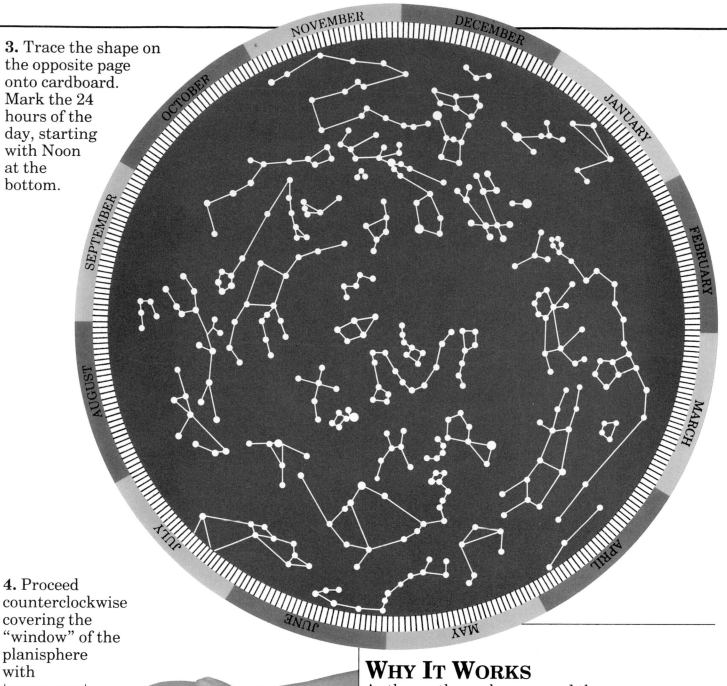

4. Proceed counterclockwise covering the "window" of the planisphere with transparent plastic. Pin it to the starchart through the center.

5. On a starry night, rotate the planisphere until the time of day, marked on the edge, is lined up with the appropriate month at the bottom of the star chart. Compare what you see with the stars in the sky.

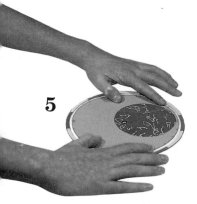

WHY IT WORKS

As the earth revolves around the sun, different constellations of stars appear and disappear in a continous cycle that can be observed. This planisphere shows where these groups of stars can be seen at any given time of the year, in the northern hemisphere. By matching up the time of day with the date, you can view the stars that should be visible in the night sky through the cut out "window." The planisphere should be held up and viewed from underneath. The stars visible through the window should match those in the sky. The Sun is a star. It is the only star close enough to look like a ball. The other billions of stars are so far away, they appear to be pinpoints of light.

177

MEASURING ROTATION

The Earth revolves on its own tilted axis, once every 24 hours. The Sun appears to rise and set. The rotation of the Earth was demonstrated in 1851, by J.B.L. Foucault, a French physicist. He realized that although a swinging pendulum seems to change direction throughout the day, it is really the Earth that rotates beneath it while the swing of the pendulum tries to remain constant. By studying the movement of the planets, astronomers have noted a gradual slowing of the Earth's rotation. They have calculated that the length of a day increases by about 1.7 milliseconds per year.

IN A SPIN

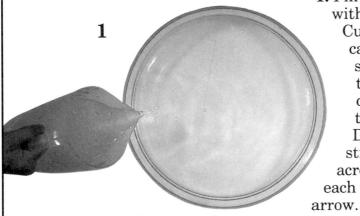

1. Fill a circular bowl with clean, cold water. Cut out a circle of cardboard, slightly larger than the diameter of the bowl. Draw a straight line across, marking each end with an arrow.

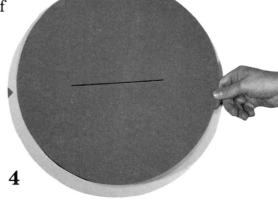

2. Find a flat surface, free of vibration. Position the cardboard on the surface, then stand the bowl of water on top. Leave it to stand until the surface of the water is still.

3. Cut another circle of cardboard, slightly larger than the bowl. Rule a line across the center. Using a matte knife, on a board, cut out a slit approximately 0.1in wide, as shown.

4. Rest the card circle on top of the bowl. Line up the slit with the marks on the card underneath the bowl, as shown. Prepare some powdered cork and keep in a dry container.

5. If the water is still, gently sprinkle the cork powder over the slit in the cardboard. It will fall through to make a narrow line of powder on the surface of the water.

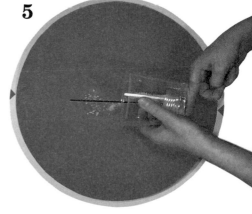

WHY IT WORKS

The line of cork dust appears to have rotated after the bowl has been standing for a number of hours. In reality, the Earth and the bowl have rotated beneath the line of dust, which remained stationary. This is because the Earth travels through 360 degrees each time a rotation is completed. Every place on Earth travels through 15 degrees each hour of the day. Artificial time zones have been created around the world to accommodate time differences.

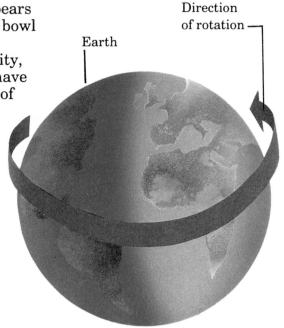

Earth

Direction of rotation

BRIGHT IDEAS

Make a pendulum by pushing a needle right through an apple and suspending it inside an empty box with thread. The thread should be just the right length to let the needle sticking out of the apple touch a plate underneath. Sprinkle some fine salt on the plate and start the pendulum swinging. Turn the plate slowly and watch the grooves form as the pendulum swings in the same plane and the plate rotates. The plate represents the Earth as it rotated in Foucault's pendulum experiment.

6. Do not touch the bowl. Leave it undisturbed for several hours. You will find, after some time, that the line of dust appears to have rotated and is no longer in line with the arrows.

6

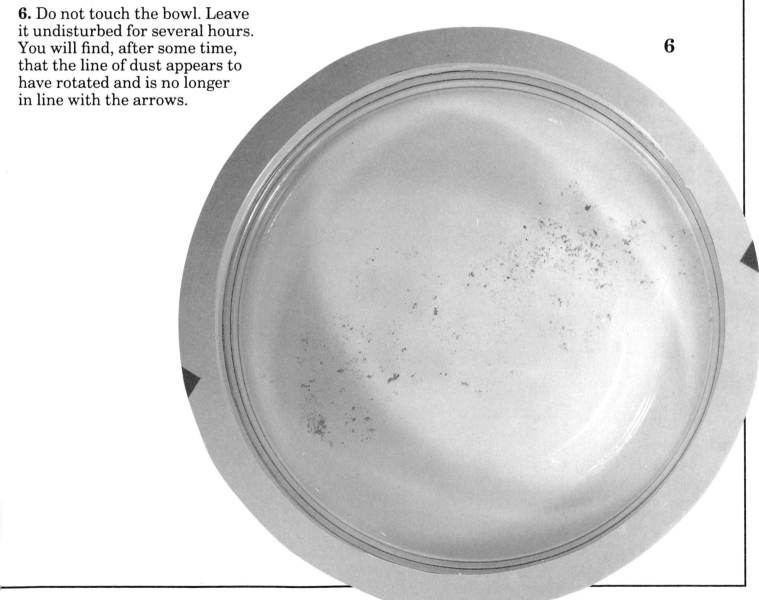

ESTIMATING TIME

Hours are artificial units of time, first introduced by the Ancient Egyptians when they observed that shadows follow a similar pattern of movement each day. Shadow clocks and sundials were early time-measurement tools. In the 14th century, the sandglass, or hourglass, was popular, but it could only be used to estimate periods of time, varying from minutes to hours. It could not indicate the time of day. On board ship, a four-hour glass timed "watch" for the crew, until John Harrison invented the more accurate chronometer in 1735. This also calculated longitude and latitude. Early sandglasses were filled with powdered eggshell or marble dust.

TIME IS RUNNING OUT

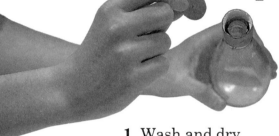

1. Wash and dry two small bottles thoroughly. Make an open-ended cylinder of cardboard and slide it over the top of one bottle. Cut out a disc of cardboard to fit inside and make a hole in its center.

2. Make sure the other bottle is absolutely dry. Now, carefully pour a measured amount of salt into it.

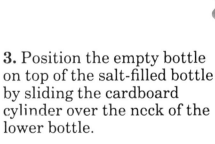

3. Position the empty bottle on top of the salt-filled bottle by sliding the cardboard cylinder over the neck of the lower bottle.

4. Check that the cardboard "seal" round the middle is secure. Carefully turn your timer over and observe what happens.

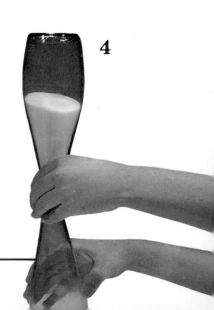

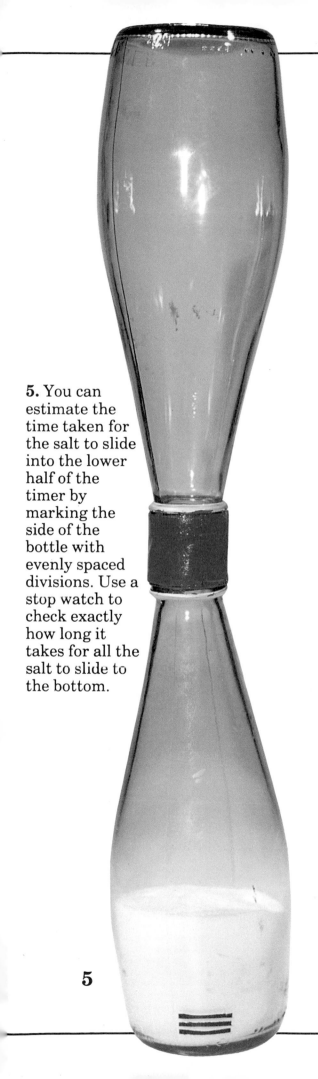

5. You can estimate the time taken for the salt to slide into the lower half of the timer by marking the side of the bottle with evenly spaced divisions. Use a stop watch to check exactly how long it takes for all the salt to slide to the bottom.

5

WHY IT WORKS

The upper vessel of the timer holds just enough salt to run through a hole, of a given size, in a given period of time. The force of gravity pulls the salt down through the hole and into the bottom container. The salt grains must be absolutely dry, so they don't stick. The size of the hole between the two vessels will determine the speed at which the grains will flow, but once established, the rate of flow will not vary. The total period of time depends on the quantity of salt. Salt

BRIGHT IDEAS

☀ Remove the regulator from between the two bottles and replace it with another, in which a hole of a different diameter has been made. Repeat this exercise a number of times, changing the size of the hole each time. What do you discover?

☀ Design a sandglass that will run for exactly 3 minutes - use it as an eggtimer when you boil an egg.

☀ Can you design another kind of sandglass that runs for a much longer period of time? Shape a funnel from cardboard, and insert it into the neck of a measuring container. Fill the funnel with sand and time how long it takes to pour through into the container below. Standardize your method of reading the scale - the top of the mound of sand will be concave.

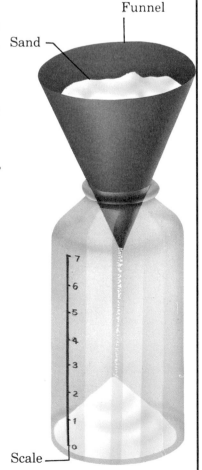

Funnel

Sand

Scale

MEASURING TIME

The accurate measurement of small units of time was not possible until 1583. The Italian physicist Galileo (1564-1642) observed the swinging of a lamp in Pisa cathedral, and by timing its motion against his own pulse, he concluded that a free pendulum was isochronous – every swing, wide or narrow, took the same time. The Dutch scientist Christiaan Huygens (1629-1695) constructed the first mechanical clock with a pendulum mechanism in 1657. In 1921, W. H. Shortt invented a pendulum clock so accurate that it was used in the Royal Observatory in Greenwich. The measurement standard for time is the atomic clock. These clocks measure time so accurately, they will not gain or lose more than a second in 300 years.

TICK TOCK

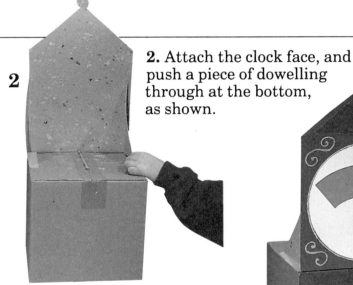

2. Attach the clock face, and push a piece of dowelling through at the bottom, as shown.

1. Cut the top off a large, square box, as shown. This will be the base of the clock. Cut a second piece of cardboard, the same width as the box, to be the clock face.

3. Decorate your clock face and design and draw a dial. Mark the indicator scale when you can observe the size of the pendulum swing.

4. The pendulum can be any length you wish. Use a dowel with a circle of cardboard attached. To give weight to the bob, put modeling clay behind the card.

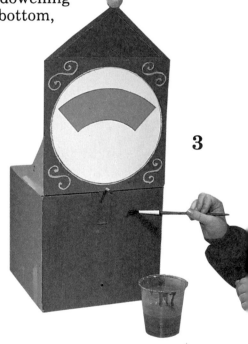

5. Balance the pendulum by fixing a short length of dowelling, with a circle of cardboard at each end, across the top, as shown.

6. Make an arrow to be the hand that points to the dial. Pin the pendulum to the piece of dowelling so it can swing freely.

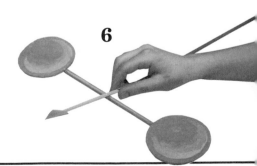

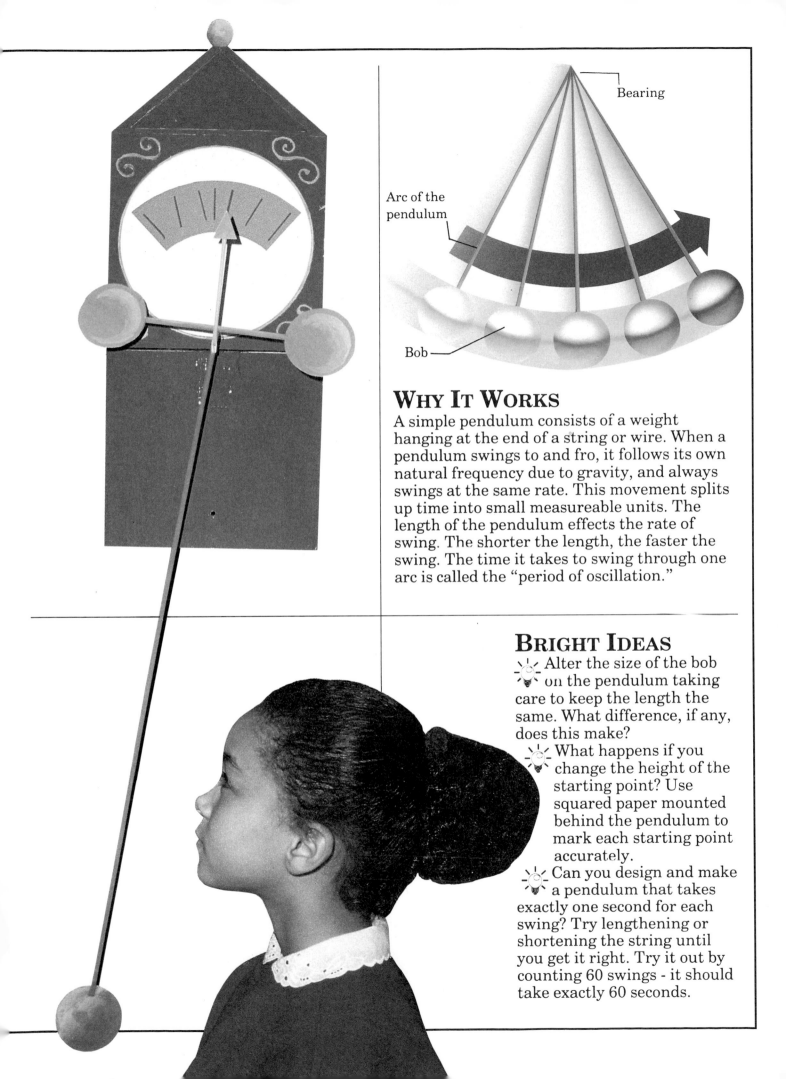

Bearing

Arc of the pendulum

Bob

WHY IT WORKS

A simple pendulum consists of a weight hanging at the end of a string or wire. When a pendulum swings to and fro, it follows its own natural frequency due to gravity, and always swings at the same rate. This movement splits up time into small measureable units. The length of the pendulum effects the rate of swing. The shorter the length, the faster the swing. The time it takes to swing through one arc is called the "period of oscillation."

BRIGHT IDEAS

Alter the size of the bob on the pendulum taking care to keep the length the same. What difference, if any, does this make?

What happens if you change the height of the starting point? Use squared paper mounted behind the pendulum to mark each starting point accurately.

Can you design and make a pendulum that takes exactly one second for each swing? Try lengthening or shortening the string until you get it right. Try it out by counting 60 swings - it should take exactly 60 seconds.

REGULATING TIME

In 1808, Sir William Congreve designed the rolling ball clock. The timing mechanism was a ball that took exactly 15 seconds to roll, in a zigzag fashion, in grooves along an inclined ramp. An accurate pocket watch was only possible after Robert Hooke discovered, in 1685, that a vibrating spring could provide a regular rhythm for a watch. The modern watch may use the natural vibrations of quartz crystal, 100,000 times per second, to keep time.

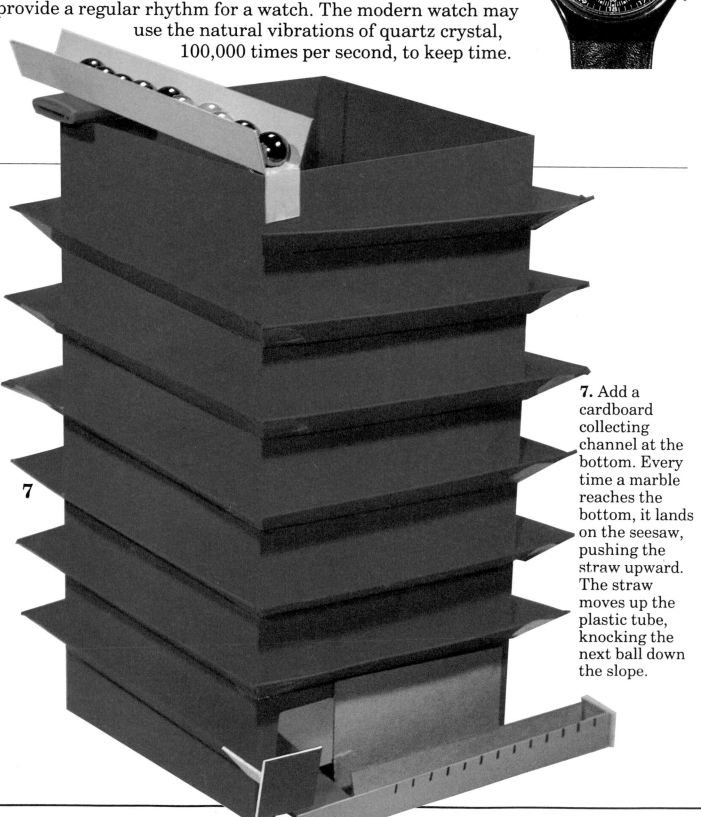

7

7. Add a cardboard collecting channel at the bottom. Every time a marble reaches the bottom, it lands on the seesaw, pushing the straw upward. The straw moves up the plastic tube, knocking the next ball down the slope.

HELTER SKELTER

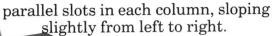

1. Take a rectangle of cardboard, 16in x 14in, and divide into four columns. Cut 6 parallel slots in each column, sloping slightly from left to right.

2. Cut a small door, as shown, and score and fold to make this 3-D shape. Tape the joints.

3. Now measure, cut and score 24 cardboard slots to fit into each of the slits. Slot them into position to make a zigzag channel for the marbles to roll along.

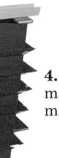

4. Make a channel for the marbles from cardboard. Cut a marble-sized hole at one end.

5. Tape a narrow plastic tube inside. Glue in place, raising it up at one end.

6. The seesaw mechanism at the bottom is a piece of cardboard, weighted underneath. A piece of tubing acts as the pivot and a straw runs from one end up into the plastic tube above.

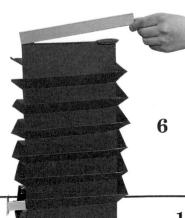

WHY IT WORKS

The rolling marble (1) is pulled down the slope by gravity. The force of gravity causes the marbles to accelerate as they fall. The marbles slow down when they are forced to change direction. Each marble takes exactly the same amount of time to roll down the slope. If this time is known, it can be multiplied by the number of marbles at the bottom (2) to calculate how much time has passed.

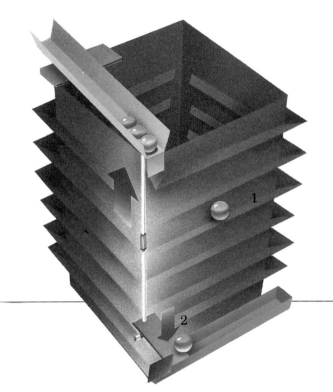

BRIGHT IDEAS

☀ What happens if you use marbles of varying size? Is it possible to time each marble's descent with total accuracy? Does each take exactly the same amount of time? What is the total time taken for all of the marbles to reach the bottom?

☀ Design and make a water clock like the one shown here. Will the flow be constant? How does the water clock compare with the sandglass? Can you design a water clock that takes exactly 10 minutes to empty?

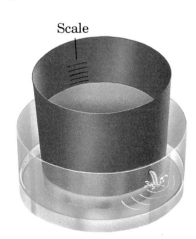

Scale

Speed and Acceleration

Speed is how fast something is moving. Velocity describes both speed and direction. When a car turns a corner, speed may stay the same, but velocity changes. Speed describes how far an object travels in a period of time. For example, a snail moves at about 0.03 miles per hour, while Concorde travels about 1,300 miles per hour. A speedometer, like the one pictured here, indicates how fast a car is moving. Acceleration is how much the speed increases in a period of time. A decrease in speed is called deceleration.

At Full Speed

1. Cut the road from stiff cardboard as wide as a shoe box, but twice as long. Secure a small piece of cardboard in the middle of one side with a paper fastener.

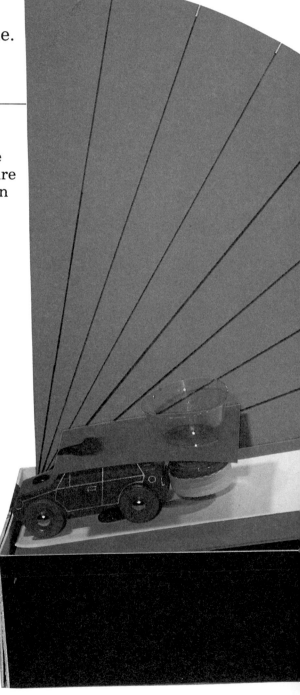

2. Tape one end of the road to the narrow end of a shoe box. It can be lifted to different heights.

3. Cut out one quarter of a circle. Divide it into angles of 10 degrees, and cut slits along the edge. Attach to the side of the box.

4. Check that the piece of cardboard on the road is in the correct position to slide into a notch. Pierce a hole in the lid of the plastic bottle. Cut off the bottom section. Tape over the hole, invert and fill with paint. Mount on top of the car.

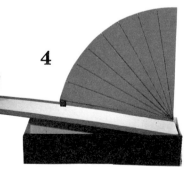

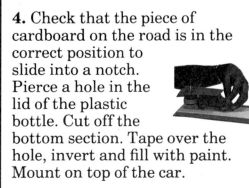

WHY IT WORKS

By observing the distance between the drops of paint on the inclined ramps you can estimate the speed of the vehicle. When they are close together, the speed is slowest. If the spaces are uniform, the vehicle must be traveling at a constant speed. If the spaces widen, the vehicle has accelerated, if they narrow it has decelerated. The bigger the mass of an object, the greater the force needed to make it move. When the slope is steeper, the truck accelerates faster. The spaces between the drops are wider apart towards the bottom of the slope. The speed can be calculated by dividing the distance by the time taken.

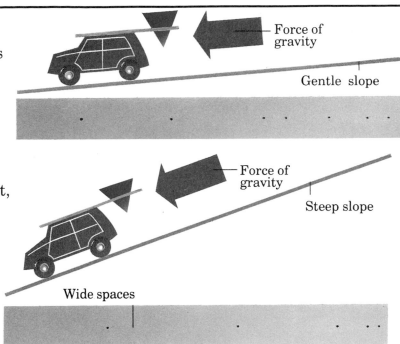

Force of gravity

Gentle slope

Force of gravity

Steep slope

Wide spaces

BRIGHT IDEAS

☀ Use a variety of toy cars on a sloping ramp and experiment with differing angles. Which car travels furthest? Did you use the same "push" each time to ensure a controlled experiment?

☀ Run the same car down a variety of angles, into a shoe box. Measure the distance that the box has moved. The distance that it moves depends on the speed.

☀ Try running on a beach at various speeds. Use a stop-watch to time yourself and measure the spaces between the footprints. Your footprints will be further apart, the faster you run.

5

5. Set the angle of the road. Place a long piece of paper over the road to record your results each time. Position the car at the top of the slope. Remove the tape just before it is released. Time each run accurately. Be careful not to push the car.

WEIGHT AND GRAVITY

Weight is due to the forces of gravity. Gravity is the force of attraction that acts toward the Earth's core, pulling us all downward. Sir Isaac Newton (1642-1727) developed the theory of gravitational pull. The Earth is held in orbit around the Sun by the pull of gravity. Gravitational pull is visible daily in the movement of the tides. They are a direct consequence of the gravitational pull between Earth, Moon and Sun. The weight of an object can vary slightly at different places on Earth.

PULL HARD!

1

1. Measure out a vertical indicating scale on a long sheet of cardboard. Space the divisions evenly.

2

2. Cut the base from a plastic bottle. Paint it a bright color. This will be a weighing pan. Pierce 2 holes directly opposite each other in the sides and attach a piece of thread, as shown.

3. Use the painted top of a plastic bottle as a holder from which to suspend the balance. Cut a flap, as shown here, and make two holes in it. These will be the screw holes through which it can be attached to a length of wood.

3

4. Tie an elastic band to the thread already attached to the weighing pan. Loop the free end to the plastic holder. When suspended the weighing pan must be level. If it is not, adjust the elastic.

4

5

5. Position the wood in a secure, vertical position. Attach a pointer to the base of the weighing pan. This will simplify the reading of the scale. Establish the position of the pointer when the pan is empty.

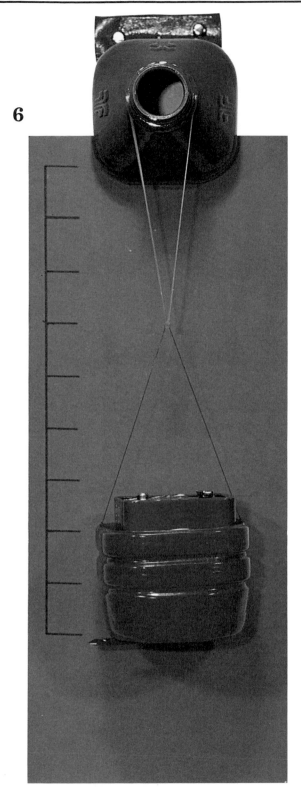

6

6. Mark the point on the indicating scale where the base of the empty pan rests. All other measurements must be taken from that point. Select a variety of objects to weigh. Place each object inside the weighing pan and read from the scale when the pan is still.

WHY IT WORKS

Robert Hooke (1635-1703) devised the theory of elasticity. Hooke's Law states that the extension of a spring is directly proportional to the force applied to it. You observed how much the elastic stretched each time you weighed an object on the "spring" balance. When the weight doubles or trebles, the elastic stretches proportionally. This is because the gravitational pull is stronger for objects containing a greater amount of matter and therefore their weight is greater.

Almost Weightless

Less heavy

Heavy

BRIGHT IDEAS

☼ Collect a variety of objects to weigh on a real spring balance. Record the length of the spring in inches. Chart these results and look for a relationship between them. The greater the force recorded, the further the spring is likely to stretch. Does the size of an object make a difference to the force of gravity acting on it?

☼ Suspend a stone from a piece of elastic. Now suspend the same object from the elastic and lower it into a bucket of water until it is immersed. What do you observe? Why does this happen?

☼ Tie a long length of string around the middle of a heavy, closed book. Now lift the book by holding the string at each end. Try to make the string horizontal by pulling hard. It is impossible! The force pulling down on the book and the angle created between the two pieces of string makes it very hard to lift.

MEASURING MASS

Mass is not the same as weight. Mass is the amount of matter in an object, measured in pounds – it is constant wherever the object is. Each civilization developed its own system of weight measurement based on mass. A Roman pound weight had the same mass as one eightieth of a cubic foot of water. Nowadays, in some countries, weighing has been standardized by the introduction of metric units of mass.
A bar of gold has a greater mass than a piece of wood of the same size. Comparing the mass of different materials can be done using a balancing scale.

BALANCING ACT

1

1. Take two plastic beakers. In the top of each beaker make two holes directly opposite each other. Thread some string through the holes, leaving the same length free on each side.

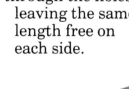

2

2. On a sheet of cardboard measure a horizontal indicating scale. Be as accurate as possible. The distance between each mark on the scale must be the same. Make the markings clear so that they can be read easily.

3. Choose a strong coat hanger that has a rigid structure. Decorate the hanger. Cut one end of a plastic straw to make a point. Suspend the straw from the center of the hanger. Ensure that it hangs vertically.

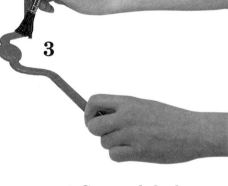

3

3

4. Suspend the hanger from a hook. Position the indicating scale so that the straw is in line with the center mark. Hang both beakers, one from each end of the hanger. Check that they are level.

4

5

WHY IT WORKS

Balancing scales work on a system of levers. When the weight on both sides is the same, the indicator will point to the center of the scale. If the indicator points to the right side of the scale, the object in the left-hand container has the greater mass.

Scale

BRIGHT IDEAS

Find the mass of a tennis ball and a baseball, or a cricket ball of the same size. Collect objects of similar size (volume).Estimate their mass, then 'weigh' them. What is the difference between mass and volume?

5. You can use marbles as weights. Ensure that they are of identical mass. Each time you weigh an item, record the number of marbles required to maintain the balance of the scales. If the straw points to the right of the center mark, more marbles must be added. When it points to the left, marbles must be removed.

Tennis ball

Cricket ball

AREA, VOLUME, AND CAPACITY

The first crude tools of measurement of length were parts of the body. Shorter units of length were measured against the thumb – the Roman "uncia" became the inch – the handspan or the foot. Longer lengths were measured against the forearm or a stride. From direct measurements of length, height and depth, indirect measurements of area, volume and capacity can be calculated. The modern unit of measurement for a large area of land is the hectare. A hectare equals 100 ares or 10,000 sq. meters. In 1794, the Cadil was established as the metric standard of capacity – it became known as the liter.

SURFACES AND SPACES

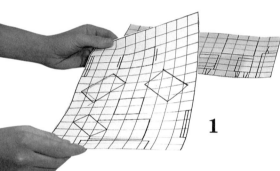

1. Use a yardstick or a tape measure to take accurate measurements of a room and the furniture. You need to know all dimensions. Scale down the measurements and transfer them to a piece of graph paper.

2. Each piece of furniture is drawn to scale on graph paper. Use these as patterns to draw round on cardboard. Score along fold lines to achieve a neat 3-dimensional shape.

3. Construct a scale model of three walls and the floor of the empty room. Draw a net, with flaps, to scale, on graph paper, then transfer it onto cardboard. Cut out the windows and glue together.

4. Arrange the furniture inside the room, so that it looks like the original room from which you took measurements.

1in
Length 1in
Volume 1in³

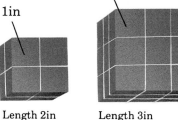
1in
Length 2in
Volume 8in³

1in
Length 3in
Volume 27in³

1in
Length 4in
Volume 64in³

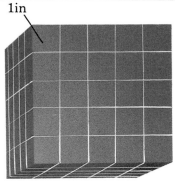
1in
Length 5in
Volume 125in³

WHY IT WORKS

Area is the size of a surface; it is commonly measured in square units. The area of a rectangular shape is calculated by measuring length times width.

Volume is the amount of space taken up by a shape. Capacity is the amount, or volume, that a container can hold. All are indirect measurements of size and space. A three-dimensional shape has length, height and depth. The volume of a regular 3-D shape, like a cube, can be measured by finding the product of these three measurements.

BRIGHT IDEAS

Make a tangram puzzle (below) by cutting up a square. See how many shapes you can make using all 7 pieces each time. Will the area be the same each time?

Use 1in plastic cubes to build a series of larger cubes. How many cubes are used on each face? What is the area of one face? What is the total surface area? What is the volume of each cube? What is the relationship between volume and the surface area of one face?

5. Observe how much space is taken up by 3-D objects. Be aware of the added dimension of depth. The scale drawings are 2-D, they lack depth. Surface area is flat, space around it can be filled.

DENSITY

Britain covers an area of about 95,000 sq. miles. France covers an area of approximately 210,000 sq. miles – an area twice as large. A similar number of people live in each. Therefore, France has a lower population density because it has twice as much space for the same number of people. Similarly, the density of a solid or a liquid can only be measured indirectly. It is dependent upon knowing the mass and the volume. Salt water is more dense than fresh water. This is why it is easier to float in the sea, particularly the Dead Sea.

How Dense?

1. Cut a length of straw and, to one end, attach a ball of modeling clay. Place it gently in water to ensure that it is balanced.

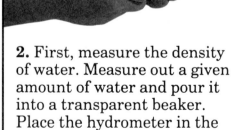

2. First, measure the density of water. Measure out a given amount of water and pour it into a transparent beaker. Place the hydrometer in the water and mark the straw at the surface.

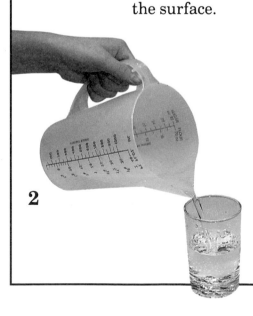

BRIGHT IDEAS

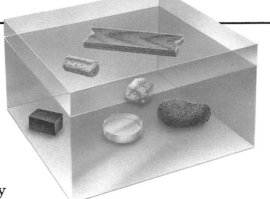

💡 Collect a variety of objects made from different materials. For example, you could use wood, cork, stone, glass, plastic, and metal. Place them in a large container of water. Do they float or sink? An object with a lower density than water will float. Those with a higher density will sink.

💡 Calculate the density of water. Find the mass of an empty beaker. Fill the beaker with a specified volume of water. Find the combined mass of the beaker and the water, then subtract one from the other to find the mass of the water. Use the formula density equals mass divided by volume.

WHY IT WORKS

You have made an hydrometer to measure the relative density or specific gravity of various liquids. This means that each measurement is compared to the measurement taken for water. The more dense a liquid is, the easier it is for objects to float. In a liquid less dense than water, the straw sinks lower. The lightness or heaviness of a given volume of any substance is called its density. Density is dependent upon how tightly the molecules of each substance are packed. If various liquids of different densities are gently poured into a transparent container beginning with the most dense first, they will settle in colored bands according to the density of each. Liquids you can use include salad oil, salt water, and colored fresh water.

3. Measure out the same quantity of oil and pour it into an identical beaker. Place the hydrometer in the oil and observe the position of the mark on the straw. Repeat for other liquids e.g. vinegar, salt water, and sugar water.

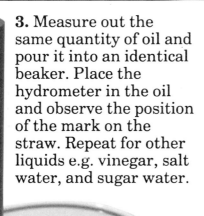

3

Least dense

Most dense

SURVEYING THE LAND

Tax gatherers in Ancient Egypt were probably the first professional surveyors. They developed a system called triangulation because it was easier to measure angles accurately than it was to measure distances. Surveyors still use the system of triangulation today – they can even use it to measure the height of mountains. The measuring tool used is the theodolite, which is mounted on a tripod like the one pictured here. Thales (624-546 BC), a Greek merchant and teacher, devised a method for measuring the height of the Great Pyramid in Ancient Egypt.

WHAT ANGLE?

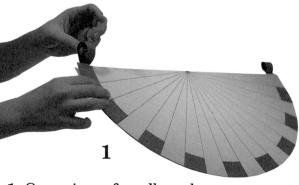

1

1. On a piece of cardboard, draw a circle, with a radius of 12in and with, the help of an adult, cut it out with a matte knife. Use a cutting board. Rule a diameter across the circle, then measure and mark divisions of 10 degrees all the way round. There will be 36 divisions, a circle has 360 degrees. Cut the circle in half.

2. Mark the divisions clearly. Make two "viewers" from rolls of cardboard. Glue them between the two semi-circles, at either end.

2

3

3. Wind a strip of cardboard round a heavy object, such as a battery. Attach this to one end of a length of string at least 24 in long. Secure the other end to the center of the straight edge of the theodolite.

WHY IT WORKS

When you viewed a landmark along your theodolite, the plumb line indicated the size of the angle at each end of the base line of an imaginary triangle. Once the distance and the vertical angle is known between two points, a surveyor can calculate the difference in height. That measurement is added to the height of the theodolite to give the total height of the landmark.

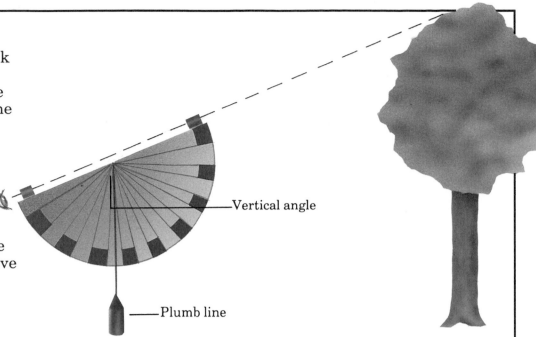

Vertical angle

Plumb line

4. To measure an angle, sight a particular point on a tall landmark through the "viewers." When the plumb line is motionless, ask someone to estimate the size of the angle from the alignment of the string.

4

BRIGHT IDEAS

You can make another kind of theodolite out of a sheet of cardboard cut to the shape of a right-angled triangle. You will also need a plumb line, a ruler and a tape measure. By lining up the longest side of the cardboard with the top of a tree or pole, so that the plumb line hangs exactly along the short side nearest to it, you can calculate the height of the tree. You will need to walk toward or away from the tree until this happens. Now measure the distance between yourself and the foot of the tree. Its height is that distance plus your own height.

Measure the height of a friend. Ask him to stand beside a tall tree, then move away until he appears to be 2in tall on a ruler. Now measure the height of the tree from the same distance. Can you estimate the height of the tree by working out how many times bigger than your friend the tree is?

READING WEATHER SIGNALS

Earth has weather because it is surrounded by a shallow blanket of air called the atmosphere. The Sun's rays pass through the atmosphere to reach the ground. The tilt of the Earth on its axis, and the curvature of its surface, create the variety of weather patterns and climatic zones experienced all over the world. For hundreds of years people have tried to forecast the weather. This is done by measuring such things as wind speed using an anemometer like this one (right), and monitoring any changes. Atmospheric pressure is measured using a barometer. The mercury barometer was invented in 1643 by Torricelli, an assistant of Galileo. The first weather station was built for Napoleon III in 1854.

STORMY WEATHER

1. Take an empty box and remove the lid. Decorate it appropriately with weather symbols.

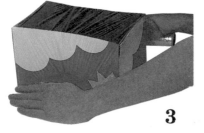

2. Measure and draw a curving indicating scale as shown. Make sure the divisions are equal. Use a marker pen to ensure clarity. Indicate "high" at the top of the scale, and "low" at the bottom.

3. Cover the box with plastic film, particularly the open top. Ensure that the plastic is taut and crease-free across this open part. This is the "drum" of your barometer.

4. Attach the indicating scale to the back of the box. Make sure that it protrudes beyond the box.

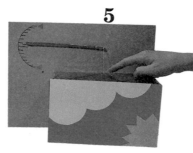

5. Secure the plastic straw horizontally to the scale card with a pin. Direct one end of the straw to the center of the scale. Fix the other pin inside as a pointer.

WHY IT WORKS

This barometer works as the air pushes down on the cellophane. When air pressure changes, the surface of the cellophane moves up or down. If air pressure falls the pointer falls – rainy weather is approaching. A rise in air pressure means the pointer will rise, indicating dry weather. The anemometer reacts to wind speed. If the wind is strong, it will push the strip of cardboard further up the scale.

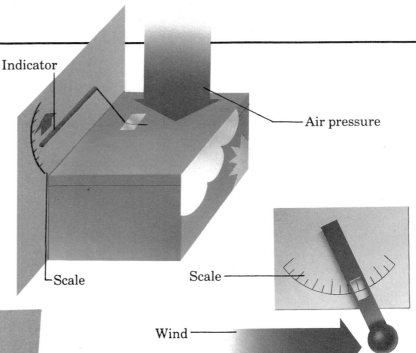

Indicator

Air pressure

Scale

Scale

Wind

BRIGHT IDEAS

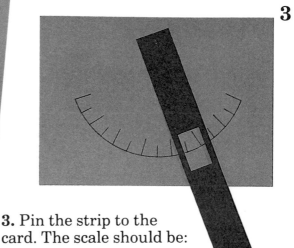

1. Design and make a portable anemometer. Use a protractor and compass to draw a scale on a piece of thick cardboard.

1

2

2. Tape half a table tennis ball to a strip of cardboard and cut a window so you can read the scale.

3

6. Use sticky tape to attach the thread to the straw. Attach the free end of the thread to the surface of the plastic. The straw must be horizontal.

3. Pin the strip to the card. The scale should be:

Angle:	80	60	40	20
mph	8	15	21	32

LOAD AND EFFORT

Imagine climbing to the top of a steep hill on a hot day. Think about what hard work it would be. Next, try to picture yourself climbing to the same height on a more gentle slope. It would take longer, but you would not find it such hard work. The gentler slope, or gradient, allows you to climb to the same height by using less effort. The slope is, in fact, acting as a simple and basic machine which makes work easier. You may think of a machine as a complicated device in a factory, but actually a slope, or inclined plane, to give it its proper name, is one of the oldest machines known to man. Stairs are a series of slopes which allow us to climb with relatively little effort.

BRIGHT IDEAS

Cut out a paper triangle and starting with the thin end of the wedge wrap it around a pencil. Does the shape remind you of a screw? A screw is a bit like a slope that is going around and around in a spiral.

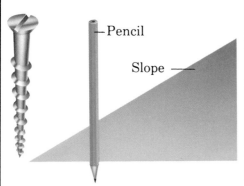

Pencil

Slope

PULLING POWER

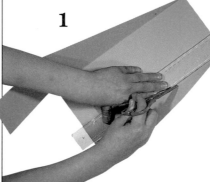

1

2. Build a solid frame from straws, and reinforce it with cardboard. Stick them together with tape and then join the frame to the ramp.

1. Make a slope from stiff cardboard. Cut out and score along the edges, as shown. Fold, and stick with glue. Put the slope somewhere safe – you will need to use it in later projects.

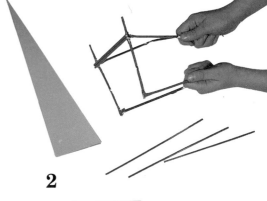

2

WHY IT WORKS

When the load (as the car being lifted would be called by scientists) is pulled up the ramp, it travels a longer distance than when it is brought up in the lift. If the weight of the car was 16 ounces, then an effort of 16oz would be needed to pull it straight up in the lift. If an effort of $3\frac{1}{5}$ oz was needed to pull it up the slope, then we say that the ramp has a mechanical advantage of 16oz divided by $3\frac{1}{5}$ oz which equals 5. In other words, without the slope you would need 5 times as much effort.

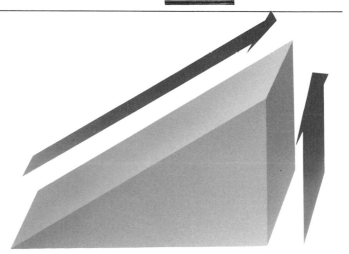

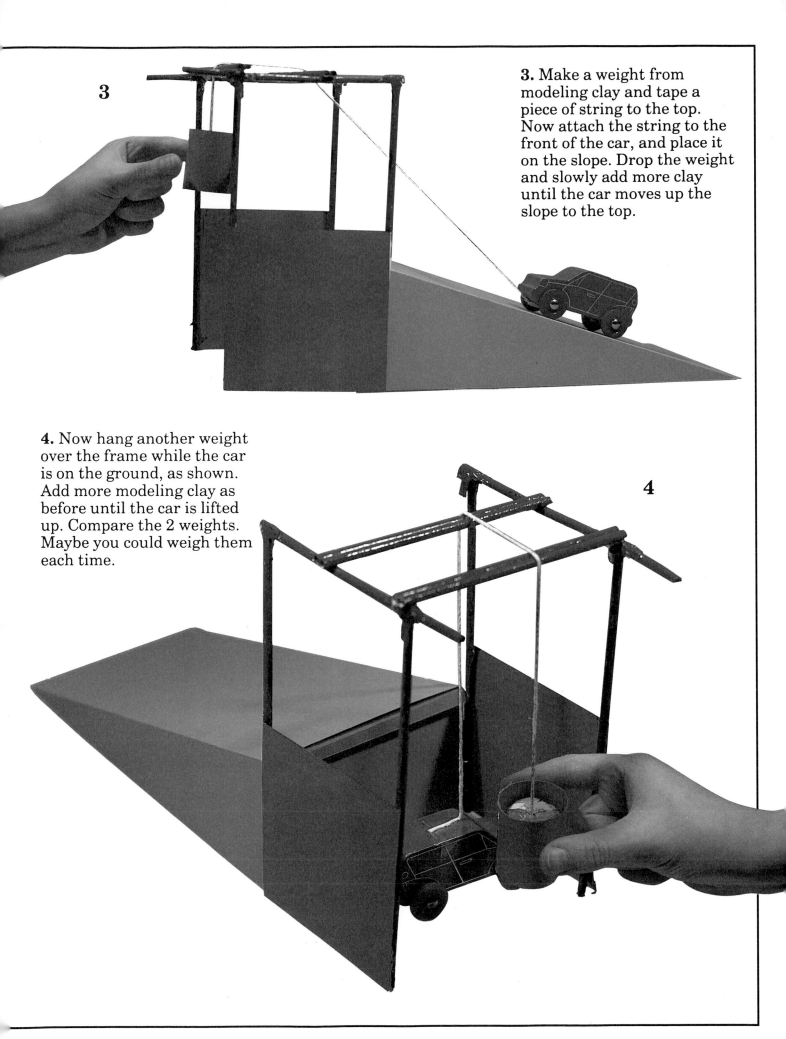

3. Make a weight from modeling clay and tape a piece of string to the top. Now attach the string to the front of the car, and place it on the slope. Drop the weight and slowly add more clay until the car moves up the slope to the top.

4. Now hang another weight over the frame while the car is on the ground, as shown. Add more modeling clay as before until the car is lifted up. Compare the 2 weights. Maybe you could weigh them each time.

201

MOVING THINGS

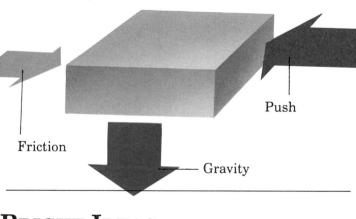

Have you ever tried to push a heavy box across the floor? If you have, you would have noticed that this can feel like hard work – especially if the box is heavy and the floor is rough. To a scientist, there are two reasons for this: the first is gravity – the force that pulls all things down to Earth and makes them feel heavy. The second reason is friction – the forces that are produced when the box begins to move and its surface rubs against the ground. Friction is a common force which stops things from moving. It opposes movement. If this force were not acting on the box, it would continue moving forever when you gave it a push!

WHY IT WORKS

To make something move, we can push it, pull it, twist it, blow it, and so on with a force larger than the one keeping it in place. When we pushed shapes with our "controlled shover," they moved a little way until the opposing force of friction stopped them. In the diagram, you can see this force acting against your push.

5. Try shoving objects of different sizes and different materials. Some objects, like a marble, move farther because their shape allows them to overcome the force.

5

Friction

Push

Gravity

BRIGHT IDEAS

🔆 Put your shover into a vertical position and try pushing the shapes again. The shapes do not have the same amount of friction working against them now. If you shoot each shape up with an equal shove, you will see there is much less difference in how far the shapes go.

🔆 Tie up a brick with string. Now pull it steadily along the floor using a spring balance. Try pulling other objects, and compare your readings.

SHOVE IT!

1. Cut out a long piece of cardboard and paint it with equally spaced stripes. Stick a piece of straw to one end, as shown.

2. Join 2 thinner pieces of straw to make your shover. Place it inside the wide straw, lining it up with the first stripe. Push a small piece of stick through the straw to keep it from moving forward.

3. Now stretch a piece of elastic around the stick, and pin it to the board, as shown. You stretch this back when you prepare to fire.

4. Use the stick as a handle to pull your shover back. Pull it as far as it will go. Place an object in front and let go.

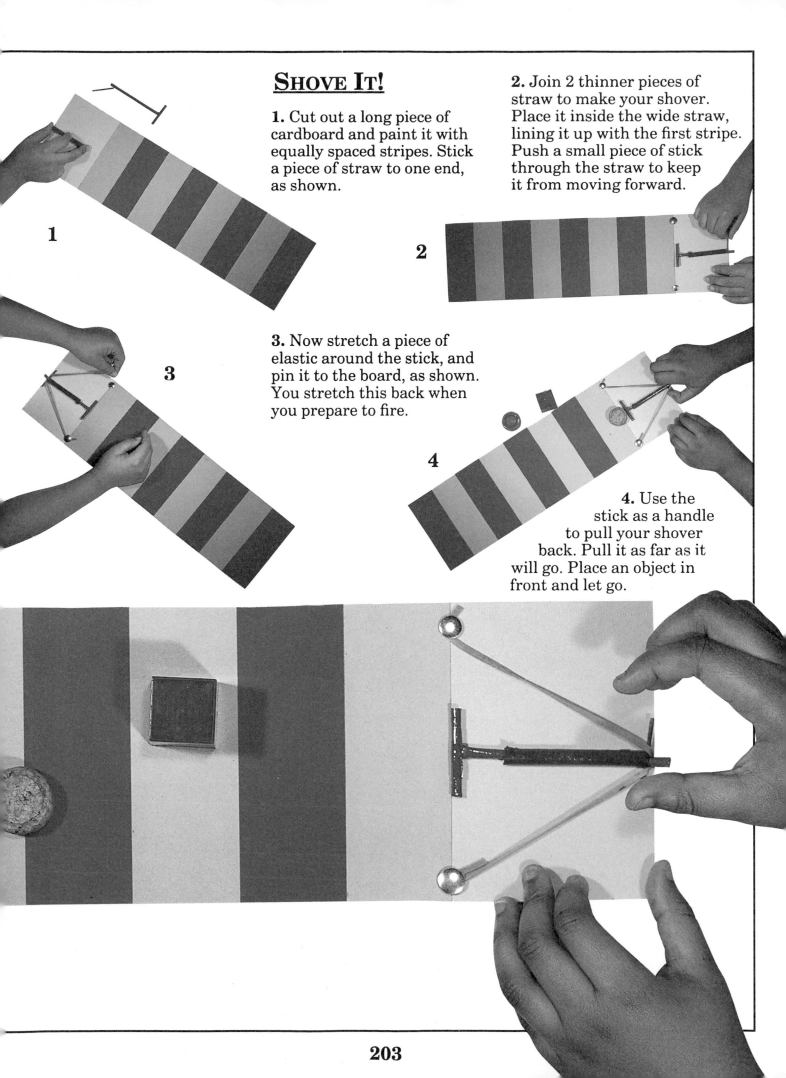

OVERCOMING FRICTION

Throughout history people have searched for easier ways to move things around. The builders of the Egyptian pyramids would have had to drag huge lumps of building stone for long distances. The forces of friction and gravity made this very hard work. They found, however, that by placing rollers under the stone blocks, they could drag the same block more efficiently. The rollers themselves would have simply been the trunks of trees. Round objects, like the ball-bearings pictured here, overcome the forces of friction and move easily.

SLIP SLIDING

1. Make a car from card, as shown. Draw windows on the sides. Make a flat container from yellow card. It should be the same width as the car and about 0.09in deep.

2. Fill the container with pieces of straw. These will behave like rollers. They should fit snuggly without being glued.

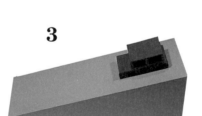

3.

3. Use the slope you built earlier. The car, without rollers, marbles or wheels, will not move. Tip the ramp until the car slides down. It will have to go quite high.

4. Holding the straws in their box, turn it upside down and place at the top of the slope. Fit the car on top and let it go. Does the car move more easily with rollers?

4.

5. Build 2 containers, wide enough for a row of marbles. Put the marbles in the containers. These will act as ball-bearings.

5.

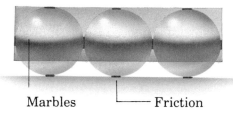

Flat
surface   Friction

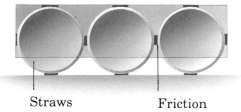

Marbles   Friction

Straws   Friction

WHY IT WORKS

The car will not slide smoothly down the ramp without the rollers or marbles because friction stops it. The amount of friction (shown in red) depends on two things: the weight of the object that we want to move, and the kind of surfaces which the object and the floor have. The greater the weight, the harder the two surfaces are squeezed together, and the rougher the surface the more friction is created. Friction can be reduced by rolling an object rather than pushing or dragging it. The rollers and marbles roll underneath your car. There will be some friction, but a lot less than when the whole of the car itself was in contact with the ramp.

BRIGHT IDEAS

☀ Try letting your car go down the ramp sideways. Does it move more easily with the straw rollers or the marbles?

☀ Change the surface of your ramp. Try sandpaper or a piece of carpet. What difference does this make to how well your car rolls?

6

6. Keeping the marbles in with your hands, turn the containers upside down and place them at the top of the slope. Put the car on top and let it roll downhill.

WHEEL AND AXLE

The earliest known wheels were made in ancient Mesopotamia around 3000 B.C. Early four-wheeled carts were not very practical, though. Their wheels were fixed rigidly to the axles of the cart which made it very difficult for them to turn corners. About 2,000 years ago, a front axle that could pivot was invented. In the Middle Ages, smaller front wheels combined with cutting away a small section of the body made steerable vehicles much better. Today, we have pressed steel and alloy wheels, pneumatic (air-filled) tires, spoked wheels, and many others.

STEER CLEAR

2. Make the body of your car from cardboard. Cut out a shape like this one, and stick the edges together. Leave a flap to cross underneath the car. This will hold the axle. Decorate with your own racing stripes.

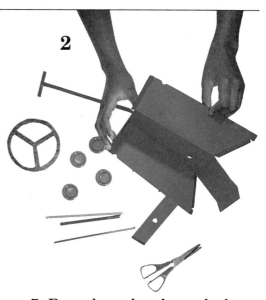

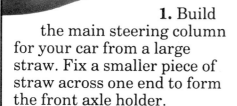

1. Build the main steering column for your car from a large straw. Fix a smaller piece of straw across one end to form the front axle holder.

4. Turn the car upside down and make a hole for the steering column to pass through. This can be reinforced with thick cardboard.

5. Pass the axles through the thick straws and attach the other wheels. You can split the ends of the straws and glue them in place. Tape the other axle in position.

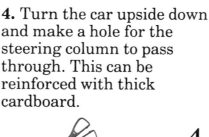

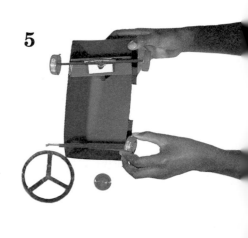

3. Make the axles from thin straws. These can be pushed through thicker straws and attached to the plastic bottle tops that are the car's wheels.

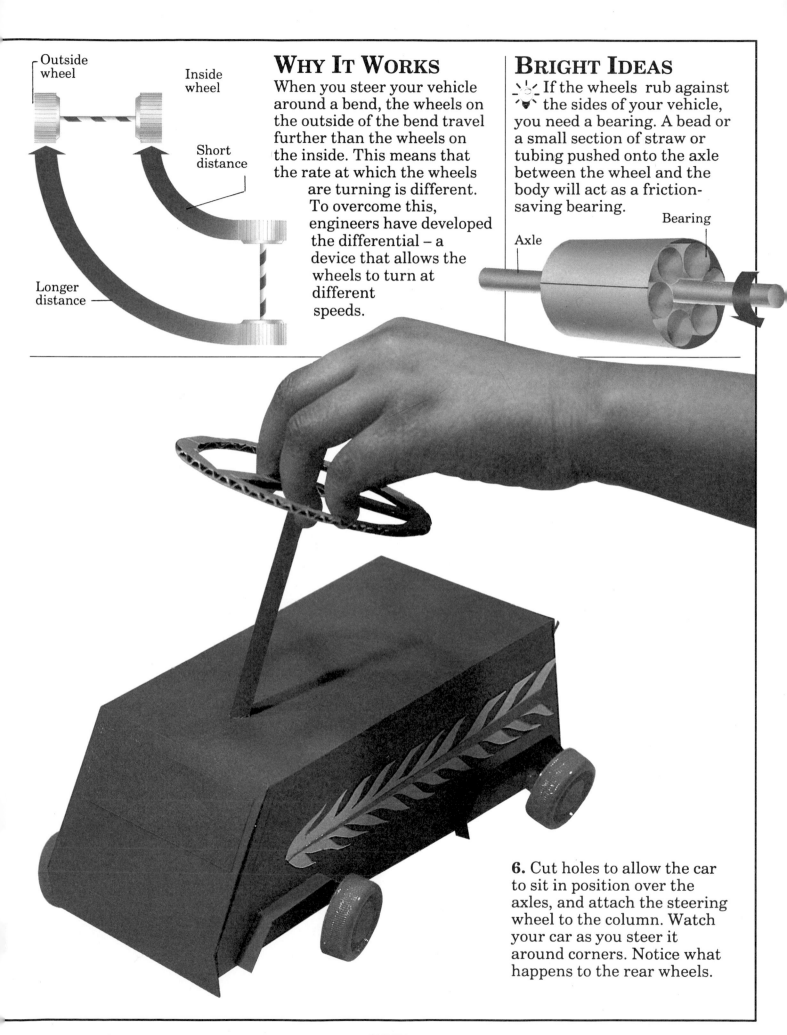

WHY IT WORKS

When you steer your vehicle around a bend, the wheels on the outside of the bend travel further than the wheels on the inside. This means that the rate at which the wheels are turning is different. To overcome this, engineers have developed the differential – a device that allows the wheels to turn at different speeds.

Outside wheel

Inside wheel

Short distance

Longer distance

BRIGHT IDEAS

If the wheels rub against the sides of your vehicle, you need a bearing. A bead or a small section of straw or tubing pushed onto the axle between the wheel and the body will act as a friction-saving bearing.

Bearing

Axle

6. Cut holes to allow the car to sit in position over the axles, and attach the steering wheel to the column. Watch your car as you steer it around corners. Notice what happens to the rear wheels.

USING FRICTION

Wheels, bearings, and lubricants, like oil, have all been developed to reduce friction between moving parts. At other times, though, friction is very useful to us. For example, think of how difficult it is to walk on a slippery surface like ice or of how cars can crash when they lose their grip on wet or oily roads. In cases like this, special shoes or car tires are designed to cause friction and so give grip. Many tires have been developed to give grip. Huge knobby tires help tractors and dump trucks to drive on rough and slippery ground.

No Obstacle!

1. Your tank will be powered by a thread spool and rubber band which can be wound up. Energy is stored in the twisted rubber band and released slowly as the tank crawls along.

1

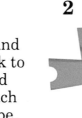

3

2. Thread a rubber band through a piece of candle and attach a small piece of stick to one end. Pass the other end through the spool and attach it to the other side with tape.

2

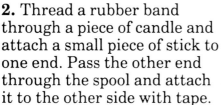

3. Cut a piece of cardboard to this shape, making sure the semicircles are big enough to fit over a thread spool. The body of the tank shouldn't touch the surface.

5. Wind a rubber band around the spool. You have provided the tank with tires. It will now grip the slope and climb up.

4. Wind the stick as tight as it will go, and place the spool at the bottom of the slope. Will it travel up quite easily?

4

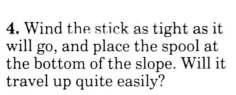

5

WHY IT WORKS

For your thread spool tank, friction is both a good and a bad thing. The material that you wrap around the spool, for example rubber bands or sandpaper, creates a large amount of friction as the tank moves up the slope, and this gives grip. Without this grip, the tank would probably slip and fail to climb the slope. When the stick rubs against the spool, however, the friction caused here makes the tank less efficient, and slows it down. The disk of candle wax comes between the rough surfaces and acts as both a bearing and a lubricant, and allows the stick to turn more easily against the reel. Surfaces with an uneven texture (1) cause friction when objects move over them. If lubricants, like oil, are applied to the surface, the valleys and holes are filled in (2). The surface becomes smooth, and friction is greatly reduced. The surface may be slippery.

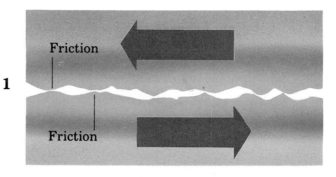

1

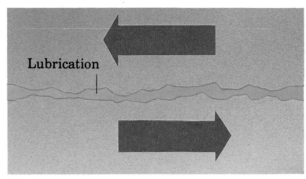

2

6. Stick the tank shape together, and carefully place over the spool. It doesn't need to be secured. A straw or pencil can be the tank's gun.

6

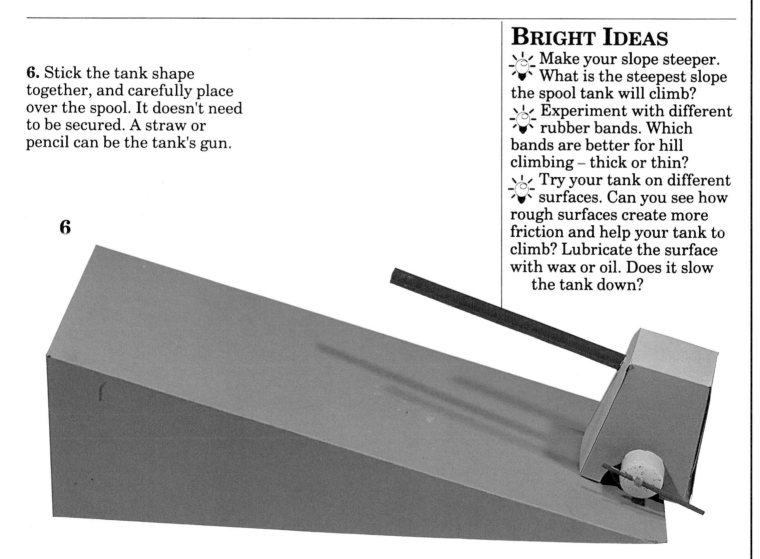

BRIGHT IDEAS

🔆 Make your slope steeper. What is the steepest slope the spool tank will climb?

🔆 Experiment with different rubber bands. Which bands are better for hill climbing – thick or thin?

🔆 Try your tank on different surfaces. Can you see how rough surfaces create more friction and help your tank to climb? Lubricate the surface with wax or oil. Does it slow the tank down?

SPINNING WHEELS

So many things rely on wheels apart from cars and other vehicles. A fairground would not be much fun without wheels. A carousel in a playground is a large spinning wheel. When a wheel is made to spin, as long as there is nothing rubbing against it, it will continue to spin for a long time. Scientists, engineers, and even toy-makers have made use of this fact in many situations. Inside a car engine, there is a heavy wheel that spins when the engine is running and even after it's turned off. This wheel is the flywheel, and it helps the car to run smoothly.

BATTLING TOPS

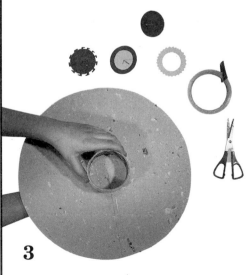

1. Cut out a large circle of cardboard about 16in across. This is the "arena" for the battle. Also cut out three small circles of 1½in across.

2. Cut a slit from the edge of the large circle to the middle. Cross the edges to make a cone shape and secure underneath with tape.

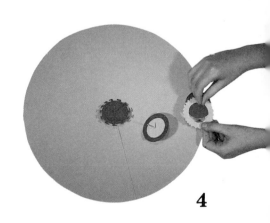

3. Turn the cone upside down, and stand the point in a circle of strong cardboard. The inside of a thick roll of tape will do.

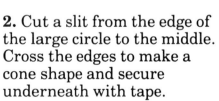

4. Decorate your tops with rings of colored cardboard, and push sharpened matchsticks through the center of each.

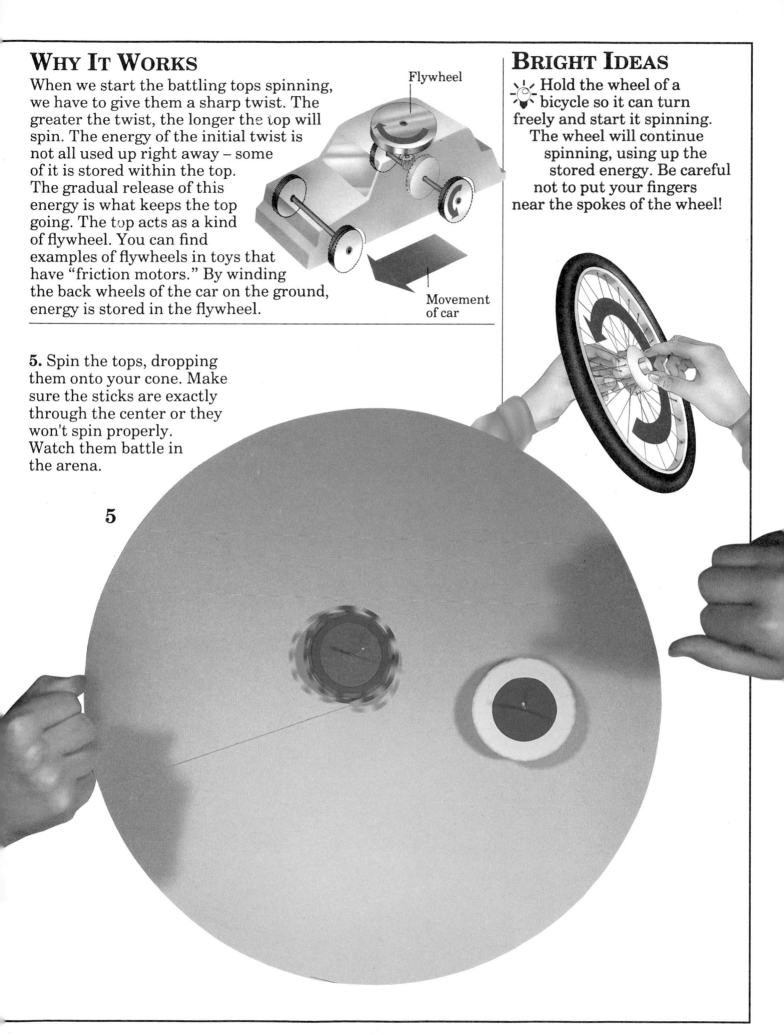

WHY IT WORKS

When we start the battling tops spinning, we have to give them a sharp twist. The greater the twist, the longer the top will spin. The energy of the initial twist is not all used up right away – some of it is stored within the top. The gradual release of this energy is what keeps the top going. The top acts as a kind of flywheel. You can find examples of flywheels in toys that have "friction motors." By winding the back wheels of the car on the ground, energy is stored in the flywheel.

Flywheel

Movement of car

5. Spin the tops, dropping them onto your cone. Make sure the sticks are exactly through the center or they won't spin properly. Watch them battle in the arena.

5

BRIGHT IDEAS

Hold the wheel of a bicycle so it can turn freely and start it spinning. The wheel will continue spinning, using up the stored energy. Be careful not to put your fingers near the spokes of the wheel!

WINCHES AND WHEELS

One important use of wheels is in harnessing the power of wind and water, and using the energy to perform useful jobs. Waterwheels, like this one, were designed to capture the energy of running water, and transfer it into energy to power machinery. Turbines are modern waterwheels that turn in streams of water released from behind dams, and generate electricity. Old-fashioned windmills used the energy of the wind for grinding corn, while modern windmills are commonly used for pumping water. Another important wheel is a winch. This is a special roller that is used to make the lifting of heavy loads an easier task.

BRIGHT IDEAS

☀ Try using your spool tank to lift up weights (below). You would have to figure out the best way to secure it to a table top first.

☀ Using a cork and four pieces of thin plastic you could make your own waterwheel. Make 4 notches in the cork and insert the pieces of plastic. If you attach it to a piece of wood so it turns, you could make a paddleboat.

☀ Have you got a toy pinwheel? If you have you could modify it to make it lift a small weight when the wind blows on it.

7

7. Wind your thread and bucket around the spool. Now all you need is the wind to raise and lower it. Produce this by blowing through a straw. You may also attach paper strips to the straws.

WHY IT WORKS

The energy which you use to blow the sails around, provides the force to turn your wind-powered winch. If you tried to move the weight by blowing underneath it, you would have little chance of succeeding. The winch, however, makes it possible to lift the weight by blowing in the following way. Pulling a weight up a steep slope will take more effort than pulling it up a gentle one. Although the force, or effort, is less, it is applied for a greater distance. In effect, by blowing onto the tips of the sails you apply the force for a great distance in order to lift the weight over a very short one. The tip of the sail will probably travel 33ft to lift the weight 4in. The work of lifting the weight is therefore made much easier.

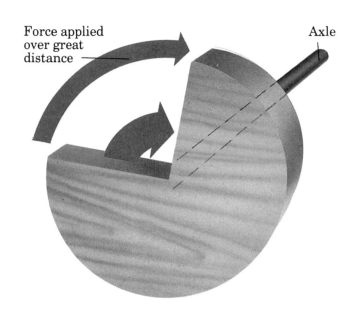

Force applied over great distance

Axle

WIND POWER

1

1. The well makes it possible to raise a bucket using "wind power". Stick 6 straws to the end of a cotton reel leaving the center clear. Secure with a piece of card.

4

4. Make a sturdy top to your wall by painting a ring of card. Make 2 holes for the upright supports.

2. Make a little bucket from card, and attach to a long piece of string. The string passes through 2 holes in the top of the bucket, so it hangs level.

2

5. To suspend your wheel between 2 posts, thread a straw through the center of the reel for your axle and fix the 2 ends through 2 large straws. Fit into the top of the wall.

5

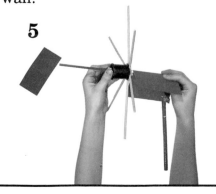

3

3. Make a base for your well from card and decorate it to give a brick effect. The top of the wall can be made by cutting slits and folding the card over.

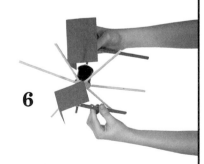

6

6. The posts should be long enough to stand in the wall, giving the wheel room to turn. Add 2 little roofs made from V-shaped pieces of card.

PULLEY SYSTEMS

If you have ever had a chance to watch a crane at work, you were probably amazed by the enormous weights that it could lift. Cranes can be seen on building sites, on ships and docksides, in railroad yards, on the backs of lorries – the list could go on. Cranes make lifting easier by using powerful winding engines and pulleys (special wheels shaped so that ropes and wires are kept in place as they move). Pulley systems can be very simple, like the block and tackle pictured here. A builder standing on the ground might use a rope and a single pulley fixed to the top of a building to lift a bucket of cement to a worker above. This would be a lot less effort than climbing a ladder with the bucket.

BRIGHT IDEAS

💡 Make a simple "fixed pulley" system of your own using thread spools, wire loops, and string.

💡 A special pulley, called a block and tackle, is used for lifting heavy loads, for example on building sites. This device has a set of pulley wheels which means the lifting force has to be applied for a tremendous distance in order to lift a load just a little way. Look at the sketch, and by using coat hangers and thread spools have a try at making your own block and tackle.

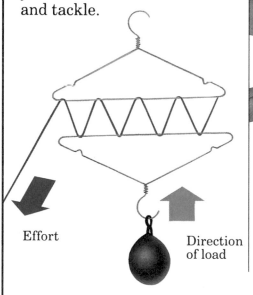

Effort

Direction of load

PULL TOGETHER

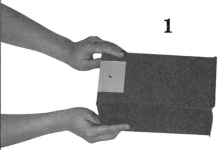

1

2. Push a thin straw through the box. At the center, suspend a thread spool with two pieces of straw on either side to keep it central.

3

4. Bend some coat hanger wire, and attach it to the thread spools as the picture of the crane on the opposite page shows. Suspend from a hook at the end of the arm.

1. Make a tall tower from cardboard, as shown, leaving it open at the top and bottom. Reinforce one side and make a hole for the winch to pass through.

2

3. Make an arm for the crane from cardboard, and fix to the main part with glue. Stick a small piece of straw underneath the arm at the end to guide the string over the thread spools.

4

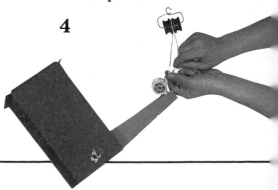

214

WHY IT WORKS

A pulley system allows a small force to be applied over a long distance. When a force moves an object, scientists say that work is being done. Work is measured in units called joules, and is equal to the force that you apply, multiplied by the distance the load is lifted. With a single pulley system (right), the load moves the same distance as the rope pulled in. It doesn't amplify (or help increase) the effort. In a double pulley system (far right), the load moves only half the distance of the rope pulled in. Distance is halved and the force raising the load is double the effort pulling the rope.

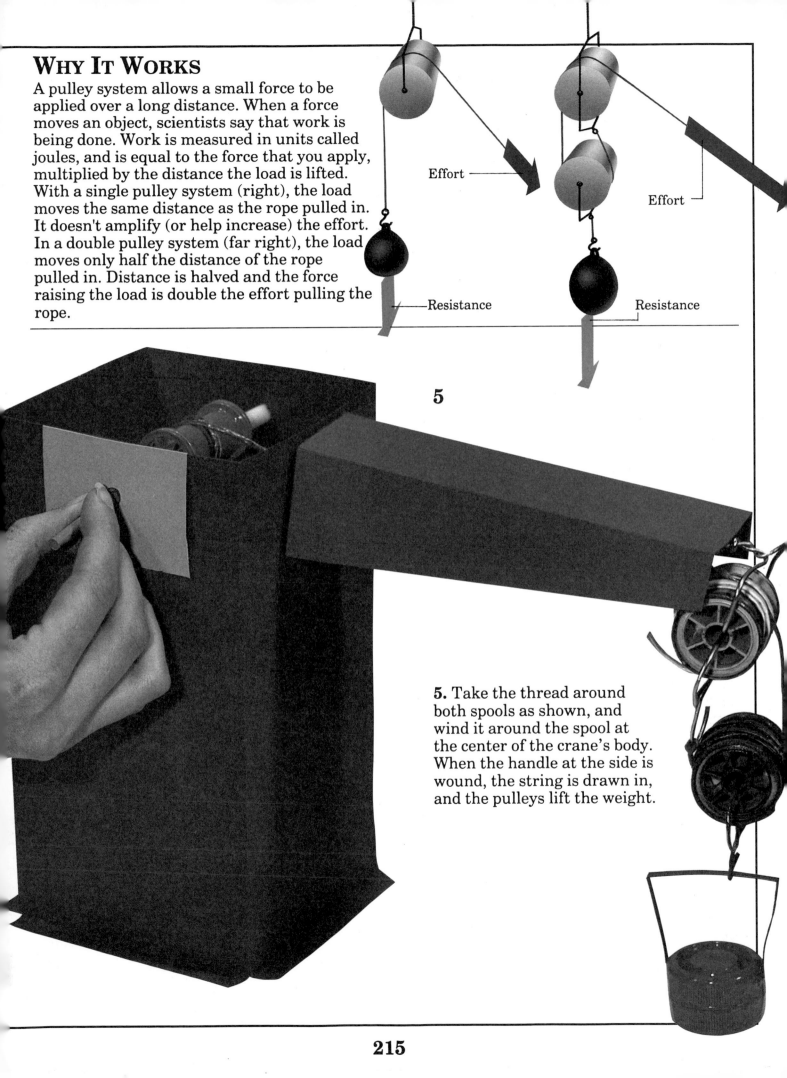

Effort

Resistance

Effort

Resistance

5

5. Take the thread around both spools as shown, and wind it around the spool at the center of the crane's body. When the handle at the side is wound, the string is drawn in, and the pulleys lift the weight.

GEARS

Today's cyclists have a much easier time than the men and women who rode the very first bicycles over 100 years ago. The draisienne was a popular bicycle in 1820 – but it was a heavy thing without pedals; you had to free-wheel along, like you would on a scooter! About 1885, J.K. Starley produced the first commercially successful safety bicycle with pedals that used a chain to drive the rear wheel, leaving the front wheel free for steering. The bicycle continued to improve, and today modern machines make climbing steep hills and traveling at high speeds possible by the clever use of special, toothed wheels, called gears.

BRIGHT IDEAS

Turn your bicycle upside down and turn the pedals slowly to make the wheels turn. Be careful not to trap your fingers. By pushing a piece of paper into the spokes when the wheel is still, you will be able to count how many times the wheel turns for each full turn of the pedals. In which gear is it easiest to go fast?

6. When both feet are attached to the bike, one leg should be up when the other is down. The left foot should be fixed to the keyhole shaped cam, not directly to the pedal wheel. The front wheel can also be fixed with a fastener.

6

216

PEDAL POWER

1. Draw a pattern of your cyclist. The body of the cyclist and the frame are one piece. The wheels and the cyclist's legs are separate.

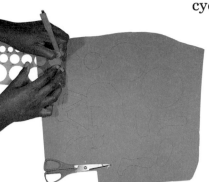

1

2. Paint your pieces realistically. The back wheel is made up of 3 separate disks of thick cardboard, held with a paper fastener. The smallest 2 are your gear wheels.

2

WHY IT WORKS

As we turn the pedals on a bike, the large pedal gear turns the smaller gear wheel on the back wheel by means of the chain. In the bottom picture, if the pedal gear has 50 teeth and the rear gear has 10 teeth then the wheel will turn five times for every turn of the pedals. This is called a high gear and would be best for going fast on flat ground. In the top picture, if the rear gear also has 50 teeth, it will only turn once for every turn of the pedals. This is a low gear and would be good for climbing hills.

Pedal wheel

Low gear

High gear

Pedal wheel

3

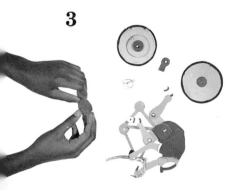

3. Join the legs of the cyclist at the knee and the hip. Cut out a thick piece of cardboard, 1in across. It should be thick enough to support a rubber band. The cyclist's foot will pedal this around.

5

4. Attach the disk to the bike with a piece of stick, so it turns. A small cam (the blue keyhole shape) is attached to the straw on the other side, and then to the other foot with a fastener.

4

5. Attach a rubber band from the back wheel to the pedal wheel. As the back wheel turns, the cyclist's legs will begin to pedal. If the rubber band is moved to the smaller gear, the cyclist will pedal faster.

TYPES OF GEARS

Gears were invented about 2,000 years ago. Today, most automated machines, as different as cars, watches and clocks, buses, trucks, drills, and motorcycles could not work without gears. Early wheeled vehicles were pushed or pulled by people and animals. When steam engines (and later gasoline engines) came along, engineers turned to gears to help to drive the wheels of trains, cars, and other machines. The teeth of gear wheels mesh together so that they do not slip. This makes them very reliable. When one wheel is turned, it will turn the other. The first wheel is called the driver, the second, the follower. A third gear, called an idler, can be placed between the two. This corkscrew makes use of a gear system called a rack and pinion.

COGS AND WHEELS

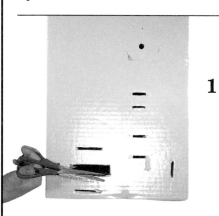

1

2. Cut out circles of cardboard of different sizes. These are the wheels. Make the 2 spur gears by cutting out 2 circles of corrugated cardboard and gluing them together.

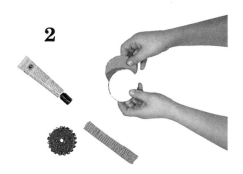

3

1. Cut slots in the top of a box to fit the different gears into it. The slots need to provide a tight fit for the pieces of cardboard that will fit into them.

2

3. For the teeth, use the inside of corrugated cardboard. Wrap it around a disk like this, glue in place, and paint in bright colors.

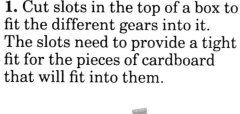

4

4. The axle for the gears can be made from plastic straws. They should turn freely, but not be too loose. Now make the U-shaped frame that supports the top gear wheels.

6

5. The matchstick gears are made from circles of 3in and 1½in across. The larger has 16 matchstick teeth, and the smaller 8 teeth. Fix them at even spaces making sure they mesh together.

5

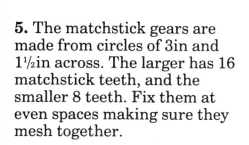

6. Cut a piece of corrugated cardboard 2½in long and ½in wide and glue to a small piece of wide plastic straw. This is glued to a toothed piece of cardboard that will mesh with the wheel below. Slide a thin straw through the larger one, and suspend from 2 pieces of cardboard.

WHY IT WORKS

Different gears do different jobs and here we can see:
1. A rack and pinion, often used in car steering systems.
2. A worm gear; the worm acts a bit like a screw and meshes with the larger worm wheel. It would be used to link shafts at right angles and on different levels.
3. Bevel gears; these would connect two shafts that are on the same plane but at right angles to each other.
4. Spur gears, the simplest form of gears used where one shaft drives another that is parallel to it.

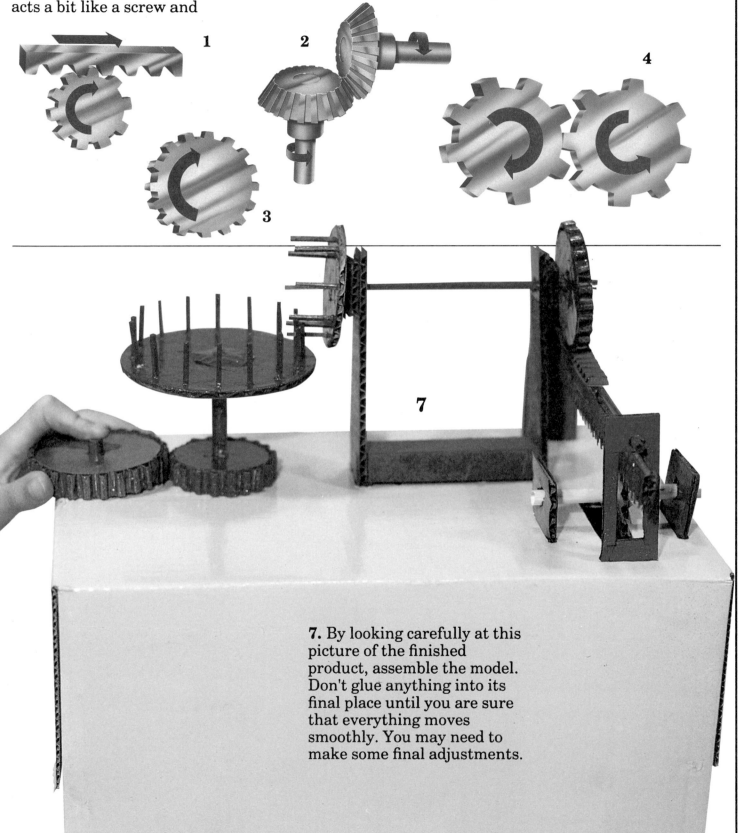

7. By looking carefully at this picture of the finished product, assemble the model. Don't glue anything into its final place until you are sure that everything moves smoothly. You may need to make some final adjustments.

LEVERS

As we have seen before, machines are devices that make work easier. There are five basic machines: the wheel and axle, the inclined plane or wedge, the pulley, the screw, and the lever. If you think about someone moving a heavy rock with the help of a crowbar, you can picture a lever making a difficult job easier. We use levers in countless ways: brake levers on bicycles, scissors, nutcrackers, a wrench, and a pair of pliers are examples of levers. In each case, levers make work easier. In our bodies too, levers are at work making everyday movements like biting, running, throwing, and kicking more effective.

FULL FORCE

5. Attach the hand and hammer to a piece of thick cardboard as shown, and make a pivot from 3 pieces of straw. Balance it as shown here. Set up all the pieces like this, making sure that when the seesaw is activated, the hand pushes the shoot up, the marble rolls down the channel and falls onto the lever. You may need to try it a few times to position all the pieces correctly. When everything is in the right place, glue the parts down and insert the paper fastener ready for hammering home.

5

1. Make the see-saw from cardboard. A piece of straw can act as a pivot. Attach a long straw to one end.

1

2. Make a tall box from cardboard, and bend another piece into a shoot for the marble.

2

3

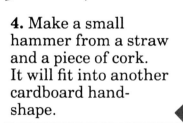

3. Glue the shoot to the top of the box, as shown, and attach a small hand to the end of the straw.

4. Make a small hammer from a straw and a piece of cork. It will fit into another cardboard hand-shape.

4

WHY IT WORKS

First class levers (1) pivot on a fulcrum (red) between the effort (blue) and the load (yellow) (like a crowbar or a pair of scissors). Second class levers (2) place the load between the fulcrum and the effort (like a pair of nut-crackers). Third class levers (3) are ones where the effort is applied between the fulcrum and the load (as in some sugar tongs or in lifting a fish out of the water with a fishing rod). The purple arrow is resistance.

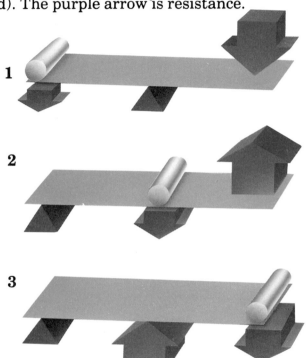

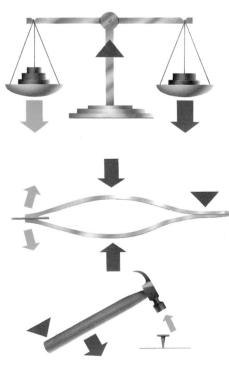

BRIGHT IDEAS

Can you tell which class each lever in the pictures fits into? The green arrows indicate resistance, the blue arrows are the effort, the red triangles are the fulcrum.

Use a lever to lift a weight. Put a small building block under a ruler for a fulcrum, and place a weight on one end of it. Push down on the other end of the ruler. Now move the brick closer to the weight and push again. You will have to push longer, and the weight will not move as far, but do you notice how it takes less effort to move the weight?

LEVERS IN PAIRS

In many tools and machines, levers work together in pairs, and the fulcrum (the place where the levers pivot) is often at the point where the levers are fixed together. Pliers, nutcrackers, scissors, and tweezers are all examples of levers working in pairs. In the human body, there are many instances of levers working in pairs. Think about the strength of a bite which is produced by your jaw muscles pulling your jaws together. Your jaws are actually working as levers. Also, when you grip something between your thumb and forefinger, look at the way they close together – your bones are levers.

GRAB THAT!

1. Cut out cardboard shapes as shown here to make your mechanical grabber. The body of the crane is made from 2 cardboard boxes. Paint it lots of bright colors.

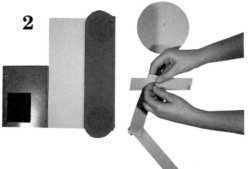

2. Make the moving arm from 3 pieces of cardboard. The top 2 pieces should be fixed together with a fastener so it pivots. Cut a circle of cardboard about 4in across for your turntable. It is attached to the crane with a pin so it moves.

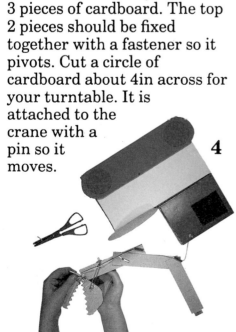

4. Take the thread down the arm, through 2 bits of straw which are guides. The end of the thread is tied to a straw which can be wound around like a handle. Staple a rubber band between the bottom set of teeth and the arm.

5. The rubber band should keep the jaws of the grabber open. When the handle is wound, the thread tightens, pulling the bottom "jaw" toward the top, closing them.

3. The teeth of the grabber are made from 2 pieces of cardboard. The top one is stuck to the arm and the bottom one is fixed to the top half with a fastener. Only the bottom of the "jaw" moves. Attach a matchstick to the top set of teeth, and tie a long piece of thread to it.

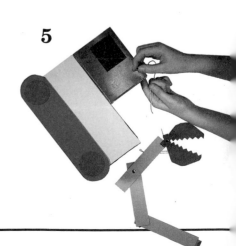

WHY IT WORKS

Levers working in a pair are most useful for gripping, cutting, and squeezing jobs. The jaws of the grabber close together like those of a pair of pliers or like those of a dog. A pair of scissors is a compound first-class lever. It produces a strong cutting action very near the fulcrum (red). The load is the resistance of the fabric to the cutting blades. The green arrows indicate resistance. In the bottle opener, pushing the handle up overcomes the strong resistance of a bottle cap. The effort is shown with blue arrows.

Effort

Resistance

Fulcrum

Fulcrum

Effort

Resistance

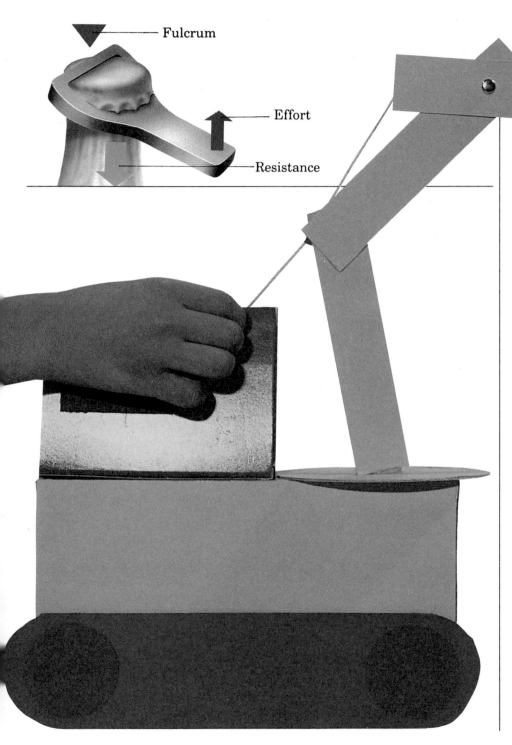

BRIGHT IDEAS

☀ Can you make your own model grabbing hand? You could make something like the grabber, but with fingers.

☀ Hold the muscles of your right forearm and clench your right fist. Can you feel them contracting and working the levers of your hand?

☀ Bend a nail with your own hands! You'll need two pieces of pipe, each one about 8in long. Put a long nail into one piece of pipe so that half of its length sticks out. Place the other piece of pipe over this half of the nail. By applying a downward force to the ends of the piece of pipe you should be able to bend the nail quite easily.

COMPLEX MACHINES

Wheels, gears, pulleys, and levers have developed over the course of thousands of years. Today, the science of engineering uses these simple machines in incredibly complex and precise ways. Many modern pieces of design use a combination of simple machines, for example, a bicycle. Spoked wheels with pneumatic tires combine with gears and chain wheels to drive the bicycle along. The pedals of a bicycle, gear change levers and the brakes, all use the principle of levers to make work easier, and the gear change cables are often guided by pulleys. Everyday objects, like clocks and watches, contain a complex series of wheels and levers.

WHY IT WORKS

At its most simple... the finger pushes the see-saw... the hand on the seesaw pushes the shoot... the marble rolls off the shoot and hits the second seesaw... this raises the box that holds the spool...the box tips as its front hits the second shoot... the spool rolls down the shoot and strikes the hammer... and the hammer hits the mouse! (Apologies to animal lovers everywhere.)

6. The bullet shape is a modeling clay counterweight wrapped in cardboard - this should balance with the bobbin and box EXACTLY. Set up your mousetrap by placing the box on the end of the small see saw and the marble on the middle of the top shoot...Now just wait for a mouse.

6

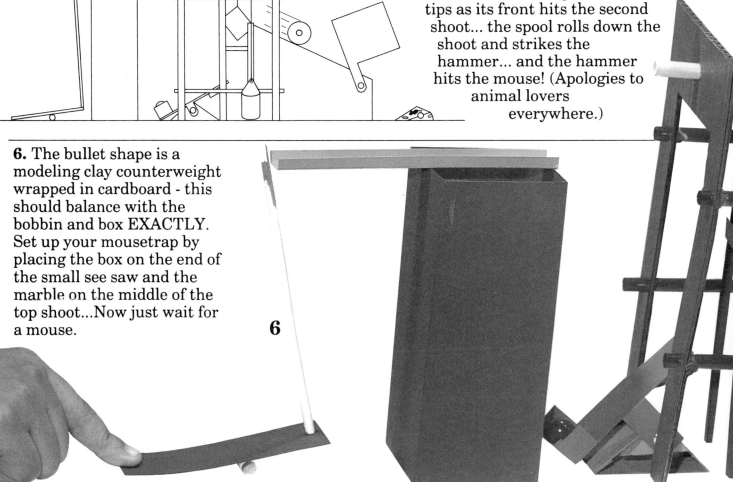

BRIGHT IDEAS

☀ Can you modify your mouse-trap so that the mouse landing on the cheese activates the mouse trap?

☀ If you have a construction set which has sets of gears, experiment and try to make a conveyor belt which will take a parcel around a corner.

☀ Convert your mouse-trap design to a burglar alarm which rings a warning (when the hammer hits a small bell) when someone enters your bedroom.

☀ Take the back off a watch or clock and have a close look at the mechanism. How many different wheels and levers can you see?

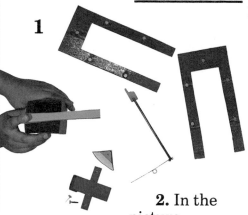

TRAPPED!

1

1. The frame for the pulley mechanism is made from two upside down U's of corrugated cardboard 8in tall and 3in across, linked together with 5 straws. The seesaw and shoot are the same as the ones you made earlier.

2. In the picture (right) you can see the basic shape for the see-saw with the cup to catch the marble. It is attached to the base with 2 paper-fasteners.

2

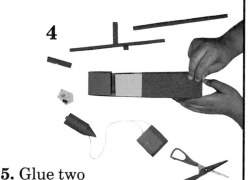

3. When you assemble the frame, first slide the four straws nearer to the bottom into their holes, then locate the top straw having already put the thread spool in place. When you are sure that the frame is rigid and level glue the straws to the frame.

3

4. Cut the corner from a cereal box to provide the ramp shown in green below. Make sure that the shoot for the roller sticks out at the top of the ramp so that it tips the roller onto the ramp.

4

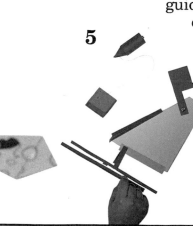

5. Glue two guides into place to channel the box which will carry the spool and attach a cardboard built hammer with paper-fasteners. The box that carries the spool up is open at one side.

5

ELEMENTS
AND
SHAPES

CONTENTS

INTRODUCTION

The world around us and everything in it is made up of 105 simple substances called elements. Some elements exist in a pure form such as particles of oxygen or copper but others are a combination of elements building simple compounds such as hydrogen and oxygen which form water. Other elements are more complex, sugar, for example is a compound of carbon, hydrogen and oxygen. The smallest part of any element is almost too small to see even under the most powerful microscope – this is called an atom. When different atoms join together, they form particles, or molecules, of new substances. By learning about elements and reactions we learn how the world around us works.

From the smallest atoms to iron girders that support the tallest buildings, structures, shapes and materials are part of our lives. It is important to understand shapes so that we can build the most efficient structures and understand which shapes are best with different materials. Throughout history our technological progress has been linked to the discovery of new materials – today one of our most useful materials is plastic in all its different forms, but we still continue to search for new and better materials.

Safety Tips

Work with an adult close by, particularly when using ovens, candles or irons to heat anything and when cutting card and wire. Remember never to smell or taste the substances you are working with. Remember plaster of Paris is very messy and shouldn't be poured down the sink. Always clean up very carefully and thoroughly.

WHAT ARE ELEMENTS?

Everything in the world is made up of elements. An element is a simple chemical substance which itself is made of tiny particles called atoms. Diamonds (right) are made from the element, carbon. There are 105 elements known to man. Some, like iron or copper, were used in ancient times, while others have been made by modern scientists. Many elements can be combined to make new substances – copper and tin can be melted together to make an alloy (mixture) called bronze. The periodic table arranges all the known elements in a special way.

PERIODIC TABLE

1. Each square contains the symbol for a different element. The symbol comes from the common name or Latin name of the element; C stands for carbon and Al for aluminum. The Latin for iron is ferrum, so the symbol is Fe.

H								
Li	Be							
Na	Mg							
K	Ca	SC	Ti	V	Cr	Mn	Fe	Co
Rb	Sr	Y	Zr	Nb	Mo	Tc	Ru	Rh
Cs	Ba	La	Hf	Ta	W	Re	Os	Ir
Fr	Ra	Ac						

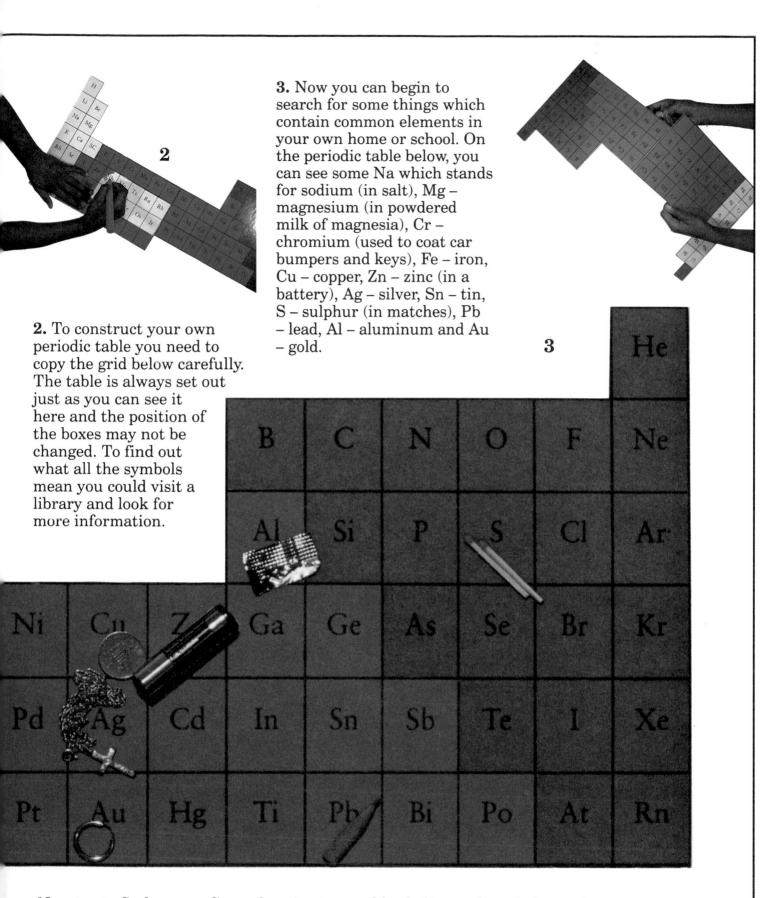

3. Now you can begin to search for some things which contain common elements in your own home or school. On the periodic table below, you can see some Na which stands for sodium (in salt), Mg – magnesium (in powdered milk of magnesia), Cr – chromium (used to coat car bumpers and keys), Fe – iron, Cu – copper, Zn – zinc (in a battery), Ag – silver, Sn – tin, S – sulphur (in matches), Pb – lead, Al – aluminum and Au – gold.

2. To construct your own periodic table you need to copy the grid below carefully. The table is always set out just as you can see it here and the position of the boxes may not be changed. To find out what all the symbols mean you could visit a library and look for more information.

Now try to find some... C – carbon (soot, pencil lead, diamonds and charcoal are all forms of carbon), Hg – mercury (the silver stuff in thermometers), Pt – platinum (a metal used in jewelry making) and Cl – chlorine (added to drinking water to kill bacteria).

STATES OF MATTER

Elements can be found in 3 forms or "states"; solid, liquid or gas. It is possible to change the state of elements; for example, by heating iron in a furnace (left) it can be melted, changing from a solid to a liquid. Oxygen, the gas which is so important for all forms of life, can be cooled down to a point where it becomes liquid. Sometimes elements join together to form new substances, known as compounds – water is a compound made from hydrogen and oxygen. Compounds, like elements, can exist in different states. Water can be a solid (ice), a liquid or it can be almost like a gas (steam).

WHY IT WORKS

If you could see the molecules (small particles) in a substance, you would notice that they seem to quiver. In a solid like ice, though, they are tightly bound and cannot move far (1). When ice is heated, the molecules quiver faster. At the point when the ice melts, they move away from their fixed place and start to slide around. The molecules are more spaced out in the liquid (2). As water is heated, the molecules move faster still and break away from each other, moving freely in the air (3). The whole process is reversed when we stop heating the water and start to cool it down.

1

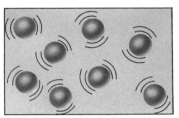

2

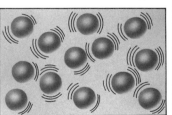

3

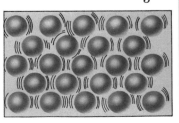

MOLECULES IN MOTION

1. We can watch the changes of state in this simple experiment with water. Empty a tray of ice-cubes into a saucepan. Put them on the stove on a low heat so that they melt slowly. You are changing a solid to a liquid.

1

2. After a while the liquid becomes hot and turns to steam. Put the ice-cube tray into a metal bowl or pan and place this next to your saucepan. Place a metal tray over the saucepan, as shown here, to catch the steam. (We've used glass here so that you can see underneath.)

2

BRIGHT IDEAS

Scientists often make models in order to show what is happening in experiments like this. You can have a go at this too. Find a small tin or box, or make a small cube from card. Next, you'll need a lid from a shoe box or something similar and a large tray which has sides. Into each, place about 25 marbles. The marbles represent the molecules of water. Now you need to make your molecules quiver just as real molecules of water do. Place the three containers on a table or a bed and shake it gently. You'll see the marbles in the cube will move only a little (like the molecules in a solid), those in the lid are more active (liquid), and the ones on the tray move around very freely (like a gas).

3. As the steam hits the tray it cools down and changes back to a liquid. Once you have collected the liquid in the ice-cube tray you can return the tray to the freezer.

3

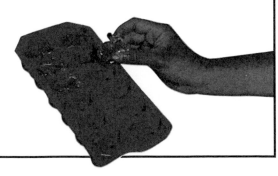

4. After a few hours, you'll be able to remove the ice-cubes from the freezer. The changes of state have now gone full circle – solid to liquid to gas to liquid and back to solid again.

4

SPLITTING MIXTURES

To form a new compound, the atoms of different elements must join to each other; for example, in damp conditions oxygen combines with iron to make rust. Rust, or iron oxide, is a new compound which has resulted from a chemical reaction between the atoms of iron and oxygen. It is very difficult to remove the oxygen and convert the rust back to iron. In mixtures, no chemical reaction takes place and it is possible to get the original elements back more easily. Salt can be obtained from the sea by evaporating the water away (left).

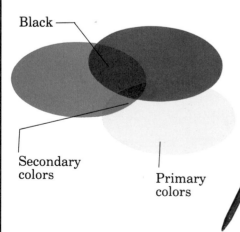

WHY IT WORKS

Most colors in ink pens or paints are not pure colors but rather mixtures of several colors. Some colors in each mixture cling strongly to the paper, while others cling less and so move through the paper more quickly. As the individual colors move at different rates they are separated out from the original mixture, and because each mixture is slightly different to start with, each strip of paper, or chromatogram, is slightly different too.

Black —

Secondary colors

Primary colors

INK-DOT DETECTIVE

1. Use three different black felt-pens and three strips of blotting paper. Draw a symbol on one end of each strip and identify each piece and the pen used with a colored dot.

1

2. Now fill a large bowl with water. It should be large enough to dangle the three pieces of paper into the water at the same time.

2

3. Stick the pieces of blotting paper onto a stick or pole and lower it until the paper just dips into the water. Watch the water move up the paper, taking the ink with it.

BRIGHT IDEAS

☀️ Mix some iron filings up with powdered limestone. You'll see that the color of the mixture is different to the color of the substances you started with; the dark grey and white have combined to make a light grey. No chemical change has taken place, however, and what you have made is not a new compound, but a mixture.

☀️ With the use of a strong magnet it is quite easy to remove the iron filings so that once again you have two pure substances.

Iron filings

Magnet

Powdered limestone

4. Look at each of the pieces of blotting paper. The black marks should have split up into separate colors. Remember which color band goes with which pen.

5. Give the pens to three friends and look away while one of them marks a piece of blotting paper. Dip the paper in the water and by looking at the band of colors you will know whose pen made the mark.

3

233

MIXING AND REPELLING

Perhaps the most common everyday mixture which we experience is the dissolving of soap in water. If you try to wash your hands in water alone, it is difficult to get them really clean. When you use soap, though, dirt and grease can be removed more easily. Often, we hear of oil spills at sea. The oil floats on top of the water forming a slick. This may spread, destroying sea-life and coastlines. Special soaps, called detergents, make the oil mix with the water so that it breaks down into smaller particles and is washed away (left).

HOW WET IS WATER?

1

1. Make this simple "soap boat" by pushing four matchsticks into each side of a cork, as shown here. These will keep the cork stable in the water.

4

2

2. A sail made from aluminum foil and a dragon's head gives rather a nice Viking look to your boat. Next, very carefully, put a small dab of soap onto the back of the boat. You could use a matchstick or a cotton bud for this.

3. Holding the boat by the mast, lower it gently into a bowl of fresh water (soapy water will not work). The boat will be drawn across the water to the other side of the bowl. To make a return voyage, you will have to renew the water.

3

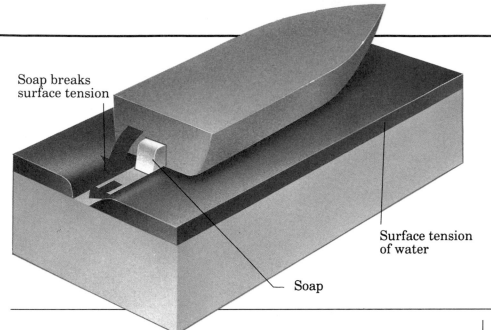

Soap breaks surface tension

Surface tension of water

Soap

WHY IT WORKS

The particles in a liquid are all attracted to each other. Particles at the surface are strongly attracted and do not easily break apart, giving a liquid surface tension. As the soap dissolves it breaks the surface tension. The water on the non-soapy side of the boat has a greater surface tension and so pulls the boat towards it and the boat moves through the water.

4. Try putting the boat into the water without any soap. Does it move in the same way? Obviously, the soap affects the way the boat moves through the water. You could also try putting a dab of soap on the back and the front of the boat before you put it into the water.

BRIGHT IDEAS

Get some oil-based paints (spray paints work quite well) and drop them onto the surface of a bowl of water. The paint will float on the water. Move the paint around with a pin or fine needle to make patterns and then lower a sheet of paper onto the surface. Remove the paper immediately. You can repeat this several times to make colorful, marbled patterns. You could use these as book covers or wrapping paper.

VISIBLE REACTIONS

Have you ever wondered why cakes rise in the oven or what the bubbles in soda are actually made of ? The answer in each case is the same – carbon dioxide. Carbon dioxide is a gas which is formed when two atoms of oxygen join with one atom of carbon. The formula for carbon dioxide is CO_2. There are actually small amounts of carbon dioxide in the air and green plants give out CO_2 during the hours of darkness. The CO_2 in cakes, however, is not drawn from the air. It is produced when acids react with carbonates or bicarbonates which are present in the ingredients.

VOLCANIC ERUPTION

1. Make a volcano which erupts with a foam of vinegar and baking powder. Form a cone shape around an old plastic cup or bowl. Glue the cone firmly to a base.

2. Cover the cone with 5 or 6 layers of newspaper and glue and leave to dry. Next, cover the base with glue and sprinkle with sawdust or sand. Paint the base and volcano.

3. When dry, a coat of sealing mixture (3 parts water to 1 part glue) will help to protect the paintwork when the volcano erupts. Once again, allow the whole thing to dry well before the next step.

4. Next, prepare the ingredients which will produce the reaction. You will need a small amount of baking powder or bicarbonate of soda and some vinegar mixed with a little red food-coloring.

5. Put a teaspoon of the baking powder into the volcano then pour in a little vinegar. The reaction should be fast and a red liquid containing carbon dioxide will foam up over the sides of your volcano as it "erupts".

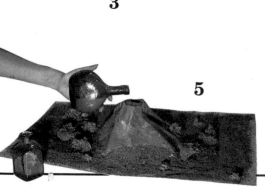

WHY IT WORKS

The vinegar is an acid and it reacts with the sodium bicarbonate (which is an alkali) in the baking powder. This reaction produces carbon dioxide gas. If you add water to baking powder you would also get a reaction, although it would be a slower one. This is because the baking powder contains acidic salts which become acids when the water is added. These acids react with the sodium bicarbonate to produce CO_2. It is partly this reaction which causes cakes to rise in the oven.

Vinegar   Baking powder   Carbon dioxide

BRIGHT IDEAS

Why not make your own fizzing lemonade? Mix the juice of 4 lemons with 1 quart of water then add sugar until your mixture tastes good. When you want a drink, pour out a glass, add half a teaspoon of bicarbonate of soda, stir and drink at once!

6. Obviously, the more ingredients you use, the bigger the size of the eruption. A fizzing noise, known as effervescence, can be heard – this is the sound of the carbon dioxide gas being produced.

6

MAKING NEW MATERIALS

Many of the materials that we use are naturally occurring elements or compounds, like iron, water or wood. Other materials are man-made, like plastics and paper. These man-made materials are generally manufactured by mixing or separating natural products – plastics are made by refining (splitting up) the compounds within crude oil, alloys are made by combining different metals together and paper is made by separating the fibers from trees and processing them to make paper. The egg carton (left), cardboard boxes, blotting paper, the book you are reading now, all these things started out life as trees!

PAPER MASK

1

1. You can recycle old newspaper to make a new material called papier mâché. Mix up a thin paste of flour and water. Then, cover a balloon with a thin coat of oil.

4. Cut out the features of your mask. This can be a bit difficult so you could ask an adult to begin. Next, paint the mask, making sure your paint is not too wet.

6. If you want, you could now recycle the mask itself. Soaking in water will reverse the papier mâché process and turn the mask back to newspaper and paste.

2. Tear up strips of newspaper, dip them in the paste and cover the balloon with 5 or 6 layers. Leave to dry until the paper is very hard.

2

3. Carefully cut the papier mâché away from the balloon. You'll find that the coating of oil will stop it sticking to the balloon too badly. Cut the shape in half.

4

5. Your mask is an example of recycling, that is, taking an old material which you no longer need and putting it to a new use.

6

WHY IT WORKS

Papier mâché is formed by layers of paper which are bonded together with adhesive paste. The flour (1) is made into a paste by adding water (2). This paste is then added to the paper (3) and soaks into the pores. As the water evaporates away (4), the molecules are pulled tighter together and the bond becomes solid.

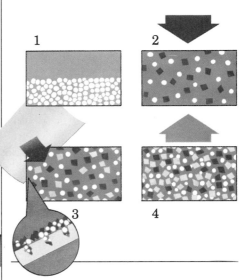

BRIGHT IDEAS

The clay and straw bricks in very old houses are made in the same way as papier mâché. Can you think of any more materials made this way?

A clay and straw brick

REACTIONS AND HEAT

To get a chemical reaction started, some form of energy is usually needed. This may simply be heat energy taken from the warmth of a room, or it may be the energy which is taken from a blast furnace where iron is taken from iron ore. Many things which we rely on have to be heated before they are ready for use. Think of a cup made of clay which has never been baked in a kiln, bricks which are still soft clay or a loaf of bread left as raw dough. Without reactions started by high levels of heat these things are not quite the same. Even the coffee that we drink gets its rich flavor when the beans are roasted (left).

DOUGH JEWELRY

1 **1.** You can make use of a reaction which involves heat to make your own jewelry. To begin with, make a thick dough with flour and water. Knead well to get rid of any air bubbles in the dough.

2 **2.** Shape the dough to give you beads and pendants like the ones you can see in the picture. You can also try your own designs – if they go wrong simply squash them up and start again!

3 **3.** It is best to work on a lightly floured surface and to rub a little flour onto your hands too. This will stop the dough from sticking. If the dough is too sticky, sprinkle it with flour and knead it for a little longer.

4 **4.** Before baking, leave each shape to harden and pierce with a skewer to give a hole. With the help of an adult, bake in the oven on a medium heat until hard. Allow to cool, paint and varnish. When dry, thread the shapes onto a necklace!

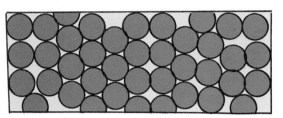
Water evaporates when
the dough is baked

WHY IT WORKS

When flour is mixed with water, it forms a dough as the flour molecules are suspended in the liquid (1). A sticky substance called gluten is also formed and the dough can be molded into all sorts of shapes. When the dough is baked in the oven, the water evaporates leaving behind the flour molecules which form a solid mass (2).

1

2

BRIGHT IDEAS

You could try changing the ingredients to get better doughs. Add a little oil and/or cream of tartare to your dough to make it more pliable.

If you enjoy this project, you could buy some specialist modeling clay and create more personalized jewelry using your own designs.

HEAT AND CHANGE

When a substance is heated, several things might happen to it. It may appear not to change (apart from the fact that it is hotter); for example, common salt which is dry and pure may change, but returns to its original state as it cools. Some substances can change permanently. Look at the burnt toast on the left – this is an example of a permanent change. When a permanent change takes place there could be a change in appearance or smell, like the toast; gases and smoke could be given off and sounds could be made, like the crackling of burning wood. There could also be changes in weight, volume or color. As you carry out this next project make a note of any changes that take place.

UNCOVER THE SECRET

1. In the past, invisible inks were used to write secret information. Onion juice and milk were often used, but we will be using lemon juice. Begin by squeezing the juice from a lemon into a jar.

2. To give your message a really original look, find a feather and trim the end to provide a quill to write with. Give your paper an ancient look by leaving it in a warm oven (which is turned OFF) until it turns light brown. Don't leave it too long or it may burn!

3. Write your message in large, clear writing. As soon as the lemon juice is dry, it will look as if the page is blank. Next, you will need the help of an adult.

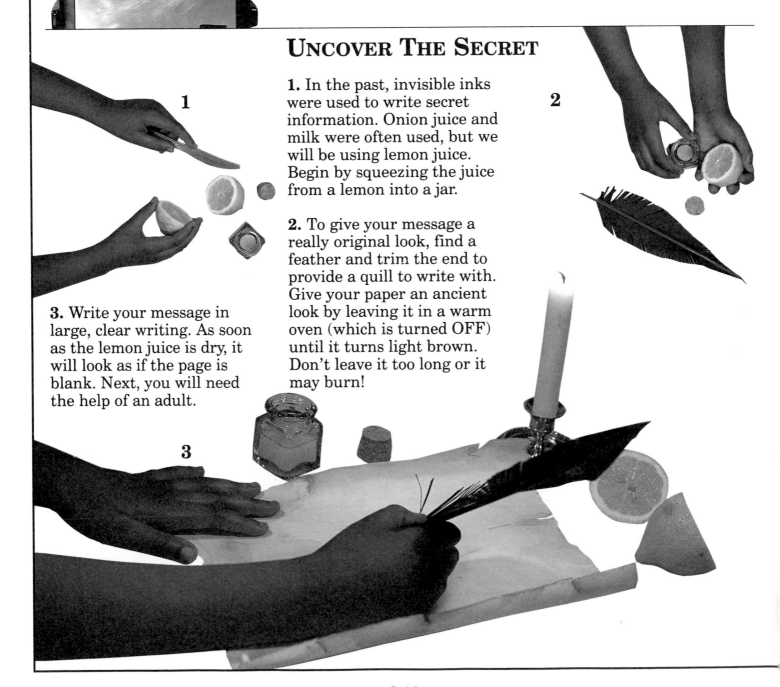

WHY IT WORKS

When the lemon juice is heated, the water molecules are evaporated away and the remaining compounds combine with the oxygen in the air. This is known as oxidization and the result is that the lemon juice turns brown. Compare this with the effect of scorching a cotton shirt with an iron. The fabric of the shirt turns brown because of oxidization.

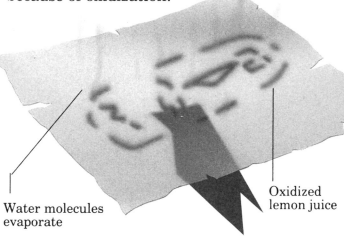

Water molecules evaporate

Oxidized lemon juice

BRIGHT IDEAS

To make honeycomb toffee put (1lb) sugar, (10oz) water and four tablespoons of vinegar into a large pan. Stir and slowly bring to the boil until the mixture reaches 280°F. Remove from heat and add half a teaspoon of bicarbonate of soda and stir. Pour into a buttered tin and leave to set. Never taste toffee until it has cooled down!

4. Heat the paper up. If you use a candle you MUST keep the paper moving or it may catch fire. Alternatively, you could iron the paper or put it in a warm oven for a minute. The effect should be the same, the heat makes the secret message appear!

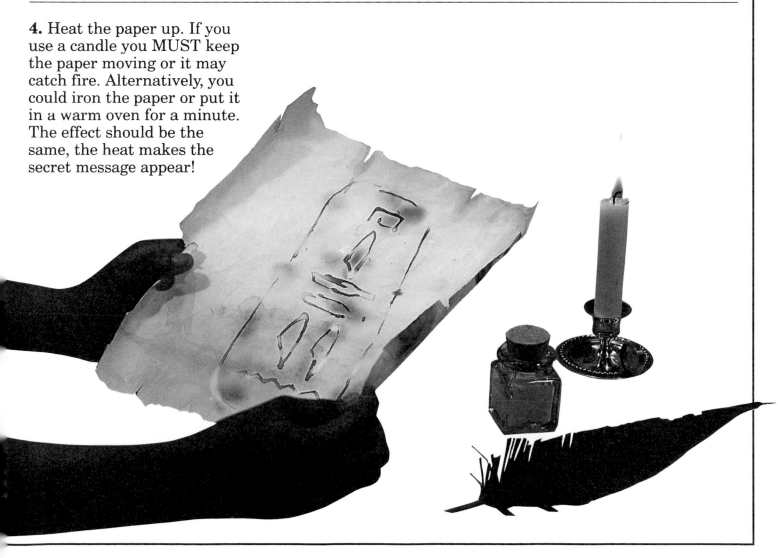

DIFFERENT REACTIONS

If you squeeze the juice from an orange or eat a slice of fresh lemon, you will find that they taste quite sour. This is because they contain acids. An alkali is the opposite of an acid. Medicines such as milk of magnesia are alkaline, and are used to cure pains caused by too much acid in the stomach. It combines with the acid and produces a mixture which is not acidic or alkaline, but neutral. Farmers use lime to neutralize the acids in soil in a similar way. On the left you can see an "electronic pH detector", this would be used by a scientist to show how acidic or alkaline a solution is.

BRIGHT IDEAS

You could try making other indicators. Blackberries, blueberries and beetroot all give a strong dye. Make sheets of indicator paper just as you did for the project.

Make solutions by dissolving different substances in a little water and then test them. Do the same kind of color changes take place? Some things to try are: sucking candies, sugar, salt, lemonade, toothpaste, fresh milk, sour milk and anteacid tablets.

COLOR INDICATOR

2. Place the cabbage in a pan and cover with water. Bring to the boil and simmer for about 10 minutes. Remove from the heat and then leave to stand for 1 hour.

1. To make your own pH detector, ask an adult to help you with the first two steps of this project. Cut a fresh red cabbage into small pieces.

3. Strain the juice and throw away the cabbage (or you can eat it). Now, dip sheets of blotting paper into the juice and then leave them to dry. This is your indicator paper.

4. Collect different inks to write on the paper. Acidic inks include sour milk, lemon juice and vinegar. Alkaline inks are fresh milk and washing soda dissolved in water.

WHY IT WORKS

Acids and alkalis produce chemical reactions when they mix with other things. In their reactions with indicators they cause color changes. The purple dye from the cabbage turns red in acids and green in alkalis. It is possible to tell from an indicator how strong an acid or an alkali is. This strength is measured on the pH scale. On the pH scale, number 1, the red color on the right, is a strong acid. Number 7, yellow in the centre, is neutral. Number 14, blue on the left, is a strong alkali.

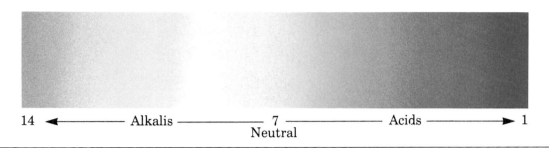

14 ◄——— Alkalis ——— 7 ——— Acids ———► 1
Neutral

5

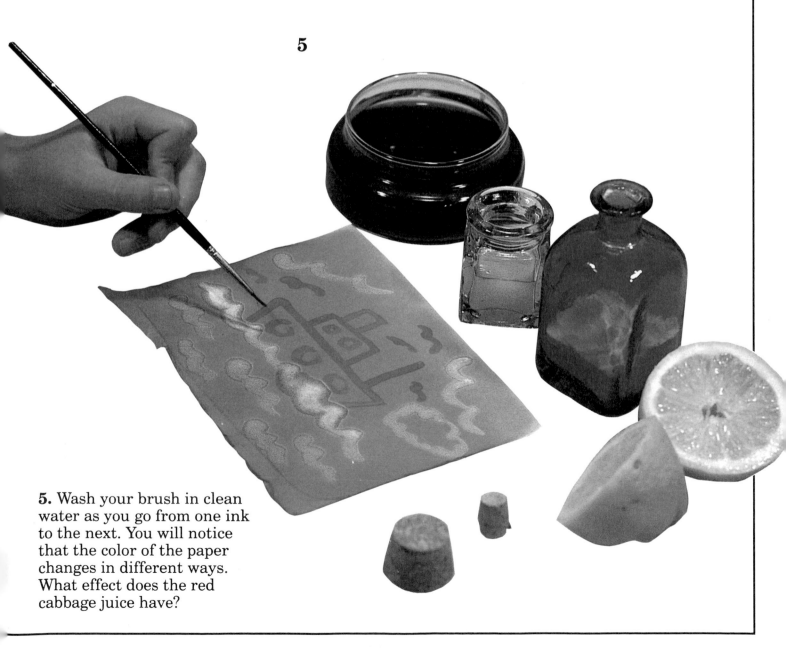

5. Wash your brush in clean water as you go from one ink to the next. You will notice that the color of the paper changes in different ways. What effect does the red cabbage juice have?

INVISIBLE REACTIONS

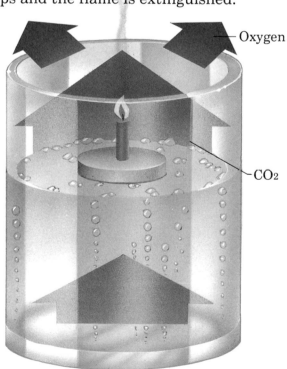

Already in this book, we have seen how ice melting, baking powder fizzing, toast burning and even washing your hands involve reactions and changes. Did you realize, though, that when a fire is burning, a chemical reaction is taking place, and to stop a fire we have to stop the chemical reaction? There are many ways of stopping a fire; we can use fire extinguishers (pictured left), buckets of sand, water, foam or wet blankets. In this project, we will see how one reaction which you have produced already can be used to fight a fire.

WHY IT WORKS

When you light the candle, you start a reaction between the wick of the candle (which is full of wax – the fuel of the fire) and the oxygen in the air. The heat of the candle burning keeps the reaction between the fuel and the oxygen going. The reaction between the lemon juice and the baking powder produces carbon dioxide (CO_2). CO_2 is heavier than the air in the jar so the air is pushed up and out of the jar by the CO_2. Without the oxygen in the air, the burning reaction stops and the flame is extinguished.

Oxygen

CO_2

4. The fizzing should carry on for a few minutes. If it does not, add more baking powder and lemon juice.

4

BRIGHT IDEAS

A good scientist would ask questions about a test like this. Was it really the carbon dioxide which put the flame out? Perhaps the oxygen in the jar was all used up anyway? Or maybe a draft put the flame out? To see whether the reaction between the lemon juice and the baking powder really did make a difference, we need to set up a control. Repeat the test in the project, but this time have two identical jars with candles burning in them. Do not add anything to the second jar after the candle has been lit. This jar is known as the control. Compare what happens as you follow the project with the first jar. If the candle in the control jar burns for longer you have proved that the CO_2 produced in the project did make a difference!

5. The flame of the candle will dim and then die completely. At this point, you could repeat the experiment to see if this always happens.

5

FIRE EXTINGUISHER

1. You'll need the soap boat that you made earlier. Remove the mast and fix a small candle in its place. Float the candle in a little water at the bottom of a deep jar. Light it with a spill.

1

2. Add several spoons of baking powder to the water and stir the mixture gently with a long spatula.

2

3. Before the baking powder and the water stop fizzing, add a good measure of lemon juice. Watch closely to see what happens.

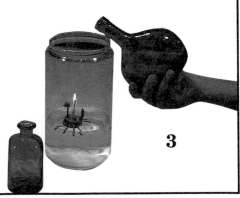

3

247

ELECTRICITY & REACTIONS

About 200 years ago, an Italian called Alessandro Volta produced a current of electricity with layers of zinc and silver separated by cardboard soaked in salt water. Later, two Englishmen, William Nicholson and Anthony Carlisle, connected the terminals of the pile to metal rods and placed the rods in water. Bubbles of gas were given off by the rods; oxygen on the positive rod and hydrogen on the negative rod – the two gases which make water! This led to the development of electroplating (left), the process of coating one metal with another metal, for example, iron is coated with zinc to prevent rusting.

SEPARATING WATER

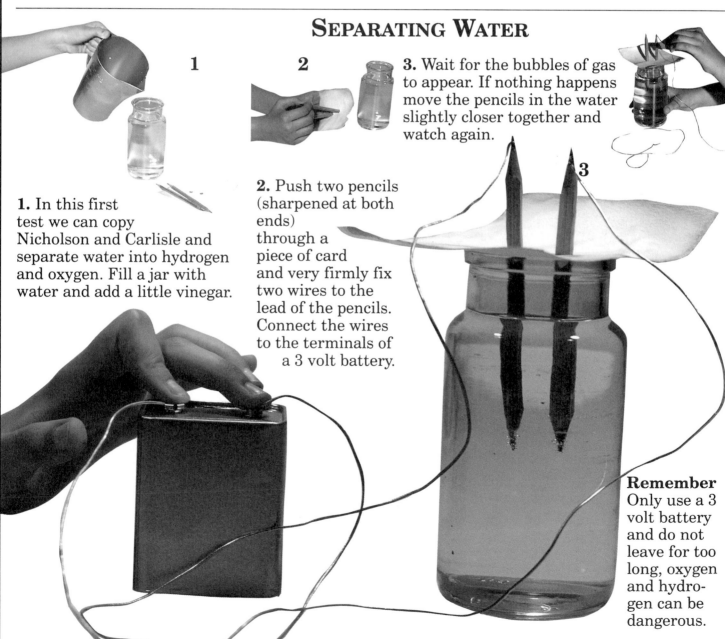

1

2

3. Wait for the bubbles of gas to appear. If nothing happens move the pencils in the water slightly closer together and watch again.

1. In this first test we can copy Nicholson and Carlisle and separate water into hydrogen and oxygen. Fill a jar with water and add a little vinegar.

2. Push two pencils (sharpened at both ends) through a piece of card and very firmly fix two wires to the lead of the pencils. Connect the wires to the terminals of a 3 volt battery.

Remember
Only use a 3 volt battery and do not leave for too long, oxygen and hydrogen can be dangerous.

248

WHY IT WORKS

In the first project, the electrical current passes from the positive terminal, through the solution, to the negative terminal. The flow of electricity causes a reaction in which the molecules of water, H_2O, are split up into atoms of oxygen and hydrogen. Oxygen is given off at the positive terminal and hydrogen at the negative. In electroplating (right), the electrical current releases particles of the metal on the positive terminal, in this case copper, and they move to the negative side coating the silver coin.

BRIGHT IDEAS

A common reaction of a metal with water is the conversion of iron to rust. Try to prevent rust by putting a nail in a jar of water (1) with another nail coated in a substance that keeps out air and water, for example, grease (2). What happens to the nails after a few days?

ELECTROPLATING

1. This project allows you to see electroplating in action. Make 2 small holes in the lid of a jar and fix 2 short pieces of plastic straw into them.

2. Thread two wires through the straws. Connect a paper clip to the end of each wire and attach a copper coin and a silver coin.

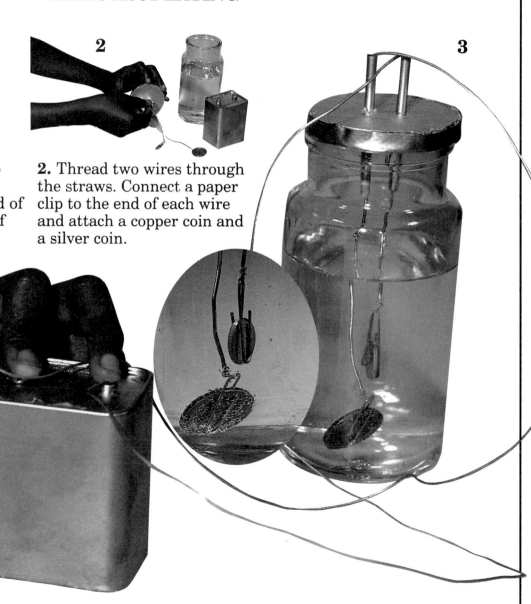

3. Suspend the coins in a jar half full of salt water and connect the copper coin to the positive terminal of a 3 volt battery and the silver coin to the negative. The silver coin will slowly take on a copper color.

ORGANIC REACTIONS

One set of reactions which we have not talked about yet are those where living things change compounds or elements into new compounds. These are called organic reactions and the most common are the ones caused by tiny creatures called micro-organisms. These include bacteria and molds. Most molds are unpleasant and unhelpful to us. One very useful mold, however, is yeast. It acts on the ingredients used in making beer (left), turning the sugar to alcohol and when mixed into the bread dough, it makes it rise. Louis Pasteur was a scientist who discovered many things about micro-organisms. In particular, he found out how harmful organisms in food could be killed off by heating, the process now known as pasteurization.

RAISING DOUGH

1. To make your own bread, mix two tablespoons of dried yeast with one teaspoon of sugar and one cup of warm (not hot) water. Leave until frothy.

2. Mix 5 cups of wholemeal flour, 2 tbs of caster sugar, 4tsp of salt and 1oz of shortening in a bowl. Stir in the yeast mixture and 2.5 cups of tepid water.

3. Remove from the bowl and knead the dough on a floured board until it becomes firm and elastic but not sticky. Don't rush this bit!

3

1

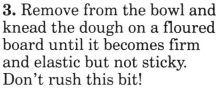

2

7. Ask an adult to help you now. Heat up the oven to 450°. Remove the clear plastic wrap and bake your bread in the oven for 30 to 40 minutes.

8. When you think your bread is cooked, remove it from the oven. Push a skewer into the bread; if it is still sticky inside it needs longer in the oven.

9. When the bread is cooked, remove it from the baking trays and place on a wire rack to cool. Fresh bread is delicious when still warm.

WHY IT WORKS

The reaction of yeast with sugar is an organic example of a chemical change which is speeded up by the heat from the warm water. Sugar is a compound made of carbon, hydrogen and oxygen. Substances in the yeast called enzymes turn the sugar into alcohol and also produce large amounts of carbon dioxide gas. The gas bubbles are what make the bread rise.

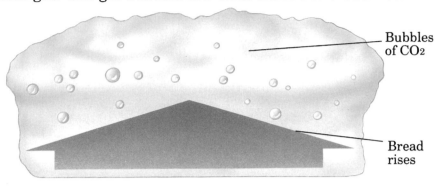

Bubbles of CO_2

Bread rises

BRIGHT IDEAS

To make some butter for your bread, put one cup of cream into a clean jar. Screw the lid on tightly and shake the jar for a long time. Eventually the cream separates and turns into a solid, butter, and a liquid, buttermilk. Remove the butter by straining through a sieve. Add a little salt to the butter and then beat it with a fork until it is smooth. Spread it on your freshly-baked bread and enjoy it!

4. Leave the dough in a lightly oiled bowl in a warm place. Cover the bowl with clear plastic wrap to keep the moisture in.

5. When the dough has risen, put it on a floured surface and knead until firm.

6. Place on lightly oiled baking trays, brush with salty water, sprinkle with a little flour, cover with clear plastic wrap and leave to rise once more.

4

5

6

REACTIONS WITH LIGHT

This final reaction is perhaps the most important one of all. It is called photosynthesis and is the process by which green plants use the energy from sunlight to help in the production of food such as sugars. Why is this so important? The cells in the bodies of animals, including human beings, are not capable of producing these basic foods. Therefore, they have to eat plants or other animals to stay alive. If the Sun did not shine and photosynthesis stopped, life would die out as the planet's food stores were used up.

BRIGHT IDEAS

The experiment with the cellophane shows how you can speed up reactions with light to create shapes. You can use photographic paper in a similar way. Get some photographic paper from a photographic supply store. Put it in a sunny, dry place with a few objects on it, for example, coins and bits of jewelry. After a few days, remove the objects and look at the effect. The paper will turn black where the light hits it, leaving white shapes where the objects were placed.

PLANT PATTERNS

1

1. To stop sunlight from reaching a plant's leaves, we can block it out with a small piece of aluminum foil. Cut out a sun-shape to stick on the leaf. Fix it to the leaf using flour and water.

2. Because you will probably have to leave your sun-shape on the plant for several days it is a good idea to strengthen the foil. You can do this by sticking it onto some paper. Treat the plant normally and leave the shape in place for two weeks or more. During this time, you could experiment further by putting similar shapes on other plants around the house. Try comparing the different effects of the aluminum foil and black pen on cellophane (see stage 3) on the same plant.

2

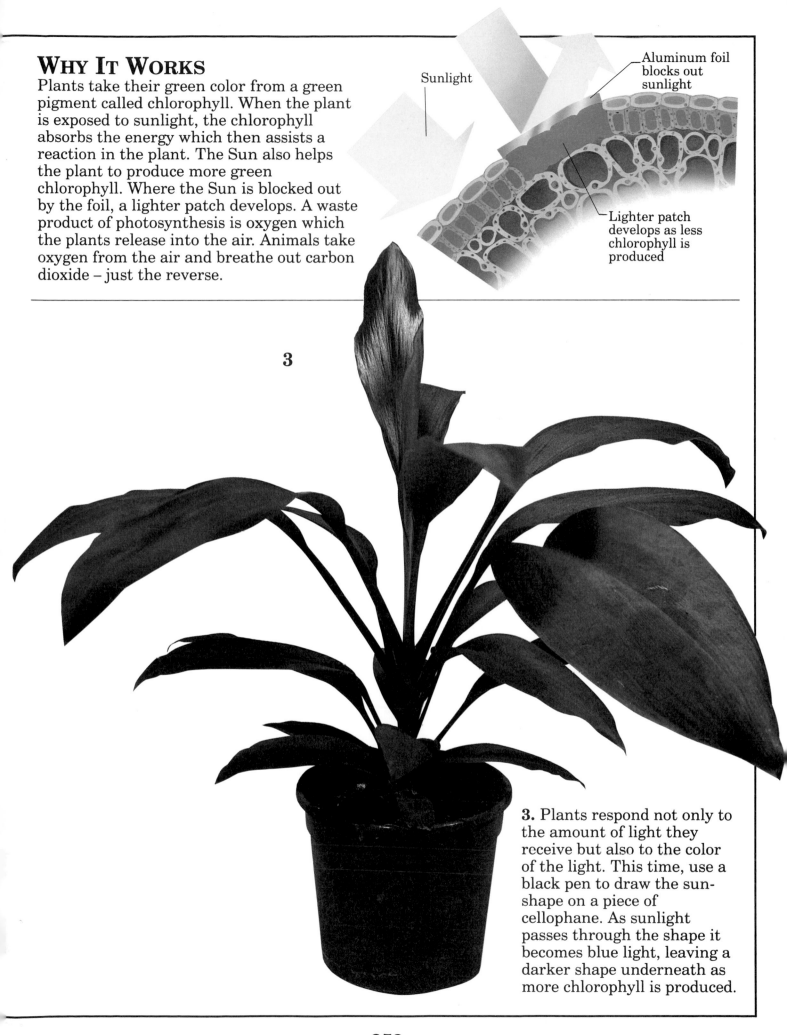

WHY IT WORKS

Plants take their green color from a green pigment called chlorophyll. When the plant is exposed to sunlight, the chlorophyll absorbs the energy which then assists a reaction in the plant. The Sun also helps the plant to produce more green chlorophyll. Where the Sun is blocked out by the foil, a lighter patch develops. A waste product of photosynthesis is oxygen which the plants release into the air. Animals take oxygen from the air and breathe out carbon dioxide – just the reverse.

Sunlight

Aluminum foil blocks out sunlight

Lighter patch develops as less chlorophyll is produced

3

3. Plants respond not only to the amount of light they receive but also to the color of the light. This time, use a black pen to draw the sun-shape on a piece of cellophane. As sunlight passes through the shape it becomes blue light, leaving a darker shape underneath as more chlorophyll is produced.

EARTH'S STRUCTURE

Diamonds are crystals made up almost entirely of carbon. The word crystal comes from the greek 'krystallos', which means 'icy cold', because it was once believed that quartz crystal was permanently frozen into rock. Gemstones crystallize within the Earth's crust, in pockets of molten rock called magma. Magma rises, cools and solidifies, only to be broken up by movements of the Earth's crust and weathering. Then it makes its way back below the surface, to melt once more. Movements of the Earth's crust happen when heat rises from the molten outer core. Molten lava erupts from volcanoes, many of which are still active today.

COOL CRYSTALS

1

When you have achieved a saturated solution, leave the jar to stand for about two days while the crystals form.

2. Mix 9oz of alum into 4oz of hot water in a transparent jar. Be very careful, you must not use boiling water. Stir the alum crystals into the hot water and keep stirring until no more crystals will dissolve.

1. To grow sparkling crystals, like diamonds, you can use potash of alum crystals. You will also need hot water, a glass jar, a sieve, some string and a pencil. If you would like to grow colored crystals, just add a few drops of food coloring.

2

3

3. After two days, drain your solution through a sieve to obtain the crystals that have formed.

WHY IT WORKS

A crystal is a solid body surrounded by flat surfaces. Each identical unit of a crystal has a structural arrangement of atoms (tiny particles). When hot water is added to potassium aluminum sulphate (potash alum), the crystals dissolve. When crystals will no longer dissolve, you have created a saturated solution. Evaporation (loss of water) causes the crystals to re-form as certain atoms in the substance move closer together. The size of the crystals will depend upon the rate of cooling.

Atoms

Crystal

BRIGHT IDEAS

Take one of your original crystals and dangle it in your saturated solution once more. Your crystal should grow even larger.

Set up two identical saturated solutions of potash alum. Allow one to cool rapidly by standing the container in ice cold water. Cool the other slowly by standing it somewhere less cold. Observe and time the formation and size of the crystals in each. Keep a record of the fall in temperature of each solution. From the results calculate the actual rate of cooling. Which produces the larger alum crystals?

Try using sugar or magnesium sulphate (Epsom salts) instead of potash alum. You can also use copper sulphate, which is blue, but be careful because it is poisonous. Create a crystalline sculpture by growing your crystals on a shaped pipe cleaner.

4

4. Each jar of saturated solution should produce quite a few crystals. You could grow one even larger in some more solution.

NATURAL STRUCTURES

The effects of weathering, erosion and deposition have created amazing natural structures all over the world. Some rocks are much harder than others; for example, chalk crumbles, but granite is very hard. A waterfall is the result of the erosion of less resistant rock by the river, so that 'steps' of hard rock are left. The Colorado River has shaped the Grand Canyon, one of the world's natural wonders — it is 3,937ft deep and 199 miles long. The sea also attacks the land, forcing air into cracks and hurling stones against the cliffs. This erosion creates fantastic arches and stacks (right).

TRICKLES TO TRIBUTARIES

1

1. With a small hacksaw, cut away one of the narrow sides of a tray. Shape some plasticine into small 'rock' shapes and position them in the bottom of the tray.

3. Now sprinkle some dry sand over the top of the soil. Put most over the highest part of the slope.

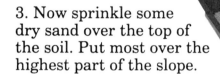

3

4. By sprinkling some green powder paint over the sand you can create a grassy effect. Position some model trees or bushes across the landscape.

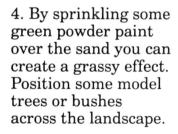

4

2. Cover the 'rocks' completely with dry soil. The surface of the soil needs to slope from the back of the tray down to the open front.

5. At this stage either take a photograph of the landscape or draw a picture. Position the tray on a raised surface with the cut-away end above an empty plastic bowl.

2

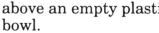

5

WHY IT WORKS

The project makes use of soft materials like sand, soil and clay, which are easily eroded. The water behaves like a real river, eroding the top layer of grass before cutting down into the soil and the sand (1). As in the natural world, the lumps of clay in your project resist the flow of the water. The water is forced to take an alternative path around the obstacles (2), forming bends. Eventually, the river changes its course to a more direct path towards the sea, depositing silt, and finally forming a crescent-shaped lake that is off from the main stream (3). This is called an oxbow lake.

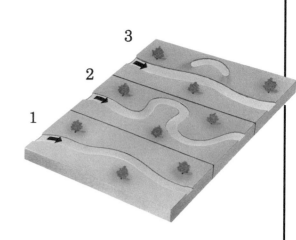

6. Fill a jug with clean, cold water and gently pour some on to the hilly area at the back of the tray. Observe and record what happens, using words and pictures. Describe the path or paths taken by the water. Which materials have been washed into the bowl?

6

BRIGHT IDEAS

Frost action can cause cracks, and stones and bricks may crumble. Fill a screw top plastic bottle to the brim with water, and place it inside a sealed plastic bag. Put it into a freezer overnight and you will find that the bottle will break. Look at the outside of a building, your school or your home. Can you see any signs of weathering? Look up at the roof from each compass direction and record what you notice.

USING MATERIALS

Natural materials are taken, not only from the Earth, but also from the air, the seas and many plants and animals. Precious metals, like platinum, are extracted from rocks in the Earth, salt is evaporated from the seas, oxygen is separated out from the air, rubber can be tapped from trees, and leather began as the skin of an animal. Cement is a mixture of limestone and clay, and concrete can be made by mixing cement with sand, gravel and water. Gypsum is a soft, non-metallic mineral. One of the places in which it is found is the Montmartre district of Paris, which is why powdered gypsum was named Plaster of Paris. The Ancient Egyptians and the Romans used gypsum, which is often called alabaster.

PLASTER PANSIES

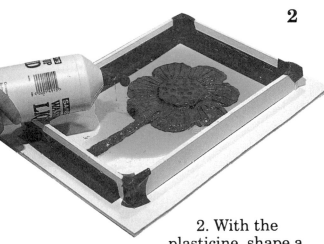

1

1. Cut away one side of a detergent box to make a frame for the mold. Place it on the craft board and seal the edges with waterproof tape. Cover all surfaces, plaster is very messy.

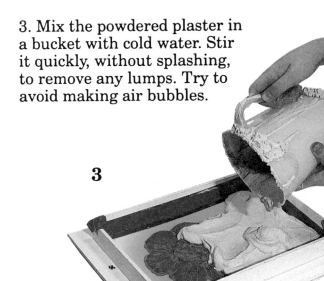

2

2. With the plasticine, shape a flower inside the frame. Add extra details with more plasticine. Squeeze dish washing liquid all over the finished shape. It will act as a lubricant.

3. Mix the powdered plaster in a bucket with cold water. Stir it quickly, without splashing, to remove any lumps. Try to avoid making air bubbles.

3

4. Immediately, pour the mixture over the plasticine flower to fill the frame completely.

4

WHY IT WORKS

Plaster of Paris is made by heating crushed gypsum. When most of the water has been removed, it can be ground to the fine powder. When water is added to Plaster of Paris, a chemical reaction takes place as gypsum is reformed. It sets hard, giving off warmth as the chemical reaction takes place.

Plaster of Paris

Water

Gypsum

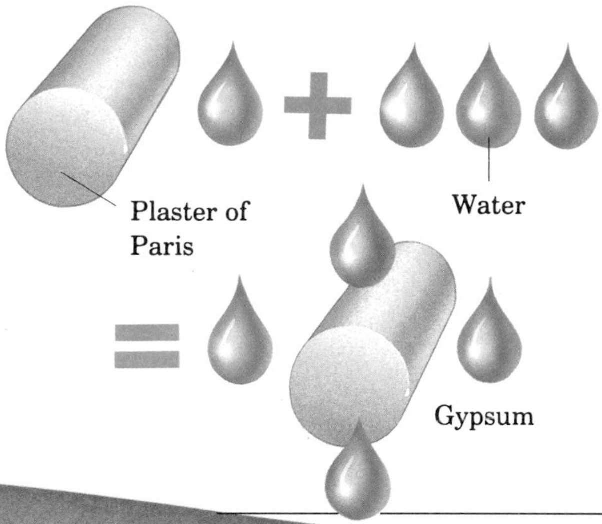

BRIGHT IDEAS

Use your plaster mold to make flower shapes from plasticine. Press the plasticine into the mold to make an imprint.

Feel the plaster model as it is setting - it will set very quickly and will feel warm. What causes this?

Shape a piece of clay to use as a mold for a plaster model animal. You can paint and varnish your plaster animal.

Use an empty detergent box to make a block of plaster. You can use this to make a sculpture. Carve a shape out of the block.

5. When the plaster is dry, gently remove it from the frame. Be careful because plaster is brittle. What do you notice about the shape of the flower? You now have a flower mold that you can use again and again.

5

PROPERTIES OF MATERIALS

Matter is anything that takes up space in the Universe. It may be living or non living. Every substance and material is made up of small particles called atoms. A material's strength and flexibility depends on the arrangement of its atoms as molecules, and the elasticity of a spring is dependent upon the interaction of these molecules. A spring is either a coil or a bending bar.

The suspension in a car depends on springs to provide a smooth ride. A door may have a spring that will return it to a closed position. An airplane's wings are built of light, flexible materials that allow them to bend and "give" in a strong wind.

JACK IN THE BOX

1

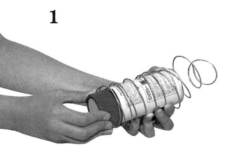

1. Coil some stiff wire into a spring shape around an empty cylindrical metal container.

2

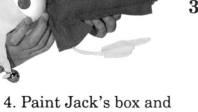

2. Design an interesting face on the ping pong ball and make a felt jester's hat to fit. Make a hole underneath the head to insert the end of a pipe cleaner.

3. The arms and legs are also made from pipe cleaners and the body is a plastic bottle. Cover the bottle with a felt coat. 'Jack' can be anchored to the top of the spring by attaching one end to the bottle lid.

5. In the bottom of the box attach a ring of cardboard around which the spring should fit snugly. Secure with Scotch Tape.

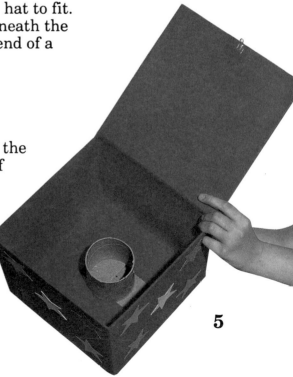

5

3

4. Paint Jack's box and decorate it with attractive stickers. Paint the outside as well.

4

WHY IT WORKS

Most materials have the quality of elasticity, which is the ability to resume their shape after being bent or pulled by an outside force. Metals can be made to have more stretch by bending them into a spring. In a spring at rest, the attracting and repelling forces between its molecules are balanced. Squeezing the spring increases the repelling forces, releasing the spring pushes the molecules apart again.

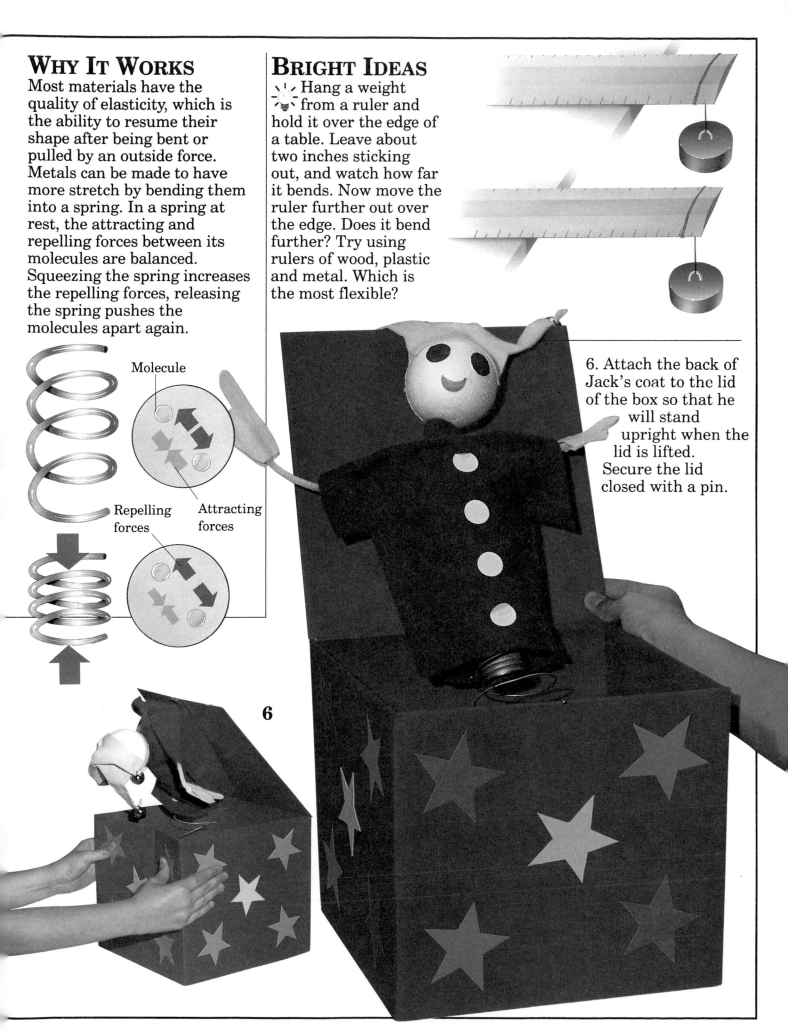

Molecule

Repelling forces

Attracting forces

BRIGHT IDEAS

💡 Hang a weight from a ruler and hold it over the edge of a table. Leave about two inches sticking out, and watch how far it bends. Now move the ruler further out over the edge. Does it bend further? Try using rulers of wood, plastic and metal. Which is the most flexible?

6. Attach the back of Jack's coat to the lid of the box so that he will stand upright when the lid is lifted. Secure the lid closed with a pin.

6

MAKING NEW MATERIALS

The properties of a material help determine its use. Physical properties, such as mass and volume can be measured, but it is also important to know how a material behaves or responds to treatment. Sometimes it is possible to change the properties of one material by combining it with another. Raw materials that are chemically changed into another substance are called synthetic, or man made, materials. Heat is often required to cause a chemical change. Bronze is a hard strong alloy (mixture) of copper, tin and other metals. Adding phosphorus hardens and strengthens bronze. Bronze is the oldest alloy known.

PETRIFIED PAPER

1

1. Using flour and water or wallpaper paste, make a mixture that has a runny consistency but is thicker than water. Tear or cut the newspapers into even sized strips. Soak each strip thoroughly in the paste.

2

2. Begin sticking around the center of the balloon, following a straight line because this will be the rim of the finished bowl. You can have as many layers of paper as you wish. The more layers, the stronger the finished bowl will be.

3. To shape the base rest the balloon inside a wide plastic lid and stick the paste strips over the plastic. Shape two handles from folded strips of papier mâché and fix them in position with more strips.

3

4. The finished shape must be left to dry out completely before the balloon is removed. The bowl can then be painted and varnished.

4

WHY IT WORKS

Each material has its own structure of molecules. In a solid, the molecules are packed closely together. In a liquid, the molecules move around more easily, and in a gas they move around very quickly. Adhesion is what causes two substances to stick together. A liquid (like the flour and water paste), can fill all the holes on the surface of the paper and then set hard forming a bond.

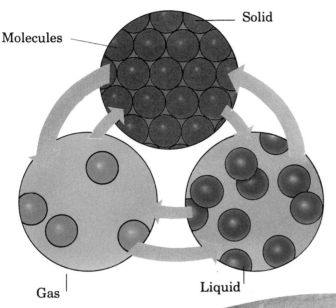

Solid

Molecules

Gas

Liquid

BRIGHT IDEAS

☀ Use a variety of materials to weave together.
💡 Choose contrasting materials for the warp and weft threads (below), such as string and wool or grasses and twigs. How strong is the new "fabric"?
☀ Use single sheets of newspaper dipped in
💡 paste and lie them on top of each other in layers until you have a 'block' of papier mâché. Cut a shape out of the block or mold over a large shape, and leave to dry.
☀ Cut strips
💡 of paper dipped in paste and wind them round a 'ball' of newspaper. Make a clay mold, brush with soapy water, and fill with the pulp mixture.

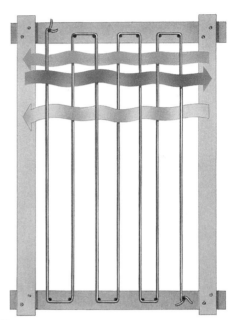

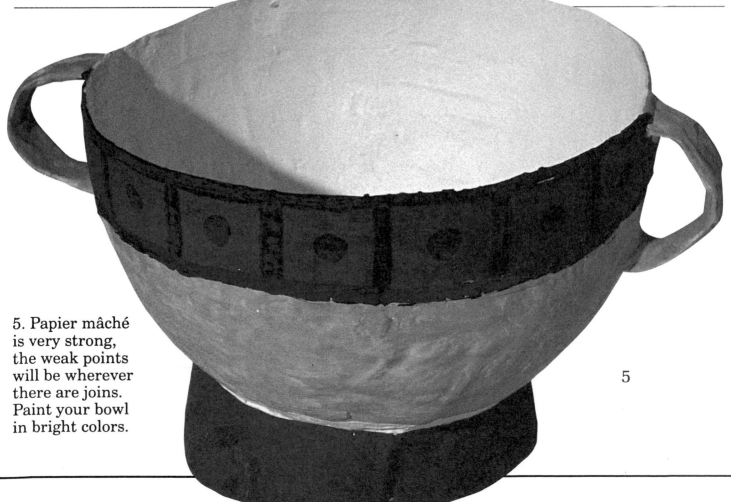

5. Papier mâché is very strong, the weak points will be wherever there are joins. Paint your bowl in bright colors.

CHOOSING MATERIALS

It's very important to choose the best material for certain jobs. Metals are good conductors of heat. In contrast, wood is a poor conductor of heat but is a good insulator. In our daily lives, we use metal saucepans to conduct heat during the cooking process, but we also need to protect ourselves from burning by using potholders. Spacecraft have heat shields that protect them from the high temperature caused by friction during re-entry through the atmosphere. The Space Shuttle, Orbiter, has heat resistant tiles. 30,000 tiles made from silica fiber must be fitted individually.

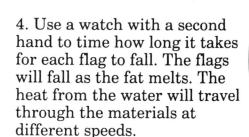

MELT DOWN!

1. Cut out three small paper flags, decorate each with a different motif and attach them to toothpicks like this. Now cut out three identical pieces of cooking fat.

1

2. Take one metal and one plastic lid. Place one piece of fat on each of the lids.

2

Now cut a piece of cork of similar thickness. Push a flag into each piece of fat.

4. Use a watch with a second hand to time how long it takes for each flag to fall. The flags will fall as the fat melts. The heat from the water will travel through the materials at different speeds.

3

3. Half fill the plastic bowl with clean, hot water. Do not use boiling water. When the surface is still, position each lid on the water, making sure that you keep a record of the precise time that each lid touches the hot surface.

WHY IT WORKS

Metal is a good conductor of heat. In a solid, the molecules vibrate continuously. When the temperature is raised, molecules begin to move around even faster. In heated metals (1), the molecules vibrate very rapidly, striking the neighboring molecules and transferring the heat through the material quickly. Heat is transferred through wood more slowly (2) because the molecules don't move about as rapidly as in heated metal.

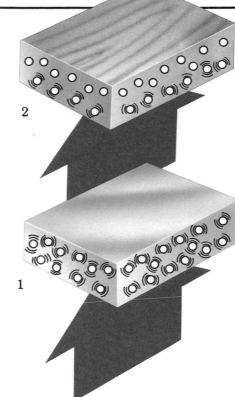

BRIGHT IDEAS

Set up an experiment to discover which type of container will keep a hot drink warm for the longest time possible. Make sure your test is fair. Use exactly the same amount of liquid each time, and start off with all of them at the same temperature. Stand a thermometer in each container and read the temperature of the liquid immediately, and then at regular, timed intervals. Record the rate of cooling on a graph.

Which feels coldest in your hand, a metal coin or a piece of wood? Why is this? Look at the handles of the cooking utensils in your home. Do the handles get hot during cooking? Find out what materials are used in the manufacture of potholders?

4

SHAPES IN NATURE

The smallest unit of living matter is the cell, which is able to divide and multiply. A plant cell has a rigid wall of cellulose, that gives it structure and shape. An animal cell is surrounded only by a thin membrane, so some animals (vertebrates) need a bony skeleton. Some invertebrates, like the crab, have an exoskeleton (an outer skeleton that protects the soft inner body). Nature has developed many strong structures. A honeycomb is a strong structure of hexagonal cells that fit snugly, side by side, without any overlapping or gaps. This is called a tessellated structure.

TOUGH TESSELLATION

1. To make this tessellation game you will need colored card. Use a stencil to cut out hexagon-shaped counters in two colors. They should be the same size.

1

2. Use the yellow card for the honeycomb design on the board. Trace the tessellated hexagons so that you have a total of 60.

2

4. There should be alternate rows of seven and eight hexagons. Emphasize the divisions by going over them with a black felt tip.

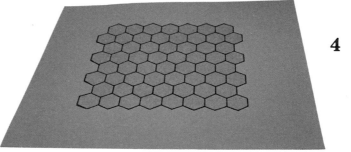

4

3. Carefully cut round the outside of the yellow honeycomb and position it centrally on more card.

3

5. Draw the net for a large cube on white card and construct a die with it. With a marker pen, put the digits 1 and 2 on the sides of the die so that there are three of each.

5

WHY IT WORKS

The complex structure of a honeycomb is a series of six-sided wax cells. Any weight on one cell in the comb is spread out over three cells below and five cells below that. Tessellating squares rest on only 1 or 2 half squares. Because regular hexagons tessellate (there are no gaps and no overlaps) less space is wasted. A six-sided framework is stronger than a square but not as strong as a circle. Circles, however, cannot be tessellated. There would be gaps left between them.

BRIGHT IDEAS

Follow the pattern below and create a spiral using nails and wool. Each point on the curve should be joined to every other point.

Look closely at a snail shell and the horns of a sheep. Do they all curl in the same direction?

Try creating a variety of tessellations using squares or equilateral triangles. You can design repeating patterns.

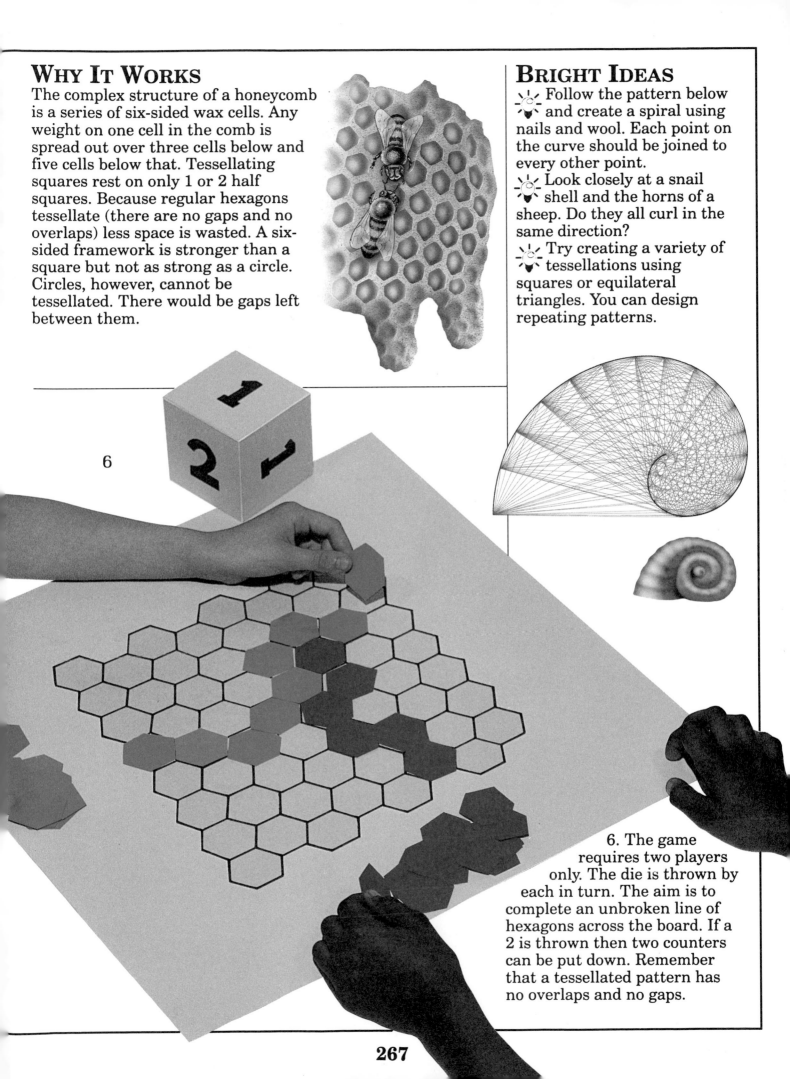

6. The game requires two players only. The die is thrown by each in turn. The aim is to complete an unbroken line of hexagons across the board. If a 2 is thrown then two counters can be put down. Remember that a tessellated pattern has no overlaps and no gaps.

STRONG SHAPES

Certain structures, natural and man made, are stronger than others. The absence of corners in round shapes, or spheres can be a source of strength, because pressure is spread around the whole surface. Domes like this one in St. Paul's Cathedral, London produce a strong ceiling to a building. The geodesic dome (left) was created by Robert Buckminster-Fuller. It is a strong, self-supporting structure. His original design had a framework of hexagons and pentagons, like some soccerballs. Transparent 'bubble' domes are now supplied as a standard system of steel cables and rods that support triangular sheets of glass.

STRONG SHAPES

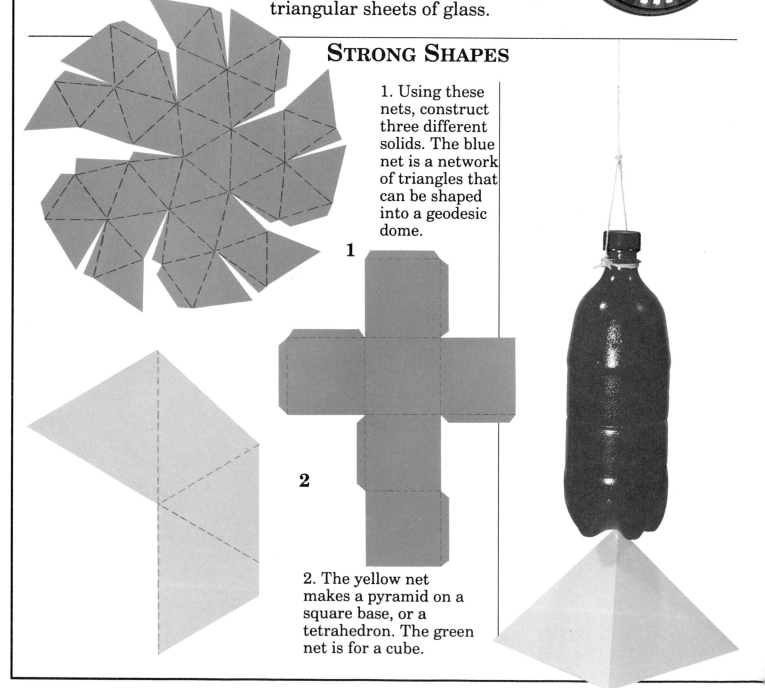

1. Using these nets, construct three different solids. The blue net is a network of triangles that can be shaped into a geodesic dome.

1

2

2. The yellow net makes a pyramid on a square base, or a tetrahedron. The green net is for a cube.

WHY IT WORKS

It is important to be aware of the effect of external forces on a structure. The spherical shape of the geodesic dome reduces the amount of stress in one particular area, and spreads pressure evenly over the whole surface. The triangular framework helps to even out any pressure on the shape and gives the structure rigidity. Hollow tubes combine great strength with light weight. A tube is equally strong all around.

External forces

BRIGHT IDEAS

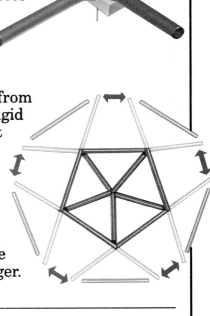

Construct a geodesic dome from plastic straws. You can join the straws as shown here using pins and small pieces of foam rubber. Will it bear more weight than a cube or a pyramid made from straws?

Design a structure from short lengths of a rigid material like wood, that will support a given weight. Start with a basic cube frame. How can you strengthen it? Try using extra thicknesses of material. Triangulating the frame will make it even stronger.

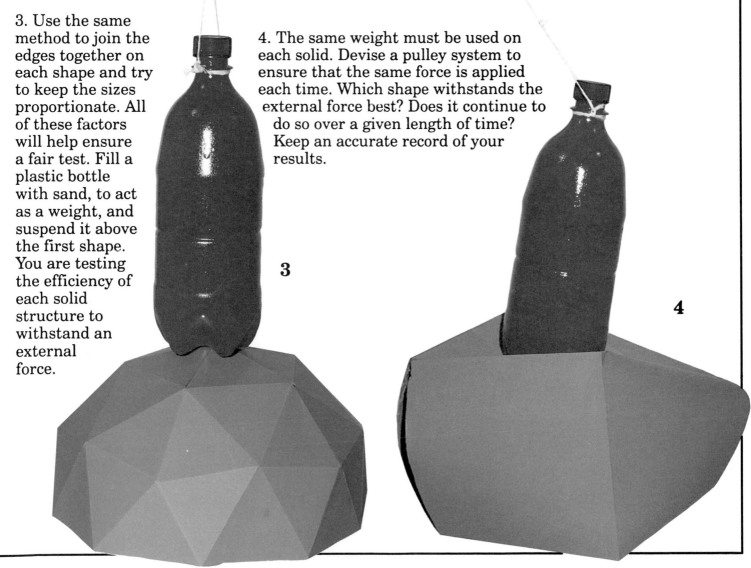

3. Use the same method to join the edges together on each shape and try to keep the sizes proportionate. All of these factors will help ensure a fair test. Fill a plastic bottle with sand, to act as a weight, and suspend it above the first shape. You are testing the efficiency of each solid structure to withstand an external force.

3

4. The same weight must be used on each solid. Devise a pulley system to ensure that the same force is applied each time. Which shape withstands the external force best? Does it continue to do so over a given length of time? Keep an accurate record of your results.

4

RIGID STRUCTURES

The human elbow joint works like a hinge. Joints work with the help of muscles fixed to the bones by tendons. Like the skeleton of a human being or any other animal, cranes have to be light, maneuverable, strong and very sturdy. Cranes are vital in the building of large structures, and they are usually built from a steel framework of thin girders. Without cranes, the building of the Great Pyramid at Giza took 100,000 men, 20 years to complete. The crane has a movable arm, or jib, that operates by combining the principles of levers and pulleys.

STRENGTH

1

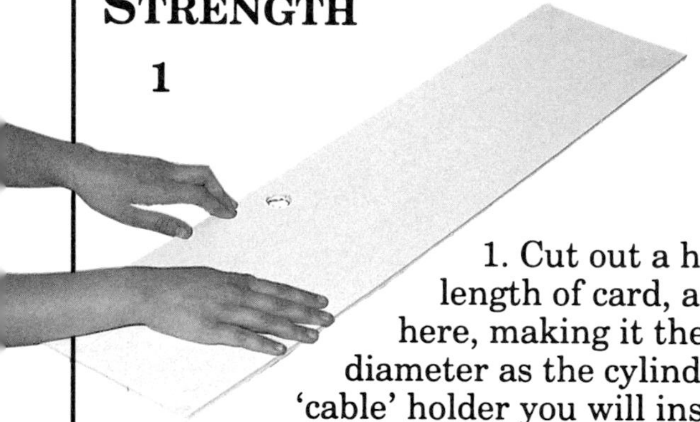

1. Cut out a hole in a length of card, as shown here, making it the same diameter as the cylindrical 'cable' holder you will insert later.

2

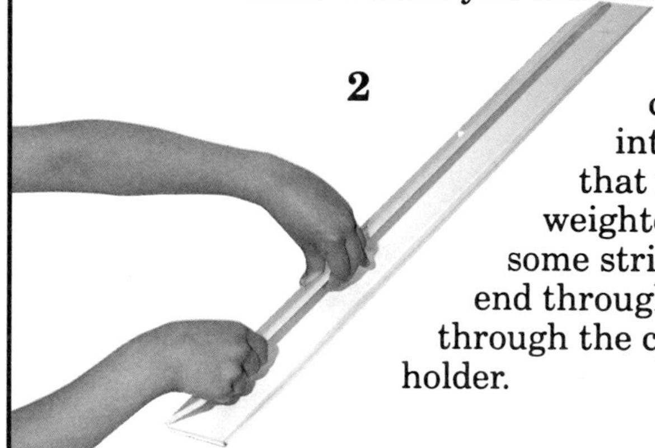

2. Divide the card lengthways into three and score along the lines. Fold to make the elongated prism shape of the jib or 'arm'. Glue the edges

3

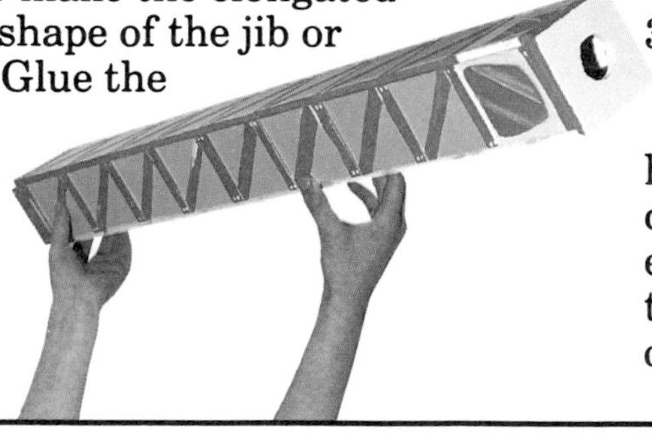

3. In one end of the aluminum foil container cut out a hole as shown. Glue down any open edges and decorate to look like the body of a real crane.

4

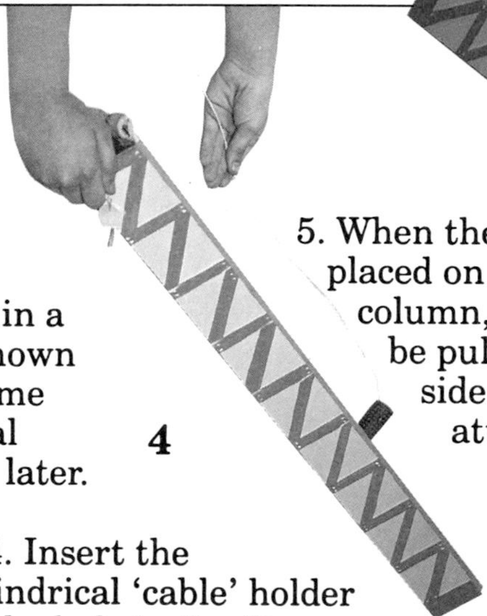

4. Insert the cylindrical 'cable' holder into the hole in the jib so that it projects. Attach the weighted hook to one end of some string and thread the other end through the arm and out through the cylindrical holder.

5

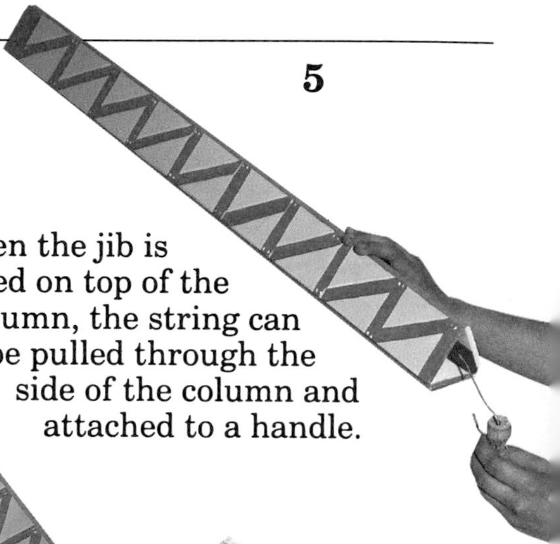

5. When the jib is placed on top of the column, the string can be pulled through the side of the column and attached to a handle.

6

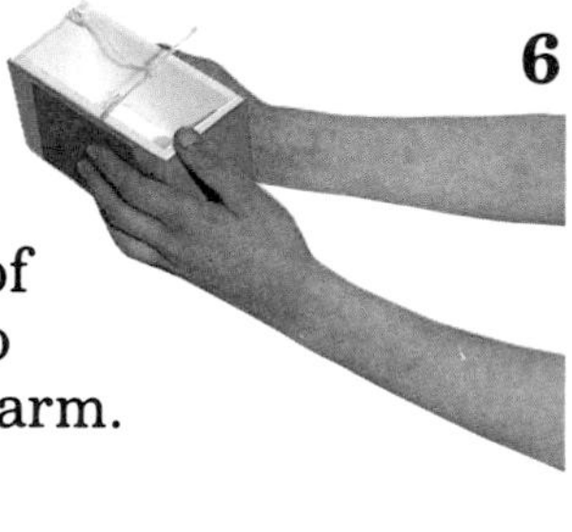

6. Make a ballast box of thick card to balance the arm.

7

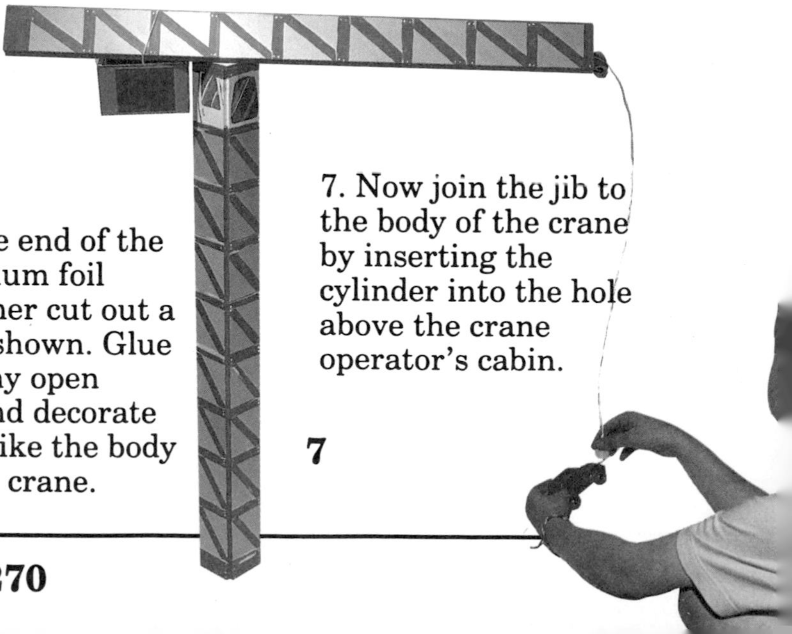

7. Now join the jib to the body of the crane by inserting the cylinder into the hole above the crane operator's cabin.

270

8. Decorate the small 'ballast' box and attach it to the jib so that it can slide along. You could weight it with plasticine.

Lower the weighted hook and attach a load. If the crane should lose balance, move the ballast box to compensate.

WHY IT WORKS

In order to maintain the shape of the structure, internal and external forces must balance. Each part of a structure is called a member. They are either under tension (a pulling force) when they are called "ties", or under compression (a pressing force) when they are called "struts."

If pressed from both sides, for example at a join, the pressing force is called "shear". Triangulation produces a stable structure, because a triangle is a more rigid shape than a square. A real crane is therefore constructed from a series of triangles (below left) to prevent movement of the joints (below right).

Joints

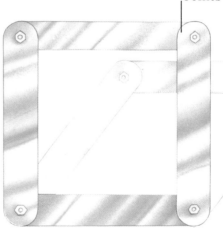

BRIGHT IDEAS

Construct a model arm from cardboard strips joined together with paper fasteners. Attach rubber bands to the paper fasteners so that they lengthen and shorten, like real muscles, when the 'arm' moves up and down.

Can you build a crane with a jib that moves from side to side as well as up and down? Is your crane

stable? Try making the area of the base larger. Does your crane need more ballast, to balance against the weight of the load?

Why are triangular struts successful? Find other ways of constructing a rigid structure. Join four plastic straws, the same length, with thread, to form a square. Is it rigid? Now remove one straw to form a triangle. Is this shape rigid?

BUILDING TOWERS

Lewis Mumford, the American city-planning historian, wrote in 1938, "The age of crustacean building has given way to the age of vertebrates, and the wall, no longer a protective shell, has become a skin." He was referring to the revolution in high-rise building that was brought about by the introduction of iron or steel frames to take the strain in buildings. Shell structures were replaced by frame stuctures. Load-bearing walls no longer limited the height of buildings, and the first skyscrapers made their appearance. The high-rise steel frame was developed by William le Baron Jenney. The Canadian National Tower in Toronto is 1814 feet high.

REACH FOR THE SKY

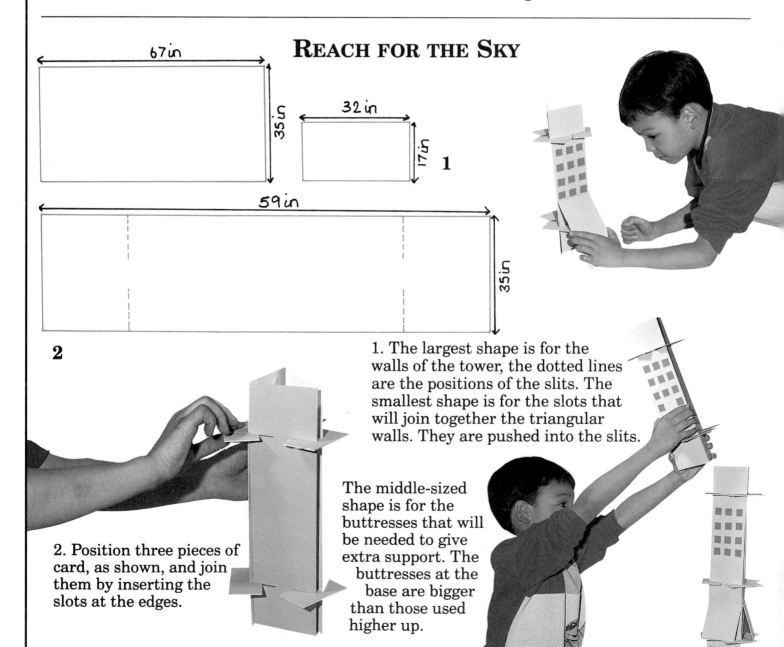

67 in

35 in

32 in

17 in

1

59 in

35 in

2

1. The largest shape is for the walls of the tower, the dotted lines are the positions of the slits. The smallest shape is for the slots that will join together the triangular walls. They are pushed into the slits.

The middle-sized shape is for the buttresses that will be needed to give extra support. The buttresses at the base are bigger than those used higher up.

2. Position three pieces of card, as shown, and join them by inserting the slots at the edges.

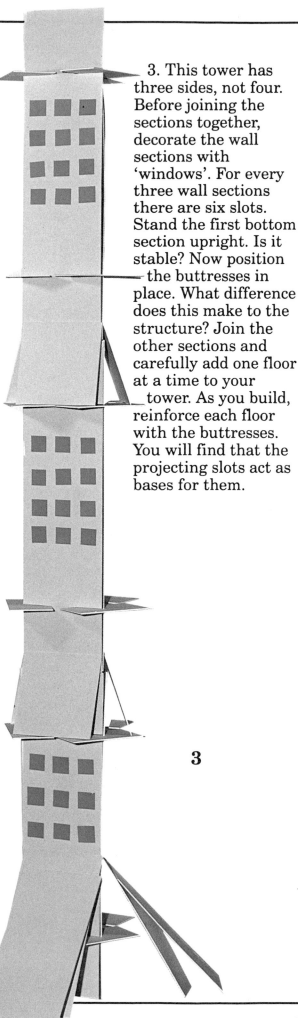

3. This tower has three sides, not four. Before joining the sections together, decorate the wall sections with 'windows'. For every three wall sections there are six slots. Stand the first bottom section upright. Is it stable? Now position the buttresses in place. What difference does this make to the structure? Join the other sections and carefully add one floor at a time to your tower. As you build, reinforce each floor with the buttresses. You will find that the projecting slots act as bases for them.

3

WHY IT WORKS

Your tower structure has stability because it has buttresses that stick out to give support in the form of a broad base, instead of foundations. The forces that the tower exerts downwards are balanced by the buttresses which exert another force upwards from the ground. The higher you build your tower the less stability it will have, and the greater the support it will need. A skyscraper built around a framework, must have foundations that support the weight of the structure – it must be stable, but flexible in high winds.

Downward forces

Upward forces

BRIGHT IDEAS

🔆 Roll a piece of stiff paper into a tube shape and fix it with Scotchtape. How strong do you think this shape is? See how many books you can balance on the top.

🔆 How high can you build your tower before it overbalances? Will it withstand a 'wind'? Try using a hair dryer to test it. Is it rigid or flexible?

🔆 Now try slotting together shapes to make a four-sided tower. Is it more stable than your three-sided structure?

🔆 What happens when you build a shell structure, like a tower of bricks? Why do you think it is unstable? How can you give it stability? Try building a tower framework out of plastic straws or pipecleaners.

SUSPENDED STRUCTURES

The first bridge was probably a fallen tree laid across a stream and early bridge-builders may have observed the strength of rock arches, carved by natural forces. There are 3 types of bridge – arch, girder and suspension. Each one displaces its weight differently. The Golden Gate Bridge, in San Francisco (left), completed in 1937, is a suspension bridge with a main span of 4199 feet. The Humber Bridge, in England, is the world's longest single span suspension bridge. It has a span of 4626 feet. The newest type of bridge is the cable-stayed, a design related to the suspension bridge but the cables are connected directly to the towers.

CROSS THE RIVER

1. For this project you will need a large board as a base. On the board, paint a river scene like the one shown here. Use a craft board and carefully cut 6 polystyrene sections for the roadway of the bridge. You will need a large ball of strong string because the 'cables' carry the weight of the roadway.

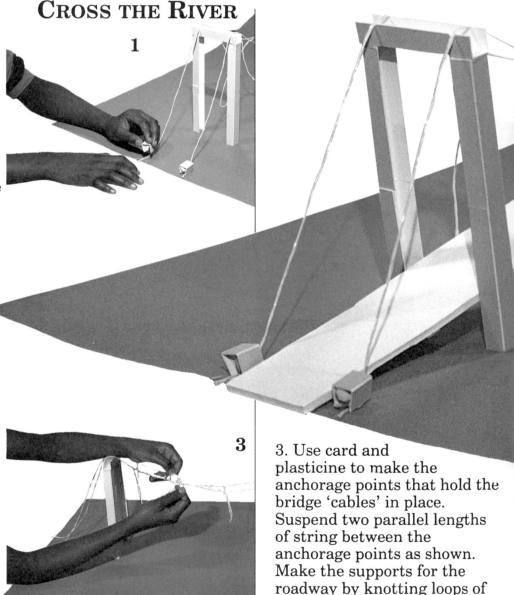

2. Cut 10 of the smaller shapes out of stiff card. Measure and mark the scoring lines. Score and fold along the lines to make the tower sections. Glue two sections together to form the sides of each tower and use one section as a cross beam. Glue the finished towers firmly to the board. Make sure that they are directly opposite each other, on either side of the river.

3. Use card and plasticine to make the anchorage points that hold the bridge 'cables' in place. Suspend two parallel lengths of string between the anchorage points as shown. Make the supports for the roadway by knotting loops of string between the cables.

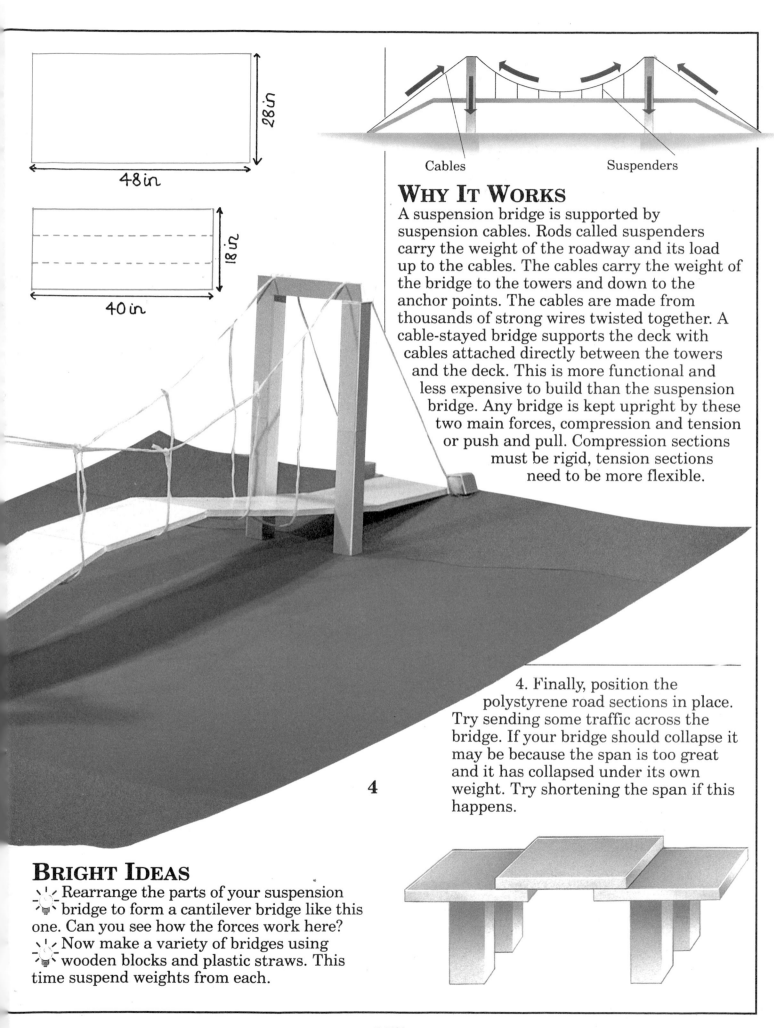

Cables   Suspenders

WHY IT WORKS

A suspension bridge is supported by suspension cables. Rods called suspenders carry the weight of the roadway and its load up to the cables. The cables carry the weight of the bridge to the towers and down to the anchor points. The cables are made from thousands of strong wires twisted together. A cable-stayed bridge supports the deck with cables attached directly between the towers and the deck. This is more functional and less expensive to build than the suspension bridge. Any bridge is kept upright by these two main forces, compression and tension or push and pull. Compression sections must be rigid, tension sections need to be more flexible.

4. Finally, position the polystyrene road sections in place. Try sending some traffic across the bridge. If your bridge should collapse it may be because the span is too great and it has collapsed under its own weight. Try shortening the span if this happens.

4

BRIGHT IDEAS

Rearrange the parts of your suspension bridge to form a cantilever bridge like this one. Can you see how the forces work here?

Now make a variety of bridges using wooden blocks and plastic straws. This time suspend weights from each.

COMBINING MATERIALS

It is possible to combine materials in such a way that the final substance retains the best properties of each. Fiberglass, for example, is glass-reinforced plastic which is light, flexible yet strong. These are known as composite materials. The idea is not a new one. Homes built from wattle and daub were being constructed hundreds of years ago. The first bricks were a mixture of clay and straw. The Inuit eskimos froze moss into ice to strengthen their dome-shaped igloos, constructed using a spiral structure. Today, concrete is reinforced with steel rods (above). Nature has its own composite materials, like wood and bone, both of which are strong but light.

TEST YOUR STRENGTH!

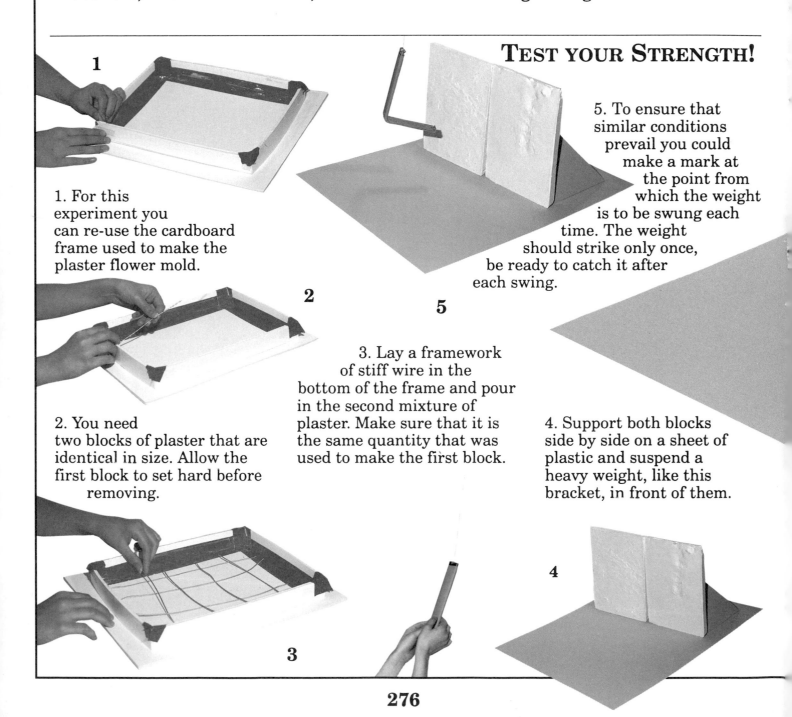

1. For this experiment you can re-use the cardboard frame used to make the plaster flower mold.

2. You need two blocks of plaster that are identical in size. Allow the first block to set hard before removing.

3. Lay a framework of stiff wire in the bottom of the frame and pour in the second mixture of plaster. Make sure that it is the same quantity that was used to make the first block.

4. Support both blocks side by side on a sheet of plastic and suspend a heavy weight, like this bracket, in front of them.

5. To ensure that similar conditions prevail you could make a mark at the point from which the weight is to be swung each time. The weight should strike only once, be ready to catch it after each swing.

WHY IT WORKS

The brittle plaster block breaks easily when an external force is applied (1). The plaster and wire block is able to withstand a greater force because it has been re-inforced with the strength of the wire (2). A composite material has better mechanical properties than any of its components. These materials can be incorporated as fibers in a weaker material, called the matrix. The matrix bonds with and holds the fibers together.

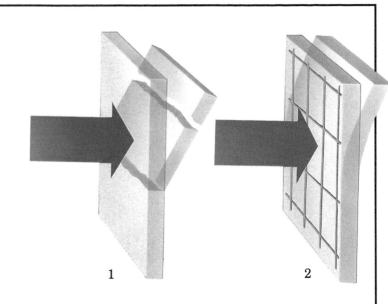

1

2

BRIGHT IDEAS

Shape bricks out of clay and leave them to harden. Now shape bricks mixed with straw and allow them to harden. Test them for strength by tapping them with a hammer. Be careful, wear protective glasses. Which are the strongest?

6

6. Eventually both blocks will crack. How many swings of the weight are needed before this happens? Draw conclusions from your observations. The best properties of the wire and the plaster have been combined in the composite.

VERSATILE STRUCTURES

Kites are named after a bird that has a ragged, flapping flight, interspersed with soaring. The Chinese saw kite-flying as an art form, as long ago as the 4th century BC. The framework was lashed bamboo, covered with silk or paper. It was not until the 16th century that kites reached Europe. Kites have been used for scientific experiments, military signalling and religious festivals. Hang gliders (left) are large kites with a very rigid aluminum structures.

FLYING HIGH!

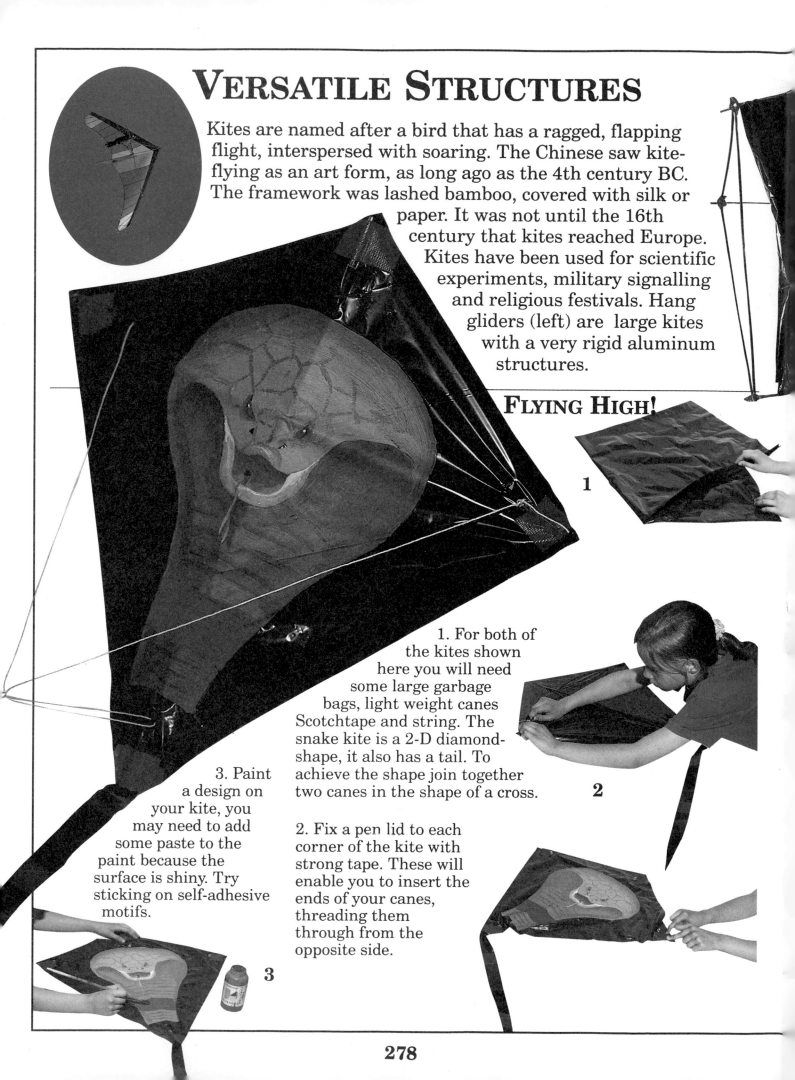

1. For both of the kites shown here you will need some large garbage bags, light weight canes Scotchtape and string. The snake kite is a 2-D diamond-shape, it also has a tail. To achieve the shape join together two canes in the shape of a cross.

2. Fix a pen lid to each corner of the kite with strong tape. These will enable you to insert the ends of your canes, threading them through from the opposite side.

3. Paint a design on your kite, you may need to add some paste to the paint because the surface is shiny. Try sticking on self-adhesive motifs.

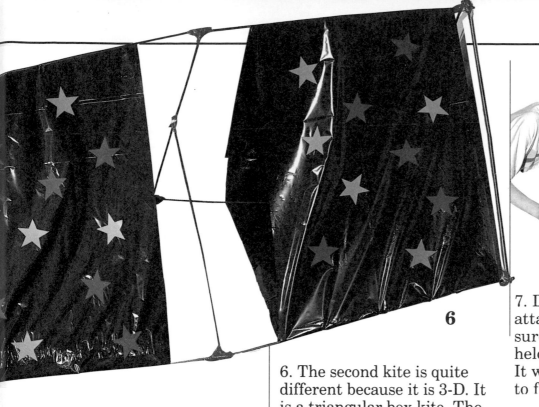

6

6. The second kite is quite different because it is 3-D. It is a triangular box kite. The framework is made from strong but light canes. Join the canes as shown here with strong Scotchtape. Large garbage bags have again been used . They will have to be cut into lengths that can be wrapped around the cane framework.

7

7. Decorate the plastic before attaching it to the frame. Make sure your frame is securely held together with Scotchtape. It will need to be sturdy enough to fly in a strong wind.

4. Secure the canes at the back and front with more strong tape and join together long, thin sections of plastic to make a tail. The tail needs to be about 16 inches.

4

5. Tie the string to three corners of the kite, as shown, fixing it to the cane itself. Now attach the handling string which must be very long. The longer your string is, the higher you can fly your kite.

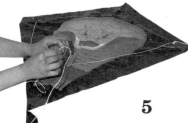

5

WHY IT WORKS
The flat kite has a tail to give it direction, the bowed kite is curved at an angle to the wind. Box kites are 3-D, the delta is triangular and the flexible kite or parafoil forms its shape when filled by the wind. The wind moves past the kite to cause a force called lift to make it rise. The forces of lift, drag and gravity combine to keep the kite in the air. When the kite is flown in such a way that its angle against the wind (angle of attack) provides maximum lift, drag and gravity are overcome. The angle is controlled by the short lines called bridles.

GLOSSARY

AEROFOIL A surface, like an aircraft wing, which is shaped to produce lift when air flows over and under it.

ALTERNATING CURRENT An electric current that reverses its direction around a circuit at regular intervals.

AMPLIFY To make sound louder.

AMPLIITUDE The height of a sound wave. The taller the wave, the louder the sound.

ANEROID BAROMETER An instrument used to measure air pressure.

AQUANANT A person who works, swims or dives underwater.

ASTRONOMY The scientific study of the Universe.

ATOM The smallest part of any element.

ATMOSPHERE The layer of air that surrounds the Earth.

BACTERIA Simple organisms which consist of only one cell and cause organic reactions.

BALLAST A heavy material used to supply extra weight or to add stability.

BAROMETER An instrument to predict the weather by measuring air pressure.

BOILING POINT 212F – The temperature at which water turns to steam.

BRITTLE Easily cracked or broken; fragile.

CAVITY WALL Two walls built with a space between.

CAPILLARY ACTION The rising or falling of water in contact with a solid.

CELLULOSE The main constituent of a plant cell.

COMPOUND A substance made up of two or more elements. It cannot be split up into its separate elements by a physical procees.

CONCAVE Curving inward like the inside of a spoon.

CONDENSATION The change of a gas, such as water vapor, into liquid drops.

CONSTELLATIONS Groups of stars visible in the night sky, recognized easily from their familiar patterns.

CONVECTION CURRENTS Movements of hot and cold air.

CONVEX Curving outward like a ball.

DECIBEL A unit of measurement for the loudness of sound.

DENSITY The heaviness of a substance for a particular volume.

DIRECT CURRENT An electric current that always flows in the same direction – like that produced in a battery.

DOPPLER EFFECT The way a sound changes pitch as it moves past you.

DRAG Air resistance, a force that holds back moving objects.

EARTH WIRE A wire used as a safety precaution, connecting a piece of domestic apparatus to the ground. If the apparatus malfunctions, the 'live' object is 'earthed.'

ECHO The reflection of a sound.

ECHO-LOCATION Using echoes to detect the distance and direction of objects.

ECLIPSE An eclipse occurs when one planet stops sun-light from reaching another.

EFFORT The amount of work needed to move an object, over a distance.

ELECTRICAL RESISTANCE The degree to which materials obstruct the flow of an electric current, measured in ohms.

ELECTRIC CURRENT A continuous flow of electrons through a conductor, measured in amperes (amps).

ELECTRIC MOTOR A machine that uses a magnet to turn electricity into movement.

ELECTRIC POWER The rate of transfer of electrical energy, such as light or heat-measured in watts.

ELECTROLYSIS Splitting up a liquid into its separate elements by passing an electric current through it.

ELECTROLYTE A liquid in which a chemical reaction, electrolysis, takes place when an electric current is passed through it.

ELECTROMAGNETISM The relationship between electricity and magnetism – one can be used to produce the other.

ELECTROPLATING The process of putting a metallic coating on a metal by using an electric current.

ELEMENT A simple substance made up of only one kind of atom.

ENERGY The capacity to do work. Energy can be stored and gradually released.

EQUILIBRIUM The state of being balanced.

EROSION The wearing away of a material by the action of weathering or a substance such as water.

EVAPORATION The change of a liquid to a gas by the escape of molecules from its surface.

FIBER OPTICS A way of sending light along very thin glass fibers.

FLEXIBLE Can be bent easily without breaking.

FOCUS The point at which light rays come together to form a sharp, clear image.

FORCE A push or a pull, equal to the product of mass and acceleration.

FREQUENCY The number of sound vibrations per second, measured in hertz.

FRICTION The force that resists movement when one surface moves relative to another.

FULCRUM The pivot point of a lever.

GRAVITY The force that attracts objects because of their mass.

GREENWICH MEAN TIME Standard time throughout most of the world, calculated from the Prime Meridian at Greenwich, London.

GYPSUM A mineral from the ground that can be heated to form Plaster of Paris.

GYROCOMPASS A compass that points to true north because it does not use magnetism.

HOLOGRAM A three-dimensional picture produced by a laser.

HYDRAULICS The technology of liquids in motion and at rest.

HYDROMETER An instrument for measuring the relative density of liquids.

IGNEOUS Rocks derived from magna or lava, on or below Earth's surface.

IMAGE The "picture" of an object produced by a mirror or lens.

IMPERIAL MEASUREMENTS Standard measurements used in some countries before they adopted the Metric System.

INCANDESCENT LIGHT Light that is produced when a solid, such as tungsten, is heated.

INVERTEBRATE An animal without a backbone, but with an outer shell, such as a crab.

LASER A concentrated beam of light of one wavelength.

LEVER In its simplest form, a rigid bar that pivots on its fulcrum or 'hinge'. Press down on one side, and the other side moves up.

LIFT An upward force that is created by the low pressure above.

LODESTONE A piece of magnetite, a magnetic rock. It was used as a compass by early explorers.

LUBRICANT Oil or other matter used to make a surface smooth and to overcome friction.

LUNAR CYCLE The time it takes the moon to travel around the Earth – around 29 days 12 hours 44 minutes 3 seconds.

MAGMA Hot liquid beneath Earth's crust that solidifies into igneous rock.

MAGNETIC FIELD The area surrounding a magnet or an electric current that attracts or repels magnetic materials.

MAGNETIC INDUCTION Making a magnet by using a permanent magnet.

MAGNETIC NORTH POLE The point on the Earth's surface where magnetism is concentrated. The magnetic north pole is about 994 miles away from the goegraphic north pole.

MAGNETIC SHIELD A magnetic material placed within a magnetic field to cancel out the effect of another magnet.

MAGNETISM An invisible force that attracts or repels magnetic materials.

MAGNETIZE Making a magnet by stroking or touching a magnetic material with a permanent magnet.

MAGNETOMETER An instrument for measuring a magnetic field.

MAINS ELECTRICITY The electricity produced by electromagnetic induction. Produced at power stations, it can reach almost every home along power lines.

MEMBRANE A pliable tissue that connects cells and organs.

MENISCUS The curved surface of water in a tube, produced by surface tension.

METEOROLOGIST A person who studies weather forecasting.

METRIC SYSTEM The decimal system of units based on the metre.

MIXTURE A combination of elements and compounds which can be separated by a physical process.

MOLECULE The smallest naturally occurring particle of a substance.

NEUTRAL POINT The point where two opposing magnetic fields cancel each other out as a result of the repulsion of like poles.

OXYGEN A gas that makes up one-fifth of the air and is essential to life.

pH SCALE A scale which measures the strength of acids and alkalis where 1 is a strong acid, 7 neutral and 14 is a strong alkali.

PIGMENT A substance that gives color to a plant or animal cell. Can be used to color paints or dyes.

PITCH The highness or lowness of a sound, depending on the frequency of sound vibrations.

PLIMSOLL LINE A load line painted on the hull of a ship.

POLE STAR The star closest to the north celestial pole. It appears to remain fixed in the sky.

PRESSURE The force exerted on the surface of the Earth by the atmosphere due to gravitational pull of the Earth.

PRISM A transparent block of glass, used to bend light and separate the colors in visible light.

REACTION A process where two substances combine to form a new substance (or substances).

REFLECTION Bouncing back of light from a surface.

REFRACTION Bending of light when it passes from one transparent substance to another.

RESISTANCE The forces, such as gravity and friction which act upon objects, making them difficult to move.

RESONANCE When a sound makes another object produce a sound because it has the same frequency of vibration.

RETINA Layer at the back of the eye which is sensitive to light.

REVERBERATION The bouncing of sound waves within small spaces.

ROLL A tipping of the wings of an aircraft in which one tips upward and the other tips downward.

SALINITY The salty taste of something – saltiness.

SHORT CIRCUIT A broken power supply, possibly due to a faulty electrical connection, causing an electric current to take a path of low resistance.

SOLENOID A cylindrical coil of wire which acts as a magnet when an electric current is passed through it.

SOLUTION A liquid into which a substance, solid or gas, has been dissolved.

SONIC BOOM A loud bang from the shock waves created by an object moving faster than the speed of sound.

SOUND WAVES A regular pattern of pressure changes in solids, liquids or gases, such as air.

STABILIZER A device used to achieve stability.

STREAMLINING Making an object smooth and rounded so that air flows easily over its surface.

SUPERSONIC Faster than the speed of sound.

SURFACE TENSION The molecular force of a liquid that pulls it into the smallest possible area, making water drops round.

SURVEYOR A person who plots detailed maps of the land.

TENSILE STRENGTH The ability of a material to withstand a pulling force.

THERMALS Currents of rising air.

ULTRASOUND Sounds with a frequency over 20,000 hertz which are too high for people to hear.

VARIABLE An aspect of change in an experiment.

VARIABLE RESISTOR (RHEOSTAT) A device to control the amount of electricity flowing through a circuit.

VERTEBRATE An animal with a backbone.

WATER VAPOR The gas evaporated from the surface of liquid water. (Vapor from boiling water is called steam).

WAVELENGTH The distance betwwen the same point on any two waves, such as from the top of one wave to the top of the next.

WHEEL A disc-shaped object mounted on a central axle. The wheel is fixed to the axle or is free to spin on it.

WORK Measured in units called joules, work is equal to the force multiplied by the distance moved.

INDEX

With thanks to the following picture libraries and photographers:

Aladdin's Lamp, British Broadcasting Corporation, British Film Institute, C.O.I. Photos, Eye Ubiquitos, Frank Spooner Pictures, Lycoming Pratt and Witney, Mary Evans Picture Library, Popperfoto, Roger Harding Picture Library, Science Museum, Science Photo Library, Spectrum Color Library, STL Designs, The Ministry of Defence, U.S. Navy Sky Photos, Roger Vlitos and Dan Brooks